)ct 2017

Schadenfreude,
A Love Story

Schadenfreude, A Love Story

Me, the Germans, and 20 Years of Attempted Transformations, Unfortunate Miscommunications, and Humiliating Situations That Only They Have Words For

Rebecca Schuman

FLATIRON
BOOKS
NEW YORK

www.flatironbooks.com

Library of Congress Cataloging-in-Publication Data

Names: Schuman, Rebecca author.
Title: Schadenfreude, a love story : me, the Germans, and
    20 years of attempted transformations, unfortunate
    miscommunications, and humiliating situations that
    only they have words for / Rebecca Schuman.
Description: First edition. | New York : Flatiron Books, 2017.
Identifiers: LCCN 2016038531| ISBN 9781250077578
    (hardcover) | ISBN 9781250077660 (e-book)
Subjects: LCSH: Schuman, Rebecca. | Journalists—United
    States—Biography. | Schuman, Rebecca—Travel—
    Germany. | Women college students—United States—
    Biography. | Germany—Description and travel.
Classification: LCC PN4874.S345 A3 2017 |
    DDC 070.92 [B] —dc23
LC record available at https://lccn.loc.gov/2016038531

Our books may be purchased in bulk for promotional,
educational, or business use. Please contact your local
bookseller or the Macmillan Corporate and Premium Sales
Department at (800) 221-7945, extension 5442, or by e-mail
at MacmillanSpecialMarkets@macmillan.com.

First Edition: February 2017

10 9 8 7 6 5 4 3 2 1

Eine Geschichte für W.R.

Contents

Author's Note

*The following is a work of nonfiction. All events are
true as I remember them, though I am unapolo-
getically prone to indiscriminate hyperbole, and
some dialogue is approximated due to the passage of
time. Most names and many identifying details have
been changed, and some individuals are composites
to further protect their identities.*

*A small number of scenes in the chapters
"Schriftverkehr," "Ereignis," and "Schadenfreude"
have appeared in a different form in* Slate *and on
my personal website.*

All translations from the German are my own.

"Give it up! Give it up!" he said, and turned away with a great swing of his body, like a man who wants to be alone with his laughter.

—Franz Kafka

Schadenfreude,
A Love Story

1.

Jugendsünde

n. teenage folly, from youth and sin.

ex. Among the most egregious of her *Jugendsünden* was the intellectual gravitas she granted to *Pinky and the Brain.*

Dylan Gellner wasn't German. He was a nonpracticing half-Jew from Oregon, just like me. But all of this is still largely his fault, or rather my fault for falling in love with him.

The first time I ever heard of Dylan Gellner was at the beginning of senior year, when he became a household name at South Eugene High School for getting a 1450 on his SATs. I realize that doesn't sound like much nowadays, when a 1450 is what you get for spelling your own name with just one typo. But in 1993, it was the best board score at my twelve-hundred-student public school—the best, in fact, I had ever heard of in real life. Certainly much better than mine.

I had already taken the test twice, the first attempt resulting in an underwhelming 1160. My parents—who met in 1965 on their

Stanford junior year abroad in Italy and married shortly before beginning joint Ph.D.s in English at the University of Chicago—had many opinions and much advice. "The only thing the SAT predicts is the *aptitude* of parents to force their kids to spend lunchtime doing practice tests," said Sharon Schuman, Ph.D., the night before my first ignominious showing. "My SATs weren't great, and I turned out fine. I got a *Ph.D.*!" She went back to grading her hundredth freshman paper of the night.

"It's like studying for a urine test!" added David Schuman, Ph.D., J.D., as he dug into his usual postdinner snack of Crispix cereal dipped in I Can't Believe It's Not Butter! My dad's own Ph.D. had been supplemented by a law degree after the English-professor employment crisis propelled him to law school just before I started kindergarten. Of course, he'd then snuck back into academia as a law professor, so he had never done anything exciting like defending murderers or helping teenagers divorce their parents.

"Just go to bed early, and do your best," he counseled. "I mean, look at Grandpa. He never even took the SAT, and he played football at the University of Michigan with Gerald Ford!"

"That's because it was 1933, Dad."

"Yes, back when they had active discrimination policies against Jews. So did Stanford when I went there, by the way. *Quotas.* Good night!"

The Schumans' laid-back attitude, it turns out, was borne not of their generation's antiauthoritarian progressivism so much as by the secret assumption that their daughter, who could talk at six months and read her alphabet at a year, was so preternaturally intelligent that she would make a 1500 and be admitted to the elite university of her choice without studying or trying. But they learned in short order that you should never underestimate the mediocrity of your own child—a mediocrity that brought about a universal change in the Schumans' conception of both my abilities and my future, and their idea of what constituted both parental involvement and a worthy extracurricular activity.

"You," proclaimed my dad some scant handful of weeks after the urine test/Grandpa conversation, thudding an onerous-looking tome in front of me on the table, "are going to SAT prep class." (I was still, mercifully, allowed to eat lunch.)

Late nights in the school newspaper office were hastily supplanted by practice tests under the semiwatchful eye of a very bored tutor at a storefront private school in downtown Eugene, which at the time consisted of a handful of record and outdoor-supply shops; my old gymnastics academy; a public library that largely served as a daytime napping station for the less-fortunate; and, of course, every drug dealer and rapist in the greater Willamette Valley. Downtown's flagship establishment, right around the corner from my new tutoring digs, was a boutique of "imports" that was the only place in town you could get Chuck Taylors in all the colors, but which did most of its business renting porn and selling bongs. The Aerie Academy, where the Schumans laid down substantial dollars to shame their oldest child back into the realm of the exceptional, was sandwiched between a thrift store run by the Junior League, which specialized in mismatched china and shoulder pads, and a place that hosted hacky-sack competitions. Obviously these were the ideal environs to develop some academic rigor at last.

After seven diligent months of drill questions and vocabulary building, the fruits of my labor resulted in a modest 100-point jump in my verbal score. "Oh look," I said to my mother after ripping open the dread carbon-paper missive from the College Board after yet more months of agonized waiting. "Slightly less mediocre mediocrity." And this was what I could accomplish with a focus I had never before applied to academics, and would not again until my first year of graduate school. So, to my parents' shock and my resignation, it was averageness that constituted (to bastardize Ludwig Wittgenstein) the limits of my language, and thus also of my college application pool. Would I be following my parents to Stanford, creating a Schuman legacy? I would not. I contented myself with the fact that my hard-fought improved score made me seem smart enough.

Until, early on in senior year, I realized that among the sea of thirty-nine other college-credit aspirants in my AP Civics class was the infamous Dylan Gellner. "When you apply to colleges, your real competition is the people from your high school," my guidance counselor had said. And there, three rows back from me, was Dylan Gellner with his damn 1450. On the first try, obviously. (Possibly as a *sophomore*.) I might as well start that correspondence degree in TV and VCR repair already.

The second thing I learned about Dylan Gellner was that he, who as a junior took all of his math and science classes with seniors, had dated Margaret O'Grady, who was a year older than we were and now went to Princeton.

"Sounds like a match made in dork heaven," I said to my friend Samantha one rainy afternoon in late September, left again to my own devices now that SAT purgatory was over and my parents had given up. Samantha was busy sifting through brochures for colleges that were now out of my league. "I bet they whispered sweet fractals into each other's ears," I said. As Samantha took careful note of Stanford's on-campus housing policy, I surreptitiously flipped through the yearbook to get a better look at Dylan Gellner—

staring during AP Civics would have been (a) rude, (b) obvious, and (c) somewhat impossible, as he normally sat a few rows behind me with his preppy ski-team friends.

"Whoa," I said to an indulgent Samantha, after I finally found his junior-year mug shot (she hadn't expected Dylan Gellner's 1450 and dating history to be worthy of an entire afternoon's discussion). "He looks like he just got home from his bar mitzvah, and like his mom lays out his clothes in the morning while he reads Dostoevsky for fun, or whatever." What I conveniently left out was my recognition of Dylan Gellner's rather arresting eyes: large, obstinate, and startlingly deep ebony. Amid the blank (often stoned) gazes of our classmates, Dylan Gellner's peepers betrayed a serious *something* that my teenage self did not yet understand but could not stop thinking about.

"What do you care?" asked Samantha, twisting her perfectly straight cocoa-brown hair into a quick bun and dipping a pita into some tzatziki. "You have a boyfriend. A nice one." This was true. His name was Travis; he was a head taller than me and perpetually shiny (but I say that in a sort of affectionate way). He had a disconcerting habit of sticking his butt out about three feet when he hugged anyone, and he was indeed very nice. He was a hip-hop superfan and computer enthusiast who got in early decision to MIT. What I was too classy to tell Samantha was that Travis's primary usefulness to me (and mine to him) was for the drawn-out but eventually successful dispatching of virginity. Still, she was right. I *had* a boyfriend, and I was *busy* with all sorts of shit, such as being captain of my noncompetitive jazz dance squad, working as managing editor of the school paper, and applying to liberal arts colleges that, like me, were too iconoclastic to care much about such conformist trifles as SAT scores. I promptly resumed ignoring

Dylan Gellner and his 1450 and his weird, penetrating stare. Until he stole my seat in AP Civics.

Advanced Placement Civics, with Mr. Rasmussen, was widely known in South Eugene High School as the easiest of all the APs (if not the easiest of all classes, period).

"I am seven months away from my pension," Rasmussen would remind us fairly regularly, with the subtext being that he no longer gave a single flying fuck about whether or not we actually understood what "social cleavage" was, or whether we got high in the parking lot before class and giggled about "cleavage" for fifty-five minutes. All you had to do to ensure an A in AP Civics was bring Mr. Rasmussen a cup of coffee now and then. Sure, technically there was no food or beverage allowed in the halls or classrooms of South Eugene High School. And yet, if one wanted to get out of even AP Civics's most basic "discussion" of American government and jurisprudence, one could get a sort of Rasmussenian papal dispensation to go off-campus and get a giant cup of Joe, to be shuttled brazenly through the proctored halls ("It's for Rasmussen!") and directly into the classroom, where college-bound twelfth-graders would be finishing a ten-minute "silent period of contemplation" (i.e., naptime). If you wanted to go ahead and take the AP exam at the end of the year for fun, you had Mr. Rasmussen's sincere blessing, but if you thought anything that transpired in that room in the preceding nine months would earn you college credit, you were gravely mistaken.

Unsurprisingly, there were no assigned seats in AP Civics. ("Sit wherever you please. Don't even come to class if you don't want to; don't do me any favors.") Still, as has been true through the ages and will be for time immemorial, in the first week or so of school, students claim "their seats" and remain more or less tethered to them for as long as the class is in session. (It's like it's their blankie, a security object that protects them from the cliques and the multiple-choice tests and the permanent processed-meat smell of the hallway.) So you can imagine my outrage when one day I tromped into AP Civics wearing my finest outfit (a Guatemalan-print vest, polar-fleece sweatpants, and Tevas), only to find Dylan Gellner's keister parked in *my* seat. Thus the first words I ever spoke to the first person with whom I ever fell in love were "Hey, that's my seat," and the first word he spoke back to me was "Tough." As he said it, he smiled a little, and those odd eyes of his flashed at me, and I had the means, motive, and opportunity to give him a good staredown in person for the first time ever. Dylan Gellner had matured considerably since his junior-year picture, and now, to my annoyance, possessed a chiseled jaw and five o'clock shadow that matched his shock of endlessly thick, jet-black hair, which in turn matched those goddamned eyes.

Hmmm. Mr. 1450 was cute—and it appeared, in a sort of fifth-grade kind of way, flirting with me. Being now in possession of a real-live sexually active relationship, I was an undisputed expert in courtship rituals, and the correct response in this delicate situation was to turn on one heel, huff to the other side of the room, and refuse to speak to or acknowledge Dylan Gellner again—until radical politics turned everything tits-up, as it has been known to do.

It was mid-February, and, according to Mr. Rasmussen, the perfect time for the students of AP Civics to learn how Our Democracy worked. And what better and more accurate way to do this than immediately bifurcate the class down acrimonious party lines? Two-thirds of us were gazing out the windows—placed just above student-head-level so that we could see outside only if we craned our necks—at the blue sky, anathema for Oregon that time of year. Ah, to be anywhere but a twelfth-grade civics classroom; to be sitting at the outdoor tables of a coffee shop, nursing the same small cup for four hours as we read the personals in the free *Eugene Weekly*. ("Solipsist seeks solipsist for rubdowns, astral projection, light anal play. No fatties.")

My friend Lisa—Travis's friend, actually (the *girlfriend* of Travis's friend, technically), who was far better-looking and more popular than I was, with supple muscular legs, pillowy lips, and what I would later learn to term "bedroom eyes"—had just passed me a note, proclaiming her desire to spend the weekend watching Monty Python movies and smoking weed.

"Rebecca," said Rasmussen, midway through a halfhearted sentence about the correct process for ratifying a party platform. "Is that a *note*? Jesus tap-dancing Christ."

"I'm sorry, Mr. Rasmussen," I said. "We were just comparing the difference between simple anarchy and anarcho-syndicalist communes." (Technically not completely false.) I shoved the note in my pocket. I thought I heard an impatient snort from the back of the classroom, somewhere near Dylan-Gellner-o'clock. "I'm sorry," I said again.

Rasmussen put both his hands on my desk and leaned down so that I could smell how recently he'd enjoyed his last cup of coffee (not very; possibly the source of his sour mood). "Rebecca?" he said. "I don't care." He returned to the front of the room and picked up a stack of Scantron forms.

"Here," he said to the whole class. "Fill out these questionnaires about your political beliefs. I don't care if you're honest or not. Just do it." This clearly had the added benefit of cutting into about thirty more minutes of teaching time, during which Rasmussen would be able to daydream about cigars.

"What are these for?" asked Jacob, who sat next to me. He was a smart-ass I'd befriended in trig sophomore year when he antagonized our teacher so cleverly that half the class got notes sent home about our behavior problems. ("Rebecca *herself* doesn't have a problem," Mrs. Kuroda had clarified to an aghast David and Sharon Schuman. "But she's encouraging the bad kids.")

"Just fill it *out*, Jacob," said Rasmussen. There were twenty-four questions, and all of them had to be answered with either full agreement or full disagreement. There was no political gray area in AP Civics, just as there was no gray area about anyone's desire to do actual work in AP Civics.

All the statements were either somewhat conservative ("I believe in limited government") or downright reactionary ("I believe there should be no restriction on firearms whatsoever"), and every time you agreed with one, you got a point. If you scored 12 or above, you moved to the right side of the classroom, toward the hall, where the AP Civics Republicans would nominate a candidate and mount a mock election campaign. Under 12 and you went leftward toward the windows, where you and your fellow AP Civics Democrats would presumably copy the Bill Clinton agenda verbatim and attempt to rerun on it. (Everyone in our class was an exact replica of his parents' politics, except without the added gravitas of having lived through the Nixon administration.) As Violet and Alyssa, the two beautiful and popular students Rasmussen "entrusted" with his "grading" so as not to have to rouse himself, returned from the Scantron machine in the teachers' lounge (and, coincidentally, a quick pit stop at a coffee shop ten blocks away), they motioned me over.

"What?" I asked. They pointed to my Scantron.

"You got a *zero*, Rebecca."

I was such a knee-jerk baby liberal that I was the first person in the history of Mr. Rasmussen's class ever to score 100 percent left-wing answers. And, it turned out, I was in some interesting company.

"And check it out," said Violet, violating every paragraph of the Family Educational Rights and Privacy Act. "Dylan got a *three*."

When it came time to split up, Rasmussen read off the names of everyone else in the class, until only Dylan Gellner and me were left.

"What about us, Mr. Rasmussen?"

"You two? You're so far toward the window that you're out on the lawn."

With the rest of the class laughing at us, Dylan Gellner and I had no choice but to make eye contact for the second time in our lives—and this time, he nodded approvingly.

"Who," he said to the other lefties, "wants to split off from the Democrats and be *Socialists*? Besides you, obviously, Rebecca."

"Dammit, Dylan, that is *not* the point of this exercise."

"Mr. Rasmussen, I respectfully disagree. We are to draft a political platform based on our actual beliefs, correct?"

"Allegedly, yes."

I cleared my throat. "Yeah," I said. "Just because it didn't work out for Ross Perot doesn't make us beholden to the two-party system! Now *who's with us*?"

"Forget that," said my friend Tamia, who worked with me on the newspaper and was one of the very few black students in extremely white South Eugene High. "I don't want to pay fifty-two percent of my money in taxes."

"But we'd get so much stuff for it, Mia!" I said. "Much more than we could buy with our own paychecks. Better roads, better *schools*—what are there, forty kids in this class? I mean—"

"Save it for the debate, Schuman," said Rasmussen.

"Really?"

"Yes, fine, you two pains in my neck win. Do your socialism. Just get to work."

Jacob defected immediately—far better chances for smart-assery in a rogue party—as did Violet, Alyssa, and Lisa (there was no socialism section in our textbook and no Internet yet, which meant an assignment with no reading).

"So," said Dylan Gellner, as we yanked a set of desks free from the false binary of the left-right continuum. "I assume you want to be president, Rebecca?"

"Are you shitting me?" I asked. "I can't take that kind of pressure. Jacob should do it. He's got charisma."

"Fine," said Dylan Gellner. "You be vice president. I'll run the campaign. Just don't fuck it up, like you fucked up your essay on *Heart of Darkness*."

I raised my eyebrows. "How do *you* know about my essay on *Heart of Darkness*? You're not in AP Lit sixth period."

"Yeah, but Bumstead put it on the overhead in third, too."

"Those are anonymous!" I said.

"I recognized your voice."

Mr. Bumstead had actually put my essay on the overhead as a good example, but I had other things to worry about, namely: What did Dylan Gellner mean he *recognized my voice*?

Dylan Gellner shrugged. "I read a couple of your newspaper columns."

I had recently sent an unsolicited set of clippings from the high-school paper to the features editor of the local daily, auditioning myself to be their "first-ever voice of a local high-schooler, talking about *our* issues from *our* perspective!" They'd bought the spiel, largely because they realized they could get away with paying a child fifteen dollars per submission—and as a result, my chubby little visage was briefly on the side of newspaper boxes, and I made the morning announcements, and so for like a week, before everyone realized that (a) high-school kids don't read the paper and (b) ripping off Dave Barry does not "current issues from a high-schooler's unique perspective!" make, I was high-school famous.

"Your Valentine's Day piece was pretty good," said Dylan Gellner, as I realized I'd been staring at him while my mind adjusted to the fact that I was on his radar. "But mostly because you made a 'Heart-Shaped Box' reference."

"I what?"

"'Heart-Shaped Box.' The song. Nirvana."

"I don't know it." I made a mental note to pick up *In Utero*, which I had been boycotting because Nirvana had (a) completely sold out, and (b) had the nerve to cancel a show for which I had tickets the year before.

"*Ahem,*" said Jacob, who, like everyone else at the table, was still present and at least somewhat interested in our socialist revolution. "Do we or do we not need to come up with a plan to beat the Democrats? They've already got a speech drafted out, and it calls us 'moochers' and 'looters.'"

We went back to our campaign, which, largely due to our successful derailment of the original assignment, won in a landslide. And, more important, Dylan Gellner and I now possessed a tacit understanding that we would work together during all future civics projects, the next of which would bring about two watershed events: Dylan Gellner would come to my house, and Franz Kafka would enter my life.

All right, technically, Kafka would *reenter* my life. My first exposure to the German language's most famous writer had been during the fall of sophomore year in 1991: on a pitch-black rainy Sunday afternoon, I'd slid *The Metamorphosis* off my parents' bookshelf and read it in one sitting. My initial reaction to the first few moments of Kafka's most famous story was shocked disbelief that Gregor Samsa, hapless star (hard to call someone a protagonist when he mostly just sits there being disgusting), worries primarily that he'll be late for work. He has an exoskeleton and a bunch of terrifying little legs, but all he can think is, "What an exhausting career I've chosen!" Why was Gregor going on about his stupid job, I wondered, when *the* only appropriate reaction in this particular moment would be this and this exclusively: *HOLY SHIT, I'M A GIANT FUCKING BUG?* My own jobs at the time were commandeering children's birthday parties at the gymnastics academy and being in the tenth grade—and, had I woken up with even the *slightest* fantastical disfigurement (really one substantial pimple would have done it) I would have forgotten immediately about school, work, everything. *I'm hideous!* I would have said. *I give up!*

I just kept waiting for Gregor to break down in horror—so I kept on reading, but to my frustration, such an emotional release never happens, not once in the entire story. Another thing that had perturbed me was that it takes Kafka about *fourteen pages* to get

Gregor to reveal his new body to his family and boss. I'd found myself simultaneously infuriated and spellbound at the methodical, unemotional pace of this narration, its wackadoodle subject matter almost an afterthought, the horror with which the family reacts to Gregor's appearance when he finally does get his door open and steps out into the living room rendered with the emotional fervor of a shopping list.

I read helplessly as Gregor Samsa's condition deteriorated, and watched just as helplessly as his family gave up on him, and, finally, I held my breath as he let himself die. *Die!* How was this possible? The story was narrated from Gregor's *perspective,* for Christ's sake—he wasn't supposed to die. But I'd never met Kafka before, and I didn't realize that authors are allowed to be completely inconsistent in their perspective. Yes, that little book frustrated the shit out of me, but I couldn't get it out of my head for weeks. I had also assumed it was the only thing of import Kafka ever wrote, and promptly moved on to other interests, such as wondering exactly which of my cutoff jeans looked best layered over just which of my pairs of long underwear. This dearth of intellectual curiosity occurred despite the minor fact that at least four of Kafka's other books were sitting on my parents' bookshelf right next to *The Metamorphosis*—one of which would two years later catch Dylan Gellner's eye during an AP Civics study party, extra light on the studying.

We'd moved on from derailing assignments about Our Democracy to derailing an assignment that purported to explicate Our Judicial System: a mock trial, in which once again Dylan Gellner was the intellectual ringleader and charismatic Jacob our star witness. However, our fake case—a breaking-and-entering—had a dizzying array of other, mostly irrelevant witnesses, and the only way to make sense of it was to call in a ringer, one Professor Dr. David Schuman, Ph.D., J.D., despite his marked lack of litigation experience. Several of my classmates came over to the house—including, of course, Dylan Gellner; I mean, he was the group leader, so he had to. It's not like I invented the study session just to get him in my house, because that would be ridiculous and desperate. But there he was: forest-green polo shirt that somehow made his eyes look blacker. Hair as thick as ever, that smelled of Earl Grey tea. (So *maybe* I hugged Dylan Gellner hello, all right? I mean, he was my friend. Travis wasn't in AP Civics, so, like, there was no reason for him to be there.)

Dylan Gellner gravitated immediately to my parents' stuffed floor-to-ceiling bookshelves and nodded after noticing the healthy representation of what he informed me were his two favorite authors: Hermann Hesse (of whom I had never heard) and Kafka.

"This," he said casually, taking out a yellowing hardcover of *The Trial*, "is my favorite book."

"Oh," I said, "I know Kafka. I really liked *The Metamorphosis*."

"*Pfft*," said Dylan Gellner. "Beginner Kafka."

"Duly noted."

"This is my other favorite author," he said, pulling off a copy of *Steppenwolf*. "Hermann Hesse." He pronounced it *Hess*, without the last *e*, despite being in AP German. "So what's your favorite book?"

If I was going to impress Dylan Gellner with my love of the literary, I was going to have to think of a favorite book that was not on the AP Literature syllabus (my standard answer before had always been *The Metamorphosis*). I settled on the one I was currently reading, *The Cider House Rules*, having always been a particular fan of how sexually instructive John Irving was, and also approving heartily of the book's prochoice message. An odd trade, yes, but Dylan Gellner agreed: I'd read "real" Kafka; he'd read Irving.

"We can compare notes," he said.

Dylan Gellner burned through *The Cider House Rules*, unimpressed, in a day; I chipped away at *The Trial* for two weeks. I was gripped at first—I mean, Josef K., a man *taken from his bed and arrested*, seemingly for no reason! By two guys who are definitely not cops! And then sent to work for the day, like nothing was really amiss! And then he gets summoned to his first hearing, and instead of being in a proper courtroom, it's in this squalid tenement building full of detritus and grime and way too many residents! And then, when he finally finds the courtroom (by *accident*), they've been expecting him, and the place is packed to the rafters—literally, guys are stuffed into this tiny balcony and have brought cushions to place between their heads and the ceiling—and in the anteroom the "law books" are actually full of amateur porn, and shit just keeps getting weirder.

The problem was that between the interrogation-in-a-filthy-flophouse scene and the climax—where K. gets summoned to a cathedral and a priest tells him his case is doomed—there are some pretty interminable chapters about a lawyer who won't allow himself to be fired and a painter who specializes in heavy-handed symbolism. (The painter has depicted the Goddesses of Justice, Victory, and the Hunt as one being. Yes, I get it, we all get it, the poor schmuck never had a *chance*.)

Now, if you *know* to read Kafka as a bone-dry humorist, those chapters are actually the best part of the book, but if you don't yet, because you are a seventeen-year-old whose primary interests are writing knockoff Dave Barry columns and watching *Reality Bites*, it is possible they might come across as a little bit boring. But this is something you might not be particularly eager to tell Dylan Gellner.

"So," said Dylan Gellner as he slid into a seat across from me in the library during our free period. "Did you finish *The Trial* yet? It's taking you forever."

"It's a hard book! The Lawyer-Manufacturer-Whatever chapter was . . . well, a little boring."

"I didn't think it was boring. I thought it was gripping the whole way through."

"Well, I liked the 'before the Law' thing," I said, referring to the cathedral scene (and thus telling the actual truth).

What I didn't know at the time was that "Before the Law" is also a stand-alone story, a parable really, a form for which Kafka is famous. Technically, it's a parable that has no answer or moral, for which Kafka is most famous of all. All I knew at the time was that the story seemed profoundly unfair. A man shows up from "the country" to get access to some mysterious Law. But "before the Law stands a Doorkeeper"—specifically, a scraggly-bearded, mean-ass jerk, who just keeps telling the man he can't go through. But the worst part is that it's not like the Doorkeeper says, *You can't go through ever; go home.* No; he just keeps saying, "It's possible, but not now." For *years.* Until the guy dies.

"I especially liked this part," I said to Dylan Gellner, and then I read aloud:

> *Given that the door to the law stands open, as always, and the doorkeeper stands beside it, the man bends over a bit to see through it, to the inside. As the door-keeper notices this he laughs, and says: "If it tempts you so much, go ahead and try to get in, despite my*

prohibition. Know this, though: I'm powerful. And I'm only the lowest of the doorkeepers. But from room to room stand doorkeepers, each more powerful than the last. Just one glimpse of the third and I can't even handle it myself."

"That's a very good part," agreed Dylan Gellner.

"But then the man from the country just keeps waiting there, like, bribing the Doorkeeper with all of his shit, just waiting year after year, even though it's completely obvious that he's never going to get in. I mean, like, why doesn't he just go home?"

"Well," said Dylan Gellner, "sometimes people want the impossible precisely because it's impossible." He cocked his head a little to the right and held eye contact.

"Yeah, well, it's pretty rough when the man from the country is about to die and he asks the Doorkeeper, 'Why hasn't anyone else come and tried to get in here?' and the Doorkeeper is like: 'THIS DOOR WAS JUST FOR YOU. NOW I'M GOING TO SHUT IT.'"

"Yep," said Dylan Gellner.

I'd only skimmed the pages between the Doorkeeper parable and the end, when the two random guys come grab K. (Note: these are *not* the random guys that arrested him; that would make too much sense; those guys do, however, show up toward the middle of the book, in a supply closet at K.'s bank, getting whipped by a court-appointed flogger.) The guys drag K. into the requisite dark alley and knife him in the gut, and his last words are "Like a dog!" But those *aren't* Kafka's last words in the story—*these* are: "as if the shame of it would outlive him." *That* part I definitely got. That part I remembered.

But what I'd skipped over—possibly the most important part of the whole book, a part that not even Dylan Gellner saw fit to explicate—was the part where the Priest and K. spend like fourteen pages arguing over what "Before the Law" is really about, like a couple of goatee-sporting poseurs in a graduate seminar. K. thinks the Doorkeeper lied to the man by giving him hope that he could *maybe* be let in, that he deceived the man by creating a door just for him and then not letting him through it; the Priest insists that the door was created for the sole purpose of keeping that particular man out (and for telling him "maybe" for all those years, which was definitely a dick move). And then the Priest says: "Understanding something and misunderstanding the same thing are not mutually exclusive."

I wish I'd comprehended that line that first time through *The Trial*. It might have led to some better life choices. But on that day in the library, my reverence for "Before the Law" was exhausted and all I could offer was deflection.

"Hey, did you like *Reality Bites*?" I asked, given that it was the fully unironic blueprint for my envisioned postcollegiate existence. (Except in my version, Winona Ryder pushes her goddamned hair out of her face and sucks it up at her job so she doesn't get fired, because even at seventeen I was a hopeless square.)

"It was all right."

"I liked when Ben Stiller was like, 'I'm a nonpracticing Jew,' and Winona was like, 'Well I'm a nonpracticing virgin.' And I was like—wow, I'm both of those things!" (Did you catch that, Dylan Gellner? I've had *sex*.)

"So? So am I," said Dylan Gellner, which as far as I was concerned was about as close to a direct proposition as a socially maladapted eighteen-year-old genius could muster. Once I realized that somebody else had had sex with Dylan Gellner—no doubt the worldly older nerd, Margaret O'Grady—his 1450 translated directly in my mind, as SAT scores so often do, into virility.

Dylan Gellner had now officially progressed from disembodied formidable mind to actual human body that I might or might not have wanted smashed up against mine. And so we joined the generations of epic literary romances that preceded us, and began exchanging stories we wrote and critiquing them via that cherished school of literary theory known as "passing notes between classes." I soon learned that Franz Kafka romanced numerous women through letters—and, later still, when I read his guarded missives to Felice Bauer and his substantially more passionate correspondence with Milena Jesenská, I realized why. Every word of Kafka's correspondence oozes two things simultaneously: the confession that the recipient alone was now in direct connection with an impossibly pensive, enigmatic soul with unplumbable depths; and, of course, longing. Shit-tons of longing.

After two or three notes from Dylan Gellner—in which, for example, he revealed that he was "essentially born when [he] read [Hermann Hesse's] *Steppenwolf*," or he contemplated the thin divide between insanity and genius, the latter best exemplified in culture by both *Mrs. Dalloway*'s Septimus and Pinky from the cartoon *Pinky and the Brain*—it seemed I was, to my delight and not insubstantial arousal, the chosen recipient of Dylan Gellner's rare-to-impossible decision to open up *his* unplumbable depths. After about a week of this, and bearing the nearly impossible weight of sexual tension, I found myself simultaneously infatuated with Dylan Gellner *and* Franz Kafka—Kafka the person, I mean, the guy who wrote thousands of pages of deep, pained, lonely diaries and love letters, not merely the author of *The Metamorphosis*. I should also probably mention that I found Franz Kafka a somewhat arresting-looking young man, in possession of a shock of thick, wavy black hair and two massive dark eyes that shone like ebony marbles. There was, as Wittgenstein might say, a *slight* family resemblance. All right, fine, Dylan Gellner was the spitting goddamned image of a young Kafka, and he had to have known it (I assume part of getting a 1450 on the SAT involves being observant).

Kafka wrote in one of his many letters that "a book should be the ax for the frozen sea within us." And Dylan Gellner, simply by taking an intellectual interest in me and treating me like an equal—someone worth debating, and challenging, and pushing past her heretofore very comfortable limits—had already axed my frozen sea to bits. Now I was primed to return the favor. But time, it seemed, was running out. "Life is astoundingly short," cautioned Kafka in his parable "The Next Village" (which Dylan Gellner quoted in a note passed off between classes). "Now in my memory everything is so pushed together that I cannot imagine why a man would want to take a journey to the next village, without the fear that—aside from accidents—the span of a normal, healthy life is far from adequate for such a ride." Despite my lackluster verbal skills, I was making an A in AP Lit at this point, so I was *pretty sure* I understood the subtext here.

Only problem was, there were two primary obstacles in the way of everlasting love with Dylan Gellner. The first was Travis, you know, *my boyfriend,* who had become as interested in smoking weed as he had become uninterested in talking about books. (I guess once you've gotten into MIT, you have no worthy intellectual challenges left; I wouldn't know.) One night, the two of us had been lolling on my Stanford-bound friend Samantha's couch. I began expounding upon my latest assignment for AP Lit, *The Birth of Tragedy,* the first Nietzsche I'd ever read and now officially the most interesting and important book in the universe. I'd gotten about two minutes into a breathless (and, likely, incorrect) exegesis of the Apollonian realm before Travis cut me off: "I *really,*" he exhaled, "don't want to talk about school right now."

I excused myself to go stare at my pupils in the bathroom, and wished that Dylan Gellner was there at this no-parents-home Christmas-break pot party, instead of reading Hegel by himself in his bedroom, or hurtling down mountains preppily with his ski buddies, or whatever Dylan Gellner did in his recreational time. Dylan Gellner would have some things to say about the Apollonian realm. Dylan Gellner would understand what a tremendous insult it was to describe talking about Nietzsche as talking about *school.*

So, back at school, I started inviting Dylan Gellner to hang out with my friends. And that is how Travis and I found ourselves giving Dylan Gellner a ride home one evening before dinner (I'd offered on Travis's behalf; I didn't have my own car).

"Do you guys want to come in and hang out for a bit?" asked Dylan Gellner.

"Uh," said Travis, at the same time I said, *"Definitely."*

We nodded hello to the elder Gellners, a tenured economics professor at the university and an artist, before traipsing down the stairs to Dylan Gellner's basement-level room—which somehow still had enough windows to catch the final extinguishing of the early-spring Oregon light, a feature of many vertiginous Eugene houses built onto the sides of steep hills, where the street entrance is actually the top floor.

"What are these?" I asked, reaching to pick up some suspicious-looking obelisks that stood in formation under a Homer Simpson poster.

"Those are polished rocks," he said, snatching one away from me, "and some of them are *fragile*."

"All right, then what are these?"

"These are my Eastern philosophy books. This is the *I Ching*, and it comes with a bunch of bamboo sticks, and you do a meditation ritual with it."

"Wow," I said. "That sounds fascinating. Can I try?"

"No."

Travis sat on Dylan Gellner's twin bed and stared out the window. He had, at this point in our epic eight-month relationship, both run out of interesting things to say to me and lost interest in the things I had to say to him (which, in his defense, were mostly about either Nietzsche or my college applications), but like any seventeen-year-old high-school boy he still recognized and honored that green-eyed demon. As we left Dylan Gellner's house, I remarked with a forced casual tone, "Boy, Dylan's *weird*."

"Nah, I don't think so," shrugged Travis—not because of Dylan Gellner's lack-of-weirdness (because he *was* weird), but because he no longer wanted to talk about Dylan Gellner at all.

But I'd already made up my mind. That night, I composed a fervent epistle full of Blues Traveler lyrics and drug references, and the next day at school, I pulled Travis aside during lunch and asked him to take a walk with me so that we could talk. He tried not to look too excited.

"I think," I said, as I handed him the note, "that we should break up."

"Oh, thank *God*," he said. "I've been wanting to for weeks, but after you didn't get into Brown Early Decision I figured you were too fragile to handle it."

"Oh, I can handle it."

We hugged and broke the news to our mutual friends, and then to our parents, who were all markedly more upset than we were. "I really liked Travis," said Sharon to Travis's mom, Phyllis, when they had a serendipitous run-in at Sundance, the health-food store down the street. "I *miss* Rebecca," said Phyllis, a middle-school sex education teacher who was a little bit *too* supportive about the circumstances surrounding her son's entry into manhood. ("I know you and Rebecca are planning to have sex while I'm out of town, so here is a variety pack of condoms. Don't use my bed!") I, meanwhile, had played up my heartbreak as high as the scale could possibly go, for the sole purpose of engineering Dylan Gellner as tear-stained confidant, an excuse for numerous earnest hand-pats and drawn-out hugs where I could again breathe in the intoxicating tea-scent of his hair and clothes.

There was only one problem left: Lisa, she of the pillowy lips and bedroom eyes, the Jolene to my Dolly Parton, except I didn't have any boobs. For she had broken up with Travis's friend Horacio, a Portuguese immigrant who was the undisputed Jim Morrison of South Eugene High. As a result, Lisa carried about her an aura of desirability I could never even begin to affect. Plus, she was much prettier than me, if I didn't mention. So not only was the school's most famous romance kaput, one of its certified *finest* girls was now a free agent.

And she'd been there the whole time: through the entire AP Civics Socialist Coup; every day in the library during free period—

crossing and uncrossing those godforsaken gams—during all the literary "discussions" that always devolved into bullshitting about when Mr. Rasmussen was actually going to crack. She'd been there, right next to me, and she was into Dylan Gellner, too. I, despite being (according to me) Dylan Gellner's long-lost intellectual soul mate, was way outgunned. There was no time to even pretend to be sad about Travis anymore. "The Next Village"! Life is astoundingly short! Go!

I made my move, need it even be said, in a note—the epistolary masterpiece of my short life, composed in the library while I was wearing my new certified-best outfit: black crushed-velvet leggings and a massive olive-green T-shirt printed with an ankh, with the neck cut out.

"I have *intense* feelings for you," I confessed, "more intense than I have ever had for anyone, least of all Travis, whose relationship with me was unofficially over long before we broke up." I knew Lisa liked him, I continued—but did she *really* like who he *really* was, or did she simply appreciate his attention, after losing Horacio's? Did *she* read his stories? Was *she* willing to enter into a place, as per *Steppenwolf* (which I had now of course read, highlighted, and annotated), meant "for madmen only"? *I* was. Before I could think better of it, I unloaded my confession unto Dylan Gellner's unsuspecting mitts, and then sat through a tortured session of AP Lit and half a tortured free period, in which I read the same incomprehensible page of *Lucky Jim* over and over again and wondered why it was supposed to be funny.

Finally, a shadow fell across my cubicle, along with a faint whiff of Earl Grey. I scarcely had time to wonder if a person's ears could actually explode from the sound of the blood rushing in them before Dylan Gellner solemnly placed a neatly folded response onto the corner of the table. His face was inscrutable, and he walked away before I could start to read.

Here was the deal. Dylan Gellner vowed to cease all flirtation with Lisa, having been only *briefly* led astray by such shallow qualities as beauty, charm, niceness, humor, and general human appeal. However, he also declared it "much too soon" to embark upon any sort of nonplatonic relationship with *another girl,* whom he pointedly didn't mention by name, who was sensitive and intelligent, but who needed "time without a boyfriend—*not* without friends." I read that noble dismissal as a full-throated endorsement of our obvious destiny. To this day I don't know how Dylan Gellner actually felt about me—but I do know that despite his highly cultivated sense of self-discipline (he woke up every morning two hours before school to read and do math for his own enrichment), he was also an eighteen-year-old boy. The spirit might resist, but the flesh would relent. I just had to time it right.

"Yes," I agreed after I tracked him down in the cafeteria. "You're right. Too soon. I'm sorry. Friends?"

"Friends."

But look, friends can *hang out* after school—especially in a group, where one friend is decidedly colder to another friend he had only recently been flirting with and decidedly warmer to a third friend, for no reason at all. And friends can drive each other home from hanging out. I mean, friends do that all the time.

At six fifteen in the evening, two and a half days after I stomped into mock-trial practice awash in crocodile tears for the demise of my union with Travis, Dylan Gellner pulled up in front of my parents' house and killed the engine of his gray 1985 Saab, in which I sat in the passenger seat. He removed the glasses he wore only to drive and placed them, folded, onto the dashboard. I was thinking: *Life is astoundingly short, motherfuckers!* I was also thinking that you don't take your glasses off *not* to kiss someone.

"So," I said. "Rebecca is duly confused about what to do." We'd developed an inside joke over the last thirty-six hours. And yes, it was the most obnoxious affectation possible: a semi-ironic use of the third person when talking about ourselves.

Dylan Gellner put his hands on his knees and pressed them. "Dylan would like to kiss Rebecca, but it's too soon."

"Much too soon," I said.

"I know."

And then somehow Dylan Gellner's face was in my face, or perhaps my face was in his. He tasted, unsurprisingly, like Earl Grey tea.

By the next day, a full seventy-two hours after the inauspicious conclusion of my relationship with Travis, Dylan Gellner and I were officially together. Lisa wasn't talking to me (I had, after all, broken the unspoken pact between all teenage girls that once a boy is "claimed," no true friend shall interfere), and Travis was, to my surprise, also not talking to me. He was over being with me, but not ready for me to be over being with him, a trait totally uncommon to mankind.

"Is there a fucking *statute of limitations* for mourning a relationship when the person you break up with refers to you as an impossible clinger he's continued to date out of pity?" I spat at Samantha over the phone.

"I don't know, Rebecca. How would you feel if Travis started dating, like, *Lisa, yesterday?*"

"That would never happen because Travis is best friends with Horacio."

"Ugh, you know that's not the point. What if he started dating me?"

"Ooh, do you like him? Why didn't you tell me before?"

"You are being impossible right now."

"Maybe, but do you know who *doesn't* think I'm impossible? *My new boyfriend* Dylan Gellner, who said I was *beautiful* today. Or, you know, he passed me a note with a quote from an INXS song about a beautiful girl."

"I'm hanging up now."

Samantha's disapproval didn't register through my thick haze of don't-give-a-fuck, because Dylan Gellner and I had just spent what I confidently deemed the most intellectually and emotionally significant afternoon of my life (possibly *anyone's* life), sitting on top of his navy-blue plaid bedspread. It was our first time alone in his room since we had made out in his car, and to celebrate, he brought down his well-thumbed Schocken edition of Kafka's *The Complete Stories*. He opened it wordlessly to the parable "Resolutions" and indicated that I should read it in its entirety, which I did:

> To lift yourself out of a miserable mood should be easy, even if you have to do it by sheer strength of will. I rise from my armchair, run around the table, make my head and throat move, bring fire into my eyes, flex the muscles around them. Work against every feeling—greet A. heartily when he comes by, tolerate B. amiably in my room, force down everything said at C.'s in long draughts, despite the pain and effort it causes me.
>
> But even then, with every mistake—and you can't

avoid them—the whole thing, easy and difficult alike, comes to a stop, and I must shrink back into my own circle again.

Thus the best advice is to take it all, to make yourself an inert mass, to feel as if you've been carried away, not to let yourself be lured into taking a single unnecessary step, to look at others with the gaze of an animal, to feel no peace—in short, to take whatever ghostly life remains in you and choke it back down with your own hand—that is, to enlarge the final peace of the grave and let nothing outside that remain.

A characteristic gesture in such a mood is the running of the little finger over the eyebrows.

What the fuck was this supposed to mean?

Interpretation A: Dylan Gellner was so brilliant and so pained, so trapped inside his own head, that he could not relate to a single other human being—how could he, when he scarcely felt human himself? Until, that is, *yours fucking truly.*

Interpretation B: Dylan Gellner was going to have some issues as a boyfriend.

But, as someone very wise (or at any rate very terrifying) once said, correctly understanding something and misunderstanding the same thing aren't mutually exclusive. And anyway, who had time for minutiae when Dylan Gellner's skin smelled like tea and sugar, and he had actual real hair on his chest, like a grown-up man?

"You remember Dylan Gellner, Mom." I'd poked my head into her study later that night to interrupt her as she prepped a lecture.

"I do?"

"You know, the guy who got a 1450 on his SAT and admired your Hermann Hesse collection."

"Oh, him."

"Anyway, he's my boyfriend now."

"Great," she said, not looking up from the copy of *Frankenstein* she was mauling with her bright green pen.

"I'm glad you're happy for me, you know? Travis is so pissed. But, like, he didn't care when we broke up! What does he want me to do, become a nun and make him a shrine?"

"Wait, what?" she asked. "I wasn't paying attention."

Things moved so fast that there wasn't time to explain the particulars to my mom—not that I would have anyway. My parents and I kept our discussions of my burgeoning sexuality on a need-to-know basis, meaning they probably knew everything, but I needed them to pretend they didn't. David Schuman, Ph.D., J.D., has a special gesture he makes, where he places both hands above his head in the shape of a sloped roof; the "hand house" is deployed during any discussions of tampons, cesarean sections, BDSM safe-word rules, and *especially* teen sexuality, which, as a teen, I would have rather impaled myself on one of my mom's infernal green pens than discuss anyway. Sharon Schuman, Ph.D., meanwhile, was so palpably uncomfortable during any talk about My Changing Body during puberty that, simply so that I would not die of awkwardness, I shut her out around age thirteen and relied on the Eugene 4J School District's comprehensive sex education curriculum to fill in the missing pieces. (This is probably why, at sixteen years old, I was still under the impression that the man finishes immediately upon entering the woman and then they wake up ten hours later wondering what happened, like in *Top Gun*.) Anyway, my parents had neither concern nor occasion to know how fast things were moving with Dylan Gellner. (I'd been taught about affirmative consent in sex ed, so I asked: "Do you want to have sex?" and although the answer was as curt as it had been to my request about the *I Ching,* it was in the affirmative.)

For a fleeting two months that I'm sure he quickly forgot thereafter, Dylan Gellner's previous ambivalence about taking on a relationship with someone openly obsessed with him was eclipsed by the oxytocin high of intercourse. Thanks to the hormones that conquered his intellect and common sense, he was, for the better part of the spring of 1994, obsessed with me back. Poems were composed, full of heavy-handed symbolism: Dylan Gellner was an island; I was a bridge that led either to it or from it, I wasn't sure (understanding and misunderstanding the same thing, etc.). Mixtapes were mixed, bequeathed, and played until they warped: Nine Inch Nails' "Something I Can Never Have"; Alice in Chains' "Man in a Box," Duran Duran's "Come Undone," Pearl Jam's "Black." Characteristically succinct sessions of coitus were followed by reverent viewings of *Animaniacs.*

When I wasn't rolling around on Dylan Gellner's polyester-covered bed, or politely turning down his mom's invitation to dinner as I scurried out through her kitchen with my shirt inside-out, I was getting serious with his literary doppelgänger. *The Trial* I was still lukewarm about, but through it, and "Before the Law" especially, I'd learned about Kafka's scores of haunting, unforgettable parables—just the right length for someone like me, equal parts very serious intellectual and person with the attention span of the first two verses of "Gin and Juice." I rushed through my AP Lit assignments so that I could savor as many of those parables as possible. I held my breath through "Bachelor's Unhappiness," which is about exactly what it sounds like, and ends with the allegedly comforting reminder from the nameless narrator that at least he still has a forehead to smack with his hand. I spent days in an existential funk about "The Bridge," the story of a man who stretches himself across a ravine and then tries to turn around to see who has walked halfway across him and then jumped up and down on his back. ("A bridge to turn around!" the narrator chides himself, before falling down onto the jagged rocks below.) The aching loneliness, the questions with no answers—these little stories climbed into my deepest speechless heart (as Rilke would say) and gave it voice.

Someday, I promised myself, I was going to read all of those stories, plus everything else Kafka ever wrote, in the language he wrote in: German. I knew by that point that Kafka had lived his whole life in Prague, which I still thought of as in Czechoslovakia even though it was the newly formed Czech Republic—and I knew they spoke Czech in Prague, but Kafka wrote in German because of something to do with the Austro-Hungarian Empire. (I had skipped AP European History.)

"You know, I like *other authors*, too," said Dylan Gellner on a glorious late-May afternoon we were spending inside watching *Pinky and the Brain*. I'd just brought up "The Bridge" again, but Dylan Gellner had moved on to *Finnegans Wake*, even though James Joyce was Irish and looked nothing like him, and thus held little interest for me. I crossed my arms and stared disconsolately out the window; obviously the subtext here was that if I had a wider array of literary interests, I probably wouldn't have just gotten rejected from five out of the six elite liberal arts colleges to which I'd applied after Brown spurned me (the sixth having yet to respond). If only I'd read fucking *Finnegans Wake* of my own volition as a high-school student, I'd probably have gotten into precious CalTech, where Dylan Gellner was headed in the fall.

"I'm late for the newspaper," I said, rising from his rec-room floor and making sure my jeans were zipped before I traipsed by his mother upstairs.

After graduation, Dylan Gellner—who, since we no longer had to see each other at school every day, had been steadfastly avoiding me under the guise of looking for a summer job—ghosted on a date to go windsurfing with his buddies, which of course is what preppy ski guys do in the summer. When at last I managed to catch him on the phone, he beckoned me over to his house, where for the first time he did not lead me downstairs to his room. Instead, he sat me on the living-room couch, took a deep breath, and said: "Look, we're leaving for college at the end of the summer anyway, and it's useless to bide time. I like you fine, but this just isn't working for me anymore."

I don't know what I'd been expecting. We hadn't had a decent conversation in weeks (well, two weeks; our whole relationship had lasted three months to the day). We'd never discussed a long-distance relationship in college, and I was, to be honest, intrigued by the potential angst-ridden Kafka fans that awaited at Vassar, a.k.a. College #6, the single institution of higher learning that had deigned to accept me into its class of 1998. But I'd pictured a summer of Sisyphus and sex-filled camping trips before a tearful, lovelorn, and mutual farewell sometime in mid-August. Dylan Gellner was still the only person who had ever really understood how I felt about reading and writing, about being different (*considerably* deeper and more profound, *obviously*) than my peers—who had actually felt the same way. I was under the impression that even if we stopped seeing each other, we'd always feel that way together, and never really stop loving each other. Instead, Dylan Gellner solemnly informed me that he'd be needing the rest of the summer to himself to practice differential geometry, and so I shouldn't call him or talk to him (he would allow one farewell meeting in the park, but *he'd* call *me*). On the way home, I briefly considered swerving off his winding street into one of the adjacent ravines.

Getting dumped by Dylan Gellner was the literal worst thing that had literally ever happened to me and so there was no hiding it from David and Sharon Schuman. As I sat in the TV room, unable to tear myself away from *Animaniacs*—I knew Dylan Gellner would be watching it, too, and he wouldn't be able to stop us from having one last shared experience—with tears splattering onto the lap of my stonewashed jean shorts, I saw my dad's lithe Semitic form fill the doorway and then shuffle to the couch, where he sat down beside me.

"Hey, Bek," he said. "I heard you and, um, Dylan? I heard you broke up."

I sniffled.

"I remember when my girlfriend in college broke up with me." Sniffle.

"I got really drunk. God, I was such an asshole." He patted me three quick times on the thigh and disappeared back into his study.

I moped through days of work at my summer job stuffing envelopes for one of my mom's friend's charities, and I moped through composing my final local-newspaper columns before leaving for college (each of which had taken an un-Barryesque melancholy turn and contained at least three veiled references to the demise of my relationship). I moped through every afternoon, sprawled on my back in the middle of my parents' long carpeted hallway, staring balefully at the ceiling.

One day in mid-July, my mom leaned over me and asked: "If you could be anywhere, anywhere at all, where would you be?"

"Dead."

"Oh, come on."

"Okay, then, camping by myself."

She bought me a brand-new tent and let me use the car for the weekend. I forgot my Therm-a-Rest pad; my stove leaked and I set a picnic table on fire; I tried to take a hike, but ended up walking down a highway alone under the blazing hot sun, and I got chauffeured back to my campsite by a mom in a minivan who assured me that God had a plan for me. (Her giving a ride to a teenage drifter that day probably counted as her Christian charity for all of 1994.)

The only person I wanted to hang out with in the festering cesspool of my heartbreak was Franz Kafka. And, unsurprisingly, he was an even worse influence than my dad. Case in point #1: I stopped eating, inspired by the title character in the short story "A Hunger Artist," about a circus performer who sits in a cage and starves himself for sport in front of an audience. I was actually thin for the first time in my life—but, as with the Hunger Artist, it took no effort, so I didn't care. *If only the spectators knew that fasting was the easiest thing in the world,* thinks the Hunger Artist, before departing a world that doesn't appreciate him, only to be replaced after his death by a slavering young panther. The Hunger Artist's problem, I realized, was not that—in his own unreliable words—he'd never found the food he liked. It was probably just that he'd been dumped.

Case in point #2: Aside from *The Metamorphosis,* Kafka is primarily known for the strange request he made of his friend Max Brod upon his demise, of tuberculosis, at age forty, that all of his unpublished writing be destroyed. (Brod famously disobeyed.) Not to be outdone, seventy years later almost to the day, I wrote a journal entry that contained only the sentence "Pain is the lasting part of love"—and then I put that journal in the family charcoal barbecue and set it on fire.

As if the shame of it would outlive me.

2.

Sprachgefühl

n. knack for language, from speech and feeling.

ex. When learning German to fluency, *Sprachgefühl* is a viable substitution for effort.

To be honest, Dylan Gellner shoulders only part of the blame for my poor life choices. (I, of course, continue to be blameless.) The rest goes to my freshman German literature professor at Vassar, James Martin. (Not to me.) I loathed Professor Martin on the first day of class, because his introductory lecture was about the expressive power of human language—and he was teaching a course on modern German literature in translation, which meant Kafka, which meant he didn't know what the fuck he was talking about, since *everyone knew* Kafka's main problem was that he couldn't talk about what he needed to talk about.

It turns out, unsurprisingly, that I was the one who didn't know what the fuck I was talking about, and Professor Martin's view on the Austrian language crisis was quite a bit more nuanced than mine—truly shocking, given that he had tenure and a Ph.D. from

Princeton, and I had a 5 on the AP Literature exam and three months' worth of twin-bed intercourse with Eugene, Oregon's foremost underage literary critic. Professor Martin was, it turns out, the best literature professor I have ever had, before or since. It is, in fact, a continuing testament to his exegetic might that he enamored me of Thomas Mann, even though Mann is a Jet to Kafka's Shark, a Rolling Stone to his Beatle, a stick of deodorant to his patchouli. German literary scholars like *either* Thomas Mann or Franz Kafka, is what I'm saying, but thanks to Professor Martin's magisterial ability to pinpoint exactly the most transcendent part of every piece of literature written in the German language between the years of 1890 and 1960, I walked out of his course liking both.

My favorite Mann story was *Death in Venice,* a novella about a curious fellow named Gustav von Aschenbach, a writer who goes on vacation to Venice during a cholera epidemic. While everyone around Aschenbach is keeling over, he spends his time pitying an old guy who's done himself up with makeup and hair dye, ostensibly to make himself look younger, but with a markedly grotesque effect instead—and then Aschenbach falls in love with a gorgeous young Polish boy named Tadzio (or Tadeusz in Polish), which is a play on *Tod,* the German word for "death."

"Every German understands that Tadzio is Death *immediately,*" explained Professor Martin in class, as he ran his hand over his stern-looking blond flattop. "Yet another reason to try to read all of this in the German."

Aschenbach never so much as talks to the boy, but love consumes him—here's a huge surprise: Thomas Mann was a closeted gay guy—and, fully obsessed with Tadzio's youth and beauty, he goes to the barbershop and gets himself done up like that pathetic old dude he mocked before. Wouldn't you know it, now Aschenbach *is himself* a pathetic old dude—and to seal his fate, so that his metaphorical reality matches his literal one, he succumbs to the sensual deliciousness of a carton of overripe strawberries, which obviously give him cholera.

When I wrote my first essay for Martin's class I got an A, which back in the dark ages of the mid-1990s was not the baseline grade of acceptability, and actually meant exceptional. (I should know, because I didn't get many after that.) On the back, Martin wrote that I'd made an "extremely fine" effort, "nuanced and rich," despite my clear misuse of the word *abhor* on multiple occasions. On the basis of this alone, I decided to be a German major midway through my first semester—despite knowing exactly that half-semester's worth of German, courtesy of Frau von der Haide, a wonderful émigré from Leipzig with a Dorothy Hamill bob, who assured us with a flip of her hand on the first day of class that no matter what anyone said, German was *leicht* ("easy").

This was an absolutely terrible idea that somebody should have talked me out of. My parents just shrugged ("It's not like there's an accounting major at Vassar anyway"), but the rest of my dad's side of the family—the Jewish side—was duly perplexed.

"A German major, huh?" asked my grandfather, during a winter-break visit to my extended family in Chicago, when I had a hard time concentrating due to the raging discomfort of my very first urinary tract infection, thanks to a stupid vanilla-flavored condom I'd gotten free from the health center and used, before it made us both burn and scream, with the curly-haired boy down the hall. "What made you want to choose that?"

My father's father had spent the better part of 1945 liberating concentration camps. "Well, it's just for the *literature*, Grandpa," I said. *"And,* did you know that pretty much every great German writer was a Jew? It's true. Plus, Kafka was technically Czech. Or Austrian. Or Czechoslovak. Something not German."

"Well, I hope you enjoy it," he said. "I didn't really enjoy college. Mostly just something to get me into law school."

"What about playing football with President Ford?"

"That was all right, except I broke my nose twenty-seven times."

Back on campus, Professor Martin had been slightly more enthusiastic to learn about my poorly thought-out scholarly choices. "Hot damn!" he'd cried, and handed me one of his own pens to fill out the paperwork. "Wait," he said. "How much German have you taken?"

"Just 101," I said. "But ask Frau von der Haide—I'm the best one in there."

Martin sent me home with a brochure for the college's summer program in a German city called Münster, a placid and picturesque university town near the Dutch border, where there were almost as many bicycles as inhabitants. To spend the summer in Germany! To leave the U.S. for the first time, and without the Schumans to cramp my style! Since Oregon was about six thousand miles round-trip out of the way, I'd leave straight from school in late May—to go where the drinking age was eighteen, the very age I happened to be! And most important of all, I'd get some of that "language immersion" I'd been hearing about since I was a kid. "You pretty much *can't* learn a second language after about the age of seven," said Sharon Schuman, whose Ph.D. is not in linguistics. "But immersion is the next best thing." I was pretty sure *immersion* was code for *magic* and involved amassing total fluency in a matter of weeks with zero effort.

That is why, instead of reading simple German stories, or listening to German tapes, or studying irregular verb conjugations, I spent the days before my departure from Poughkeepsie packing up my dorm room and constructing a homemade travel journal from scratch—like a veritable angst-ridden MacGyver—out of a cardboard box, an old pillowcase, rubber cement, thirty sheets of leftover printer paper, and the sewing kit my mom had insisted I bring along to college in case any of my trousers of choice (men's wide-wale cords four sizes too big) sprung a leak. I decorated the cover with a curlicued EUROPE '95 and an artistically rendered ankh, before tucking it safely into my navy-blue JanSport backpack, right on top of my stupid pouch of Drum tobacco (I'd recently started smoking roll-your-own cigarettes, just like that excellent role model, John Travolta in *Pulp Fiction*), and my hulking "compact" German-English dictionary, which I'd won as a prize for being the year's top-achieving freshman.

After stuffing the contents of my incense-reeking dorm room into a storage trunk for the summer, I parted my fluorescent-yellow hair—recently shorn into a scraggly pixie and bleached in the dorm bathroom—and fastened it down with two little-girl's plastic barrettes. I lugged my bulging suitcases onto a Metro-North train to Grand Central, then a bus to JFK, where I disembarked breathlessly at the international terminal for the first time in my life. At the gate, I made out the silver-gray Peter Tork coif of Herr Neudorf, the jovial seventy-two-year-old from Bamberg who had been heading up the Münster program since shortly after the erection of the Berlin Wall.

"Oh, *Webecca!*" he said in his accent as thick as the Black Forest. "I can tell you've been up to NO good! NO good! I call your *muzzah*, and I tell her EVEWY-SINK! Come, come. *Evewy*-one else is *alweady awwived!*"

It turned out Herr Neudorf's charms were universal, for he'd secured for our group an out-of-use first-class lounge while we waited. He led me in and motioned for me to take my place in the circle of young people already seated on the floor. (You can always locate the group of American college students at any international gate in the world, for they will be the ones sitting in a circle on the floor.)

I recognized Anneke, the Dutch girl with the milky-white skin and ethereal smile who sat next to me in Frau von der Haide's class. I waved, and she scooted over to make room for me. "We're going to be roommates at the youth hostel in Cologne!" she said.

"Is it going to be weird for you to change planes in Amsterdam and not stop?" I asked.

"A little," she said, "but it's a great airport. You'll like Schiphol." She pronounced it *SCKGGGGCKHIP-pl,* which I surmised was the correct way to do so.

"German is going to be so easy for you," I said. "I mean, isn't it pretty much just Dutch but meaner?"

"That's a sweeping generalization, isn't it?" said the guy sitting on the other side of me, a petite but elegant-looking hippie leaning against an army duffel and a clarinet case. He'd been in Frau von der Haide's class, too, but he'd sat on the other side of the room.

"Oh, hey, Fernando," I said.

"You can call me Freddie," he said. "Frau von der Haide called me 'Fernando' on the first day of class, and it sounded so nice in her accent I never wanted to correct her." It was true; even the way she said *Schlumpf* (Smurf) sounded charming. (*Die Schlümpfe,* huge in Germany, was originally a Belgian cartoon, which in retrospect makes a tremendous amount of sense.)

Just then, another latecomer ambled in—a handsome Korean kid wearing a baseball cap that looked like it hadn't been washed since the 1986 Mets won the World Series. Freddie turned to greet him. "What's up, Justin?" he asked. "You ready for a valuable immersion experience in German language, history, literature, and culture?"

"I'm ready for a nap on the plane."

That wasn't a bad idea, of course—but who could indulge in such trivialities as *sleep* on her very first ride on a 747, where the towering blond flight attendants changed outfits in the middle of the night, and they served dinner and then breakfast, both of which were somewhat edible? If I napped, I might miss the free white wine, or a hot towel, or the end of *Disclosure,* the movie where Demi Moore sexually harasses Michael Douglas, which KLM Royal Dutch Airlines played in its uncensored entirety. By the time we disembarked on the other side of the Atlantic, I felt like my teeth were growing hair, and due to sheer exhaustion I almost keeled over and fell out of my seat into the aisle of the much smaller plane that flew us from Amsterdam to Düsseldorf, but I could sleep for all of 1996. Now was the time to see if I could do some of that magic "immersion" and get myself fluent before the bus docked in Cologne, our first stop in the whirlwind two-week bus tour that was to serve as a general introduction to all things Teutonic.

I mean, I'd *definitely* been practicing my German. Or at any rate, I'd continued to be the best student in my German 101 class. Every test, quiz, and one-page "mini-essay" (about such prescient, intellectual topics as whether I owned a cassette player—I *did!*) had come back scrawled with As. There had never been a class-time exercise that I had not been able to master. So although I had never so much as read a single sentence of Goethe, Mann, or even the great unassailable Kafka in the original—nor had I ever had a single conversation with a German, other than the beloved and overly enunciative Frau von der Haide—as far as I was concerned, I was pretty much a native speaker, especially given that anything I didn't already know I would acquire through magic.

This is not what happened. What happened is that I spent the next two weeks speaking very loud English on the bus and making a general *Arsch* out of myself on the few occasions I had to speak to an actual German. This wasn't magic at all. It was, like, *hard!* The thing is, Frau von der Haide was still right. German's not a categorically difficult language. (Really, check the five-point scale of difficult languages for native speakers of English. Spanish and French are ones; German ranks a two; the fives include Mandarin, Arabic, and Korean.) And yet, German's ease comparative to Farsi and Uzbek (both fours) notwithstanding, the dulcet vernacular of Nietzsche and Wagner has the undeniable characteristic of sounding mean and nasty to the untrained ear, and of requiring a near-total grasp of some voluminous grammar conventions to communicate even simple concepts. This can make it seem hard when everyone around you is talking at Autobahn speed, and you have no idea what they're saying, but it sounds like they might be ordering you to murder a kitten, *immediately.*

To say in German something as banal as "I live in the red house," you have to use the dative case, which gives special endings to the words for "the" (*das* becomes *dem*) and "red" (*rot* becomes *roten*, unless you take away the "the," in which case it becomes *rotem*, which in and of itself is enough to send most reasonable English-speakers screaming away, *rot* in the face). If you use the wrong word ending, the person you're addressing may think that a red house lives in you, or that you are trying to *be* a red house, or that you are pondering both your own existence and that of red houses in general. At the very least, it will be abundantly clear that you are suffering from some sort of acute intellectual malady, one that can only be cured by your interlocutor switching into heavily accented, questionably ordered English ("Are you not meaning that you instead to school will go?").

So instead of magic, this is what happened during my first week in Germany after one year's worth of study, all of which took place in a heavily controlled environment, requiring only the regurgitation of a finite set of (TOTALLY USELESS) vocabulary words, recited on cue and only after substantial inner-monologue rehearsal, all with the context of less-apt classmates fucking it up spectacularly to make me look like a genius by comparison. The first time I attempted to utter a full sentence to an actual German in her actual native land was on the day our group landed in Düsseldorf and then drove to Cologne. I needed to inform the tiny-spectacled receptionist at the Cologne Youth Hostel—where the door handles looked like toilet flushes and the toilet flushes looked like door handles; where the first floor was actually the second floor and sixteen-year-olds could get beer at reception—that my fold-up bunk bed was stuck in its "up" position, and thus locked to the wall.

I broke out in a cold sweat despite the day's heavy, almost tropical warmth (air-conditioning, or *Klimaanlage,* is dismissed by most Germans as an indiscriminate typhus factory). I shuffled down the stairs and repeated in my head, over and over, the most accurate description of my situation that I could muster: *Mein Bett ist geschlossen,* a sentence that literally means "my bed is closed," but whose erroneous use of "is," rather than the (INCOMPREHENSIBLE)

German passive voice, conveys a more permanent, existential, perhaps *sensual* state, rather than the bed's actual state of being temporarily lodged vertically; and, furthermore, whose use of "my" conveys one's permanent, actually owned bed, rather than one's transient accommodations in a youth hostel. A more accurate rendering of the state of affairs would have been *Das Bett in Zimmer 405 geht nicht auf* ("The bed in room 405 won't open"), which at the time I could not have come up with if I'd had two months. So, "my bed is closed" would have to do, and I repeated it over and again in my head, in Frau von der Haide's effortless, melodic accent: *Mein Bett ist geschlossen, Mein Bett ist geschlossen, Mein Bett ist geschlossen.*

I tiptoed to the front desk, where the back of the receptionist's spiky blond head was currently turned to me as she made a harried intercom announcement in fluent French, for the benefit of the chain-smoking Francophone schoolchildren currently sharing the hostel with us.

The word for *excuse me* in German, *Entschuldigung* (literally, "apology"), is long and difficult enough that a native speaker can tell from its first syllable just what kind of rube she is dealing with—especially given that there exists some sort of physiological conspiracy in my throat in which it *knows,* instinctively, that I'm attempting to communicate in a foreign tongue and thus at *the exact moment* I attempt a word, fills with phlegm. So, despite—or perhaps because of—my intense staircase journey of rehearsal, what first came out to the German receptionist was *ENTSCHBLURG-HUNK,* followed by a coughing fit. (It did get her attention, and so was a successful utterance according to today's more progressive language-pedagogy approaches.) Throat half-cleared, I then managed to eke out *Mein Bett ist geschlossen,* heavily Americanized and utterly without context, which resulted in the first of what would, in my life, be hundreds—thousands—of quizzical German *what in the ever-loving fuck just happened here* looks.

Unlike the Germans I'd meet who would immediately and sanctimoniously switch to English without prompting, however, this receptionist was patient—knowing, as she did, that my group was at least trying, unlike those degenerate French *enfants*. So she nodded with increasing amounts of comprehension as I sputtered out the word *Wand* ("wall") and then made what I hoped was the universal hand gesture for verticality; she then managed to extract my room number and informed me that her colleague would be right on it. And, bless her spiky little soul, she did this all based on my effectively proclaiming to her, unprompted, that the bed I owned back at home was shut like a door.

So, while it was possible to be understood in German even if I didn't speak it well, not everyone was patient enough to allow that to happen. This is understandable, given that rather than a week's worth of magic, it takes years of protracted study and immersion to develop what the Germans Germanically call *Sprachgefühl*, or a "feeling" for what "belongs" to a certain linguistic situation— such as when a bed is actually yours, rather than simply located in a room in which you're staying. What's more, two seconds spent thinking about whether that bed is in motion toward the wall or stationary against it (and thus whether to use the dative case), and your conversation partner has (patient hostel receptionists aside) already gotten bored and started yelling at you for buttering your bread incorrectly.

Once the receptionist's colleague had been dispatched to unlock my bed, I resisted the urge to collapse into it and instead embarked on a series of wholly banal activities that, given that they were banal things happening *in Germany*, took on monumental significance: I boarded my first S-Bahn, short for *Schnellbahn*, or "fast train," the commuter rail that links the bucolic towns that surround almost every major German city with the center. (The *Jugendgästehaus Köln* was located, as most youth hostels are, far from anywhere anyone could get up to any sort of good trouble.) I learned the hard way that the doors of a German train do not open automatically at every stop; rather, you have to push the giant flashing button, one that says, coincidentally, PUSH HERE TO GET OUT. (Even in thwarting me, the Germans were unassailably efficient.)

I walked down my first certifiably old street ("Julius *Caesar* twod on these cobblestones!" said Herr Neudorf). I saw my first Gothic cathedral close up—the staggering Kölner Dom, which took over six hundred years to build, measures 134,000 square feet, and was pretty much the only part of Cologne left standing after the Allied bombing. I saw my first German street signs (the font, bold and sans-serif, was so *precise*!), my first German traffic light (so *stern*! No wonder Germans don't jaywalk), my first German trees (so *erect*!), my first German German people, from a safe distance away (*please don't say anything to me, please please please*). And, most important of all, I sat my corduroy-clad ass on a splintering wooden seat in my very first German *Biergarten*, and ordered and consumed my very first legal beer. Frau von der Haide had explained to us that every region in Germany has a local specialty, and Cologne's is the *Kölsch*, which Herr Neudorf took great pains to tell us was *klein, aber stark* ("small, but strong"). I didn't see why we needed a warning—just because I hadn't slept in thirty hours and was too chickenshit to order any food, and those teeny tiny "strong" beers cost two deutsche marks each, *which*, I couldn't help but notice, was actually less than it cost to buy a thimble-sized glass of room-temperature mineral water. Halfway through my second *Kölsch,* I chanced a look up at the sky and almost fell backward off the bench.

"*Vorsicht,* Webecca!" said Herr Neudorf. "*Klein, aber stark.*"

"The stars here!" I said. "They're brighter than they are at home. I swear they are."

"*Aber auf Deutsch,* Webecca!"

"*Die . . . Sterne? Hier?*"

"*Ja . . .*"

"*Sind . . .* um, SEHR, uh, *stark. Starker. Stärker?*"

"*Gut! Aber das ist das Bier, Webecca. Das Bier.* The beer is stwong as well!"

My inaugural entry into my artisanal travel journal that night, in overly careful penmanship that matched the affected prose:

> *25.05.95* [I'd already adopted the German backward dating system.]
>
> *Köln.*
>
> *This room is small and odd, but adequate. I am rooming with Anneke, who is a delight as always. I do believe the two of us will be great friends. Also befriended Freddie, the earnest Peruvian guy with the goatee from the other side of the room in v.d.H class, and Justin, who was supposed to graduate this year and is doing some experiment where he doesn't wash his hair for a month. Ordered beer in German; did passable job. May take a few more weeks before I am fluent, though.*
>
> *Freddie had to pee and so he went into a bar called*

Zippys, which turned out to have a clientele consisting
only of gay men over 60. Köln is center of German
gay culture, and Freddie could have gotten a lot of free
drinks, but he didn't want to give anyone the wrong
impression because he is straight; already making
moves on this very cute tiny little girl from another
college who speaks way better German than all of us;
didn't get her name.

   Tonight I saw the Dom. Latticework spires against
the darkening sky, lit up green. Bats flying around.
Understand, finally, why some people believe in God.

What I didn't commit to posterity was that so moved by the Dom's
sheer immensity and intricacy had I been that I laid out fifty pfen-
nigs for a votive candle—which, like the other thousands of Catholic pilgrims who come there to marvel and pray, I was supposed
to light for someone, but which instead I slipped into my backpack
as a very cheap souvenir, unsure whether that counted as a mortal
or venial sin.

   And then, religious contraband stowed safely in my JanSport,
I was off on a two-week crisscrossing expedition through the Federal Republic, employing what all ethnographers would agree is
the best form of cultural immersion: fourteen days sequestered on
a tour bus with a bunch of other Anglophones, taking heavily curated tours of churches and museums, given either in English or
in halting, gesticulation-heavy beginner's German. The first two
weeks in a new country are normally when you get out all of your
most significant cross-cultural faux pas, which then either devolve
into permanent faction or resolve themselves in mutual enrichment and understanding. There is, however, little opportunity for

culture clash when the new culture can't puncture the rarefied bubble of American eighteen-to-twenty-one-year-olds with similar interests, who dip in and out of tourist attractions at predictable intervals and never go anywhere without each other. *Here's a baroque monastery! Here's another one! Put on these special slippers so you don't blemish the five-hundred-year-old floorboards! This is a painting by Caspar David Friedrich! Martin Luther preached a sermon here! These two castles built on opposite sides of the Rhine were occupied by warring brothers who shot at each other all day long!* The bus tour was beautiful, and exciting, and provided a tremendous amount of enrichment, by which (as Dave Barry would say) I mean beer. But it also felt like watching 3-D television.

Sometimes we would get a peek of Germanness if we were staying far enough in the boonies to opt for a *Gasthof* (inn) instead of a youth hostel—the strange "double" beds that were made of two singles pushed together, with their massive feather pillows and their duvets folded down the middle instead of spread out; the showers next to the beds and toilets in the hallway; the staggering breakfast spreads of rolls, cheeses, cold cuts, and mounds of butter; the squat, unsmiling ladies who would walk around the table asking *Möchten Sie Kaffee oder Tee?* (*Kaffee.* My answer was always *Kaffee;* it, like the beer in Cologne, was small but potent.)

But no matter where we went, the specifics of the tour-bus culture meant that just about the only conversations I had with Germans were the brief, rehearsed *Mein-Bett-ist-geschlossen*–type exchanges that took place at restaurants and bars. The only way to go off-script was to tether myself to one of the German heritage speakers (people with German parents or grandparents) in the group, who spoke with the sort of idiosyncratic conversational

fluency that came from speaking a language at home but never taking classes in it. Our group's most charismatic heritage speaker
was a Bavarian kid named Henrik, who, about one week in, taught
me, Freddie, and Anneke how to say *eine Flasche Weißwein zum
Mitnehmen,* or "one bottle of white wine to go," which the proprietor of a quiet pub was all too happy to grant each of us, one at a
time, even so much as uncorking them so that we could take them
into an empty town square and down them under the low summer sky, giggling into the night, surrounded by empty bakeries
and butchers in half-timbered houses that looked like the Seven
Dwarfs' vacation homes.

"You guys," I said, two-thirds of my *Flasche* deep. "You guys.
You *guys.* What if the white wine in this village is infected with
some deadly disease, and that's why the guy at the *Kneipe* sold us
each a bottle for three marks fifty? And everybody knows it but
the tourists? And then all the tourists will start keeling over, and
there will be a really good-looking kid at our next hostel, and I'll
fall in love with him but never say anything to him, and then I'll
die of the wine disease, and I wear too much makeup and my hair
looks ridiculous?"

"Well, your hair does look ridiculous," said Freddie. "I've been
meaning to tell you since the airport. I liked it a lot better before."

"Tadzio," I said.

"What the fuck are you talking about, Schuman?" said Henrik.
"That doesn't even—whoa, *Katze,* dude!" A stray cat skittered
across the cobblestones and ducked behind one of the fake-looking
adorable buildings.

"Rebecca *really* likes *Death in Venice,*" explained Freddie.

"Venice?" said Henrik.

"Tadzio!" I cried, and took another swig of wine. Nobody understood me. Nobody would *ever* understand me, really. It was the most poetic loneliness. If only I'd had someone to share it with.

The cat yowled. Awash with longing—general longing, random pangs of specific longing for the early days of Dylan Gellner, and also for the affections of a person I hadn't met yet, somebody who would want to talk about *Death in Venice* at two in the morning in a tiny German village whose name I didn't know, over cheap German white wine consumed directly from the bottle in the out-of-doors—I grabbed one of Freddie's cigarettes. I lit it and took a massive pull of burnt filter fumes before I noticed I'd put it in my mouth backward. *"Tadzio!"*

The next morning, I almost missed the bus, and as I scrambled on, hair askew, green of face, pores reeking of vinegar, Herr Neudorf turned the tour-guide microphone up to its highest setting.

"OH, WEBECCAAAAAAAA," he said, as I attempted to open my window as wide as it would go and stick my head out like a dog. "I SEE YOU! I CALL YOUR MUZZAH! I CALL HER *WIGHT* NOW! Now, *meine Damen und Herren,* today we're going to see a wonderful old town that dates back to the *Mittelalter,* Rothenburg ob der Tauber. We go to a special medieval torture museum, where we see devices invented to torture women who were too loud! Speaking of which—*Webecca,* the things I will tell your *muzzah!"*

Rothenburg ob der Tauber is indeed an old-fashioned walled town, with old-German signage and old-German houses and old-German winding narrow lanes—which are accordingly crammed with modern-day international tourists with not an actual German in sight. It's arguably the least authentic of all Germany's "authentic" old-German attractions: in fact, a good 70 percent of the historical sites I shuffled through in my hungover haze were replicas, which Herr Neudorf pronounced *weplica,* erected out of the war's rubble, which he pronounced *wubble.* But it was there, of all places, that I had my first true encounter with German culture.

My white-wine-to-go hangover had just begun to abate when the group sat down to dinner at a rustic pub in a small village near Rothenburg. As an adornment to my beer, I—a vegetarian since the age of ten, much to the Schumans' annoyance—was brought the *vegetarische Speise* on offer: broccoli with melted cheese, on top of which had been sprinkled a generous portion of cubed ham. I was ready to remove each speck manually; growing up in an uncooperative carnivorous family, you embrace the pick-it-off method. But Layla—that was the tiny beautiful girl's name, the one from another college that Freddie had the hots for—in addition to being tiny and beautiful and good at German, was also a stricter *Vegetarierin,* and she was adamant: *"Es gibt aber Fleisch darauf!"* ("But there's meat on it!")

To which the astonished waitress replied: *"Das ist doch kein Fleisch—das ist Schinken!"* For emphasis, she repeated it in English: "Theht's not meat—it's hehm. *Hehm!"*

After a week of castles and churches, after a year of adjective endings and Thomas Mann, my first real and substantive German cultural learning experience was the discovery that until a unit of meat reaches a certain size, it counts as parsley.

That size, by the way, is the size of a *Wurst,* which in 1995 I described as "a cardiac-infarction-provoking mixture of gristle, innocent baby cows and the last place a hog's food visits before it leaves his body," thus making me loads of new friends on the bus. (I couldn't say anything besides *Ich bin vegetarisch* in German, which means "I am suitable for a vegetarian to eat.") The "actual meat" on offer for the normal people in the Münster group that night was *Knackwurst,* which gets its name ("cracking") because it swells during cooking, and then when you bite into it, it "cracks" and spooges sausage-juice all over you, which I guess is supposed to be a positive? I tried not to watch the carnage—and also tried not to be consumed with Aschenbachian longing for my dearly departed broccoli with cheese—as I tucked into the plate of mushy spaghetti and ketchup I was brought after Layla cowed the wait-ress. I was lucky, though—we were in Bavaria, and if our hosts had wanted to treat us to something really special, they would have made *Weißwurst,* or "white sausage," which is made from veal and fatty bacon, and so perishable that, so the saying goes, such a treat shouldn't live to hear the church bells ring at noon.

As the tour bus continued its zigzag through the Fatherland and Herr Neudorf continued in his threats to call my *muzzah,* I realized that, in the words of Goethe's Faust, from the play *Faust* (which I had not yet read, being an eighteen-year-old idiot inter-ested only in Kafka and, very recently, Thomas Mann), two souls dwelled in my decidedly unvoluptuous breast.

Part of me drank in every difference, every drop of German history, which seemed equally majestic and abhorrent (I finally figured out how to use that word). That part of me enjoyed the ache of solitude as I looked out the window at the verdant land-scape whizzing by, protected from a country full of strangers by a bus full of strangers. I was having, I insisted to myself, a transfor-mative experience, changing into a grown-up thanks to a much-needed change in perspective brought on by the hundreds of years of history around me (at a safe distance, *natürlich*). The other part felt monstrous in my alienation—stuffed so far down into myself that nobody could reach me there, regarding the world, as Kafka wrote, with the gaze of an animal, trapped inside my own disgusting shell of otherness. The alienation was twofold: both from the language, which had the gall not to be immediately and magically understandable, and from the new American friends who shared this experience with me and yet didn't understand the profundity of my deepest soul the way they should have after two weeks drinking beer together.

It was a good thing, then, that I was so excellent at German by the time I stumbled off the bus and into the perplexed non-embrace of my new host family, the Herrmanns, because I had no trouble using my powerful arsenal of language to express the many nuances of my inner Sturm und Drang. Wait, no: I was functionally illiterate, perpetually confused and resentful—and I imagine even all of that would have been *akzeptierbar,* had I not also committed the unforgivable misdeed of losing track of select personal belongings.

3.

Lebensraum

n. habitat, from living *and* space

ex. Rooming with Germans in their natural *Lebensraum*
gives a person ample opportunity to remind them, in
various subtle ways, how the Nazis perverted the
word *Lebensraum* (among other things).

As I stepped off the bus into the Münster parking lot where our
host families were to greet us, Herr Neudorf, with one final threat
to call my *muzzah*, motioned me over to an enclave of very tanned,
very blond Germans. I watched the father's bronzed brow compress,
as he said: "You *don't* look like your picture."

Du siehst ja ganz anders aus, echoed the woman I assumed was
my new mommy, regarding me like a show dog who turned out to
be so inbred that he had one really short leg.

It was true. Not about my legs, both equally short, but the rest.
We'd been asked to supply a photo so that our host families would
recognize us, but in the age of the film camera, the most recent snap
I had was one of my senior portraits from high school: pre–pixie

cut, pre-bleach, pre–freshman-fifteen, and pre-cigarettes, and thus depicting an altogether different girl in a far more innocent (or at any rate marginally less obnoxious) time.

The Herrmann family had been expecting an earnest-faced child with chestnut ringlets that cascaded down to her elbows. I didn't know the German for *bait and switch*, but judging by the looks on my new family's *Antlitze* that was one bit of cross-cultural communication that didn't need words. They had, it turns out, chosen me largely because of my supposed physical similarities to their previous and much-beloved exchange student, Kelly, also in possession of long brunette waves, a pale complexion, and light gray-blue eyes, which stared at me daily from the large soft-focus picture of her they kept on the mantel in their lushly appointed foyer. Kelly, I would learn, was so adored that Herr Herrmann thought of her as a "third daughter." Apparently they had been in the market for a fourth, but clearly wanted to exchange the goods that ended up stumbling off the bus reeking of Riesling sweat and stale Drum.

Indeed, it didn't help matters that the day I met the Herrmanns was the day after Herr Neudorf's notorious bus-tour sendoff: a wine-tasting party, at which he was not satisfied until every participant "tasted" two liters of syrupy German vintage and belted out *"Du, du liegst mir im Herzen"* in a perfect accent, while linking arms and swaying back and forth.

The Herrmanns, it turned out, had never seen anyone who embodied the postgrunge aesthetic quite like me. The prevailing fashion in my subculture—dresses straight from the Elaine-from-*Seinfeld* collection, baggy jeans held up with huge belts, vintage polyester bowling shirts, dark-purple lipstick, massive Doc Martens, short hair plastered down with little-girl clips—differed greatly from the flowing flaxen locks, snug, brightly colored pants, and modest fitted tees covered in nonsensical English logos ("Feel It Easy!") favored by mid-nineties German youth. And this is how I came to present myself to the uniformly unimpressed Herrmanns, all decked out in my finery, and sporting a short, straw-yellow coif that—especially juxtaposed with their staid Aryan real-blondness—appeared to be the result of a minor nuclear accident.

The Herrmanns lived in a small village outside Münster called Wolbeck. They drove BMWs and they had a tanning bed (or *Solarium*) in their house, a fact painfully evident from the matching tangerine complexions that set off the luminous flaxen locks of the children and Frau Herrmann, and the platinum-silver hair of Herr Herrmann, who was both the oldest and the shortest member of his family, and whose substantial potbelly and jaunty legs looked tailor-made for *Lederhose*. He looked like an imp who'd made sound financial investments. Frau Herrmann had remarkable posture and a disarming glare; her makeup was immaculate; her lips were pursed in a perennial straight line; her hair, blond as that of her progeny with the help of an upscale *Friseur* (stylist), was set in an immobile Princess Diana coif. The two Herrmann daughters, Lisette (seventeen) and Gisela (fifteen), were in high school, which I was astounded to learn was in session all through July. Lisette, a head taller than me with hair down to her waist, was studying to be a ballet teacher and was correspondingly willowy. She was also charmingly cavalier about cheating at school: the sole ironclad rule about our homestays was that our family was not to speak to us in English, but it was a rule Lisette broke a few times in private, in exchange for me doing all of her English homework. (I wonder if her teacher noticed a strange but temporary uptick in the word *random* and the term *having issues.*) She was also enrolled in *Fahrschule,* or driving school, so that she would be ready to take her driving test at eighteen, and when she found out I'd been driving (poorly) since I was Gisela's age, she was aghast. "But don't worry," I said. "When you turn eighteen in America, you can buy a gun."

Gisela, meanwhile, was identical to her sister save for a prodigious set of curves, every centimeter of which was on display in her American jeans that had gone out of style shortly before the sexual revolution, which she pronounced *Levees fünf null eins.* ("Why do you wear your pants so large?" she asked. Unable to explain the nuances of body dysmorphia *auf Deutsch,* I just told her it was the style, which was also true, but largely because most of America suffered from body dysmorphia.) There was also a third Herrmann child, Christoph, who wasn't a child at all but a twenty-four-year-old student who still lived at home (not abnormal for a German), but I didn't see hair or hide of him for weeks.

I would glean most of these Herrmann-related facts via hand gestures and low-level snooping in my early days *im Herrmannshaus,* but all I knew for the first two hours of our acquaintanceship was that they did not approve of my heavily cultivated look, nor were they impressed with my preferences in literature.

"So, Rebecca!" bellowed Herr Herrmann from the front seat of one of the Beemers, as he screeched around the bend of a narrow village road at approximately a billion kilometers per hour. He pronounced it like most Germans do, which is sadly not *Webecca*: the R rolled in the back of the throat, then a long, stressed first *e. Rrrrrreeeeey-beeeeeeeey-kaaaaa.* I dug my hands into the sumptuous leather interior and hoped they wouldn't leave a mark. "Where does your interest in German come from?"

Delighted to have understood the question in German, I cleared my throat (I'd learned some preemptive phlegm-avoidance tactics during my stilted conversations of the past few weeks) and said: "I love the literature of Franz Kafka. I would like to read Franz Kafka in the original."

Frau Herrmann snorted. *"Er war aber kein Deutscher!"* (He wasn't a German!) "He was from Czechoslovakia!"

"I think it's just called the Czech Republic now, Mama," said Gisela. "I've never read anything by him," she said to me. I wanted to tell her that I was *exactly* her age when he changed the course of my life forever (kind of), but I didn't know how.

"He wrote in German, though," I said.

"You should read some real German authors!" said Herr Herrmann. "Goethe. Schiller. *Echte Deutsche.*"

"Münster has a famous poet who comes from here, you know," said Frau Herrmann.

"Annette von Droste-Hülshoff," mumbled both daughters in unison, in the tone I use when I say *dental X-rays.*

Herr Herrmann took another corner like a Formula-*Eins* driver, and his wife let loose a guttural stream of invective I didn't come close to understanding.

"Mein Gott, Mädchen!" he answered. (He'd called his wife "girl," and I was pretty sure that was an insult.)

When the Herrmanns pulled their gleaming black *Bey-Emm-Vay* into their driveway and gave me the grand tour of my new digs, I did my best to play it cool—like, *I've seen rich people before, obviously.* But I hadn't, really. Not up close. Not in their natural environs. The Herrmanns, for example, had a swimming pool in their basement, albeit a petite one. (Right next to the tanning bed, obviously.) They also had their own ballet studio down there, which, since I had listed "dance" as one of my *Interesse* on my application, was why I got placed with them at all. The basement also contained a sauna, an elaborate party room with a wet bar, and an entire autonomous one-bedroom apartment with its own entrance—residence of Christoph, and primary reason for my not seeing him for weeks. The main floor of the Herrmann house was somewhat less opulent, as was the top story, where the girls and I had our bedrooms. My little room was modest—dorm-sized, with a twin bed and a small skylight instead of a window—but it did have *its own television,* a luxury I had never before experienced. Despite my growing stack of flash cards and the magic of two entire weeks of immersion, I was still very much a beginner, so my German hindrances meant the dizzying array of channels was lost on me. As a result, I ended up watching many hours of VIVA (at the time Germany's answer to MTV), due to its English-language videos. This primarily involved prolonged exposure to boy bands, which hadn't yet experienced their renaissance Stateside. On my first night with the Herrmanns, Lisette commanded me to sleep as long as I wanted. I took her literally, stayed up half the night watching the tube, and then didn't pad back downstairs until one the next afternoon.

"Oh, there you are!" said Frau Herrmann. "I thought you'd died."

The next day, our group began language class in two unused classrooms of a high school near the Prinzipalmarkt, Münster's main town square. It's a beautiful plaza, all cobblestones and postcard-perfect triangular medieval façades, but one of the first things I learned about it was that it was fake. The original had been destroyed in the Second World War, and in its place the West Germans, in West German fashion, built an exact replica, down to the three alarming baskets that hang from the steeple of the central church, the originals of which once displayed the corpses of the Anabaptists who had briefly overtaken the region in the sixteenth century.

At school, Herr Neudorf's first conversation assignment for us was to describe our host families to the best of our limited abilities. Since my rudimentary skills precluded tact, I simply proclaimed, "*Sie sind reich*" ("They're rich"). I wondered if they were nouveaux-riche or old-money types. If it had been about two hundred years earlier, there would have been no question: either they'd have a nice *von* in their name to signify an aristocratic family, or they wouldn't. And if they were aristocrats, even if I was cash-loaded and they were cash-poor, as a commoner I would have been considered a different and inferior species of person. In the eighteenth century, in fact, there was an entire genre of drama called the *bürgerliches Trauerspiel*, the "bourgeois tragedy," which was usually about a common woman falling in love with a man from the nobility and getting pregnant, and the man attempting to avoid the ensuing disgrace of a *Missheirat*, or "mismarriage." The "tragedy" part of the bourgeois tragedy was almost always death: of the infant, the woman, or both. One play from 1776 dispenses with all subtlety and is just called *Die Kindermörderin* (*The Child-Murderess*); it depicts a girl puncturing the skull of her newborn with a knitting needle. Back in the "bourgeois tragedy" days, in fact, infanticide was so common that authorities who suspected a girl of secretly bearing and then killing a baby had a method of *force-milking* her to prove she'd recently been pregnant. It was a fun time for all, I'm sure, and the Herrmanns' tanning bed and *Schwimmbad* didn't seem so bad in comparison. Still, even in the cosmopolitan nineties, it kind of did still feel as if we were different species.

I never did figure out how they got their money. When I asked what the dad did for a living, the girls said a word I'd never heard (and don't remember), and then defined it by explaining: "He helps people with [something something] money [something]," which I took to mean that he was an accountant. Alas, despite all of my As and my flash cards and my Freshman Achievement Award, I did not understand upward of 90 percent of what went on in that house at any given time. *Is the mother angry about something, or is that just the way Germans talk? Is she talking about me?* (The mother's job, incidentally, was a word I knew: *Hausfrau*.) At any rate, soon after my arrival, some sort of calamity whose exact nature I never figured out befell Herr Herrmann's workplace. Robbery? Flood? Fire? Once again, it was described using a word I didn't know and I was too ashamed to ask about. But whatever happened, the Herrmanns were distraught about the irreplaceable valuables that had been lost, and this, along with Herr Herrmann's odd private antique money collection, led me to believe that perhaps he was not an accountant, but some sort of top-level numismatist.

Either way, his line of money-related work resulted in enough money for him that he could reward himself with a well-deserved dip in his very own pool whenever he liked. I discovered this in the least-comfortable way possible, when, one Sunday afternoon, I tiptoed down the basement stairs to visit the ballet studio and sensed that I wasn't alone. A quick peek to my left confirmed this suspicion and seared into my retinas the indelible image of Herr Herrmann's bronzed and bare rear end, as he plunged into his hard-earned pool in the nude (the state in which he obviously also used the *Solarium*). I thanked every possible deity that the splash covered up the sound of my pointe shoes clattering to the floor, then grabbed them as fast as I could and scuttled back up the stairs.

"Is Papa still swimming?" asked Lisette as I surfaced, wondering if she could see on my face that I'd just seen her father's naked butt cheeks wobbling as he sprang into the water. I managed to creak out a *ja* before hustling back upstairs to the safety of my pocket-sized prudish enclave, whereupon I cleared a path through the discarded garments on the floor and looked briefly at the tiny, yellow German Reclam paperback edition of Kafka short stories I'd recently bought. Despite the seven-point type and Kafka's hundred-mark vocabulary, I now understood the *entire first two sentences* of "Das Urteil," which I supposed pitiful non-German-speakers such as not myself would still call "The Judgment" in their monolingual ignorance. This was an excellent development—but that story had a naked dad in it, too, so it made for a poor distraction.

Heart still pulsing in my temples, I flopped onto the bed and watched a video by the British boy group Take That for the seven hundredth time to calm myself. The squat lead singer, Gary, was promising me that whatever he said or did, he didn't mean it. He just wanted me back for good. *Christ, Gary,* I thought, *you should know what you did.* But these boy bands, they never stopped being huge in Germany, even as America rejected them for Pearl Jam and the like. "We don't understand the words to any of the English songs," Lisette had explained to me. "But we like them anyhow." I suppose that would explain the gem that played directly after "Back for Good," a truly obscene American song about cunnilingus called "Lick It" that no German understood, bless them. Then, as "Common People" by Pulp came on (which I had the good sense to recognize as one of the best songs of that or any decade), I heard someone futzing around outside my room and held my breath. Frau Herrmann, back to do her *Sauberkeitspolizei,* her cleanliness policing.

I may have been scandalized by Herr Herrmann's adoption of the universally accepted German preference for *Freikörperkultur,* or nudism (literally "free body culture"), but that was nothing compared to Frau Herrmann's terror at how I kept my room. Despite being well off, the Herrmanns did not employ a housekeeper, and instead every Herrmann was a fanatic and constant cleaner-upper. The Herrmann daughters' rooms—suites, rather— were spotless at all times. Whereas for me, one of the most joyous aspects of moving out of my parents' house at the age of seventeen had been breaking free of the constant bellyaching of Sharon Schuman, Ph.D., in regards to the state of my own quarters, in which a few square inches of floor were visible on a good day. I had reveled in my college dorm's dearth of neatness policing, so much so that even when my habit of leaving bags of Top Ramen on the floor resulted in an influx of loud, MSG-sated mice, I simply—to the horror of my neat roommate—picked up the half-empty, gnawed-apart packages, threw them away, and shrugged. I tried my best to be considerate about common spaces, but I was an adult, goddammit, and my adult autonomy would be expressed through squalor. Given that I was unable to articulate this philosophical stance to my hosts, the state of my tiny bedroom became a constant source of tension between Frau Herrmann and myself.

On my seventh day of school, I came home to find that the dirty clothes in my room had been washed, dried, and folded; the bed had been made (the "correct" way, with the duvet folded sideways); even my Aschenbachian collection of eyeliners and hair dye had been arranged on a vanity tray in an orderly fashion. When I came back downstairs to get a glass of water—straight from the tap, which prompted a gasp and *"Aber das ist ungesund!"* ("That's unhealthy!") from Gisela—Frau Herrmann looked up from scrubbing the kitchen counter and said: "I hope you don't mind that I straightened up your room. It was *a little bit* messy in there."

"*Nein,*" I said. "*Oder . . . ja. Nein, kein Problem? Ja, es ist OK?*"

I can't even do passive-aggressiveness in English, so this was not going to end well. And anyway, instead of taking the hint and cleaning up my act, I took her entry into a room in her own house as a gross violation of my personal space, my *Lebensraum,* my habitat, the little closet-sized cushion of sovereignty I needed around myself for just a few hours every day, in order to feel safe. Of course I wasn't about to say that to the Herrmanns—and definitely not with the word *Lebensraum,* which, like the word *Arier* (Aryan) or the last names *Himmler* and *Goebbels,* had been co-opted by the Nazis enough to taint them during everyday usage (many Germans with those surnames, not to mention You-Know-Who's, changed them after the war). In the case of *Lebensraum*—once a rather harmless word popular in the natural and social sciences— Germans started using it around the turn of the twentieth century to describe the way they "needed" to "settle" (i.e., colonize and oppress) some of the surrounding countries in order to "survive" (I'm not sure they knew what that word meant). During the Third Reich, the Nazis invoked the term to justify the annexation of everything they could get their *Sieg Heil*–ing little paws on, so as to possess enough agricultural riches to create a pastoral idyll for the *Übermenschen* (another word, courtesy of Nietzsche, that can't be used without invoking Nazis). Since I possessed neither the chutzpah nor the linguistic facility to discuss the nuances of *Lebensraum* with Frau Herrmann, I made the other logical choice: I smiled and nodded at her all day long, but started referring to her in my artisanal homemade travel journal as *die Drachenfrau* (a literal and inappropriate translation of "the Dragon Lady"). And then, rather than be subjected to more mild criticism, I proceeded to shut the entire Herrmann family out, to treat their house like a really inconveniently located hotel. I stopped going home for lunch, or *Mittagessen* (literally, "midday-food") which is traditionally Germans' biggest meal, and which would have been my primary venue for linguistic immersion, a.k.a. magic. I didn't think I would be missing much, really, since from what I could tell it mostly involved Frau Herrmann immersing potatoes in béchamel sauce and frowning at me while everyone else enjoyed a nice *Wurst* and I went at the potatoes one-handed with fork only, barbarian that I was. (I'm sure *Kelly* ate the "correct" way, two-handedly, with a deftly brandished knife *and* fork.)

Instead of interacting with actual Germans, the ostensible purpose of this expensive study-abroad program, I hung out on the Prinzipalmarkt every day with Freddie, Anneke, Layla, and Justin, smoking cigarettes and drinking beer and coffee. Outside of our strictly delineated German study sessions (during which we admittedly studied pretty hard), we spoke mostly English with each other, and usually had our lunch picnic style in the vicinity of the corpse-baskets, which then bled into hours of "hanging out" at *Der bunte Vogel* (The Colorful Bird), a pub where we honed our beer-ordering skills and pilfered the colorful cardboard coasters as souvenirs. Anneke downed gargantuan ice-cream sundaes every afternoon and still managed to keep her comely, translucent-skinned bod (obviously something to do with the Dutch metabolism); Layla insisted we all crush our soda cans and hand them to her, so that she could add them to the recycling station at her host family's house; Justin seemed to survive entirely on Guinness; and Freddie often brought his clarinet to school so that he could half-busk and half-practice in the park on nice days. I was sure this counted as cultural immersion somehow. I mean, Anneke was *Dutch,* for fuck's sake, and since we were less than a hundred kilometers from the Netherlands in a town where everyone and his dog had a bicycle, she was pretty much a Münster native.

I could afford to while away my days in this decadent fashion because for lunch, it cost me less than a dollar to procure a *Käsebrötchen* (a roll with cheese baked into the top of it) and a warm can of Schwip Schwap, a mixture of cola and orange soda that sounds like it would be vile but is actually delicious. Indeed, I scarcely even noticed the fact that I was missing out on a good 90 percent of what Germans consider acceptable food, so enamored was I of the grocery store and *Bäckerei,* purveyor of something the Germans referred to with a cognate I knew—*Brot*—but which relegated everything I had heretofore defined as "bread" to the status of aggressive glue. Germans' *Brot* has about as much in common with American bread as the Hubble telescope has with squinting really hard at what you think is Orion. Our bread is so paltry in comparison that Germans call it *Toasts,* because they know the only way to camouflage its glutinous mediocrity is to char it beyond recognition. I was duly enamored with everything the bakery had on offer, from my daily *Käsebrötchen* to the dense, tender whole-grain bread, in constant supply at the Herrmanns', which I would slather in Nutella for my midmorning "break snack" at school, a German tradition I'd adopted with aplomb.

It was, however, in my failure to adopt other important German cultural mores with similar enthusiasm that my real conflict with the Herrmanns soon emerged. In my defense, much of my failure was rooted not in malice, but in my propensity to smile and nod when spoken to, in all situations—with, perhaps, a wider smile and a more enthusiastic nod for conversations in which my comprehension ranged in the single-digit percentage. It is *possible*, then, that I *was* technically told that local land-line calls in Germany are charged by the minute, *before* I got in the habit of gabbing in English with my friends every night. I'm sure Herr Herrmann watched the time click by and counted it off in antique Nazi Reichsmarks (which he collected and kept in a binder, and showed me one day when he found out I was selectively Jewish). As did he, I'm sure, every time I showered—which, unlike Germans, with their far more reasonable twice-weekly bathing schedules, I did every single morning, oftentimes to such extravagant lengths that I would disrupt the girls' routines and make them late. (I'm sure *Kelly* was so naturally floral that she did not need to Bath & Body Works raspberry-cassis-exfoliate to keep herself fresh, and just emerged every morning from her immaculately kept room looking dewy and smelling like fucking gardenias.)

Again, all of this was an accident. How was I to know that a phone call to Herr Schmidt two houses away cost damn near as much as one to my parents in Oregon? How was I to know that ten minutes of hot running water cost almost as much as the down payment on one of those sleek black Beemers in the driveway? Just because they *told* me? That would have involved actually admitting that I did not understand what was going on in the house, which would have meant admitting that I didn't speak German very well, which was in stark contrast to how I was doing in my now-*intermediate* classes, in which I was still the tippy-top student, which was supposed to count for something. Granted, I had one class where all we did was learn idioms and vernacular phrases— from a book written in 1969, effectively rendering our conversational speech dangerously close to Wild-and-Crazy-Guy levels of cultural soundness. To this day I have never found the occasion to say *Ich hab' mein Schäfchen ins Trockene gebracht,* which literally means "I've brought my sheep in from the rain."

So I smiled and nodded at things I did not understand:

"Do you [verb preposition noun article preposition article article] Amsterdam [endless compound noun] dirty [verb verb verb]?"

"[nod]."

"Did you [verb verb] with the [either two nouns or a compound noun] in the [noun] by the [noun]?"

"[nod]."

And in this way, I accidentally ran up a massive tab on this unsuspecting family—in possession of such a spectacular abode probably due to their frugality—all while openly resenting what I took more and more to be their intractable, unapologetic Aryanness. I wasted their money, I messed up their rooms, I scoffed at their food—and aside from a few amused family viewings of *Die Simpsons* dubbed (episodes I knew by heart, so had no trouble following), I scarcely spent two minutes partaking in the hospitality they had specifically signed up to give. And yet, all of this would have been easily dismissed as quirk, had I not also—once again without intent—*maybe* put their house and all of its trappings in some *eensy weensy* danger of being robbed.

It all started because Freddie's host family left town, and he invited Anneke, Layla, Justin, and me to come hang out at his house. I still don't know why a bunch of adults of legal drinking age, in a welcoming, inexpensive city with innumerable parks, fountains, cobblestoned pedestrian squares, and reasonably priced purveyors of *Eiskaffee* (which is not iced coffee, but the far better coffee with a giant scoop of ice cream), felt the need to go "hang out" at some random German house in the suburbs, but there's no accounting for the caprices of youth. Getting to Freddie's required me to transfer buses, and it was either in the confusion of the transfer process (again, the "why" of this is lost on me, as German bus timetables and maps are unsurprisingly well-organized), or the distraction of riding with my friends rather than my Walkman and *Pulp Fiction* soundtrack, that my Stash Sacks purse, made of 100 percent hemp, disappeared from my possession.

Was it stolen? Did I just up and lose it? I don't know—but I do know that it wasn't until I was halfway up Freddie's walkway that I even noticed it was gone, and that I only ended up getting to "hang out" at his house for forty-five minutes anyway, because then this happened:

A leathery, middle-aged German woman wearing a visor stormed into the house without knocking and began unleashing a diatribe as she grabbed the nearest window shade, which was up, and yanked it down—with an amount of violence that would have been right at home at Dachau, come to think of it. "[something something something] not [preposition verb verb verb] every day!!!" she screamed. Layla was the only one in our group who could even begin to understand her, and attempted to defend Freddie against whatever window-dressing-related transgression he'd committed: "He didn't [something something noun preposition verb verb]!" The woman just glared at us and then stomped back out the door.

"Who the fuck was that?" I asked.

"The neighbor," said Freddie, and took a fortifying swig from his room-temperature mineral water.

"What did you do?" asked Justin, as he removed his putrid baseball cap and gave his head a rub.

"I have no idea," Freddie said. "I have *got* to stop smiling and nodding when my host-mom says shit to me."

"I'm guessing it had something to do with the windows," said Justin.

"No kidding. I think you guys should probably take off."

I no longer had my bus pass, nor any currency or identification, but I could ride the bus anyway, because much of German public transportation operates on the honor system. Riders who already have passes are actually encouraged to board a bus by its rear doors to minimize traffic, and a plainclothes ticket agent (or *Kontrolleur*) will pop up at random intervals to check passengers' passes and fine offenders (called, uncomfortably, *Schwarzfahrer*, or "black riders"). So for a treacherous forty-five minutes, I "rode black" back to the Herrmanns', where I was to face their wrath. (Let's just say that *Kelly* somehow managed to live an entire month in their midst and not lose anything important or jeopardize their very hearth and home, like some sort of magic goddamned sorceress.)

"Wie war's?" asked Frau Herrmann, as I scuttled into the kitchen. (How was it?)

I answered, in my best German, *"Nicht so gut.* My purse is getting stolen gotten on top of the bus."

She set down her tiny glass of room-temperature mineral water in alarm. *"Und dein Schlüssel?"* She wanted to know if my house key was in there.

"Ja," I answered mournfully.

"Und dein Pass? Für den Autobus?" Yes, my bus pass was in there as well. Upon which was written, in that near-indecipherable curlicue German script, the address of the well-appointed and now fully vulnerable *Lebensraum* of the Herrmanns. Frau Herrmann was distraught all right, but not about my lost eighty deutsche marks, or the Oregon driver's license that still had a picture of me as a high-school junior, or my Stash Sack, which I am pretty

sure was limited edition. She wasn't upset for me—in a great exercise on German dative prepositions, she was *sehr, sehr böse mit mir*, with me, given that I had just imperiled the swimming pool, sauna, wet bar, and creepy antique Nazi money collection. She called me every compound word beginning with *dumm* in my compact German-to-English dictionary, and then a few new ones. Mercifully, after a hastily convened family summit ("[something something something] done [verb adverb preposition verb verb] so stupid [adverb adjective] and dangerous!" "But [something something verb verb] not [something]!"), it was determined that the Herrmanns would not need to change their locks, as they lived so far out in the boonies, and in such a quiet and uptight neighborhood, that anyone up to no good would be immediately recognizable.

No one ended up robbing them. In fact, the only real result of the kerfuffle was that I fully (and understandably) lost my key privileges, and thus, for the remaining days of my stay, I was forced to buzz myself into the house every time I came home. This was awkward, because although I had no curfew, the buzzer went directly to an intercom in the elder Herrmanns' boudoir, meaning that for several nights in a row, in order to be let back into the house I'd put in danger, I had "no choice" but to rouse from slumber the very family who continued to house me, despite my acting with all of the consideration and un-Kelly-like foresight of an active heroin addict.

Eventually Christoph, in a rare cameo, showed me where they stashed their hidden key, and all was right with the world once again—until, that is, I was given the assignment to interview the Herrmanns about something interesting having to do with

Germany, and without the slightest bit of hesitation (indeed, with more than a slight bit of sanctimony), I chose the Holocaust. To my selectively Jewish self, the Germanness of a person, whether one wanted to be born that way or not, was an immediate call for a lifetime of somber self-reflection, of grave shared responsibility, of *Gewissensbiss*, remorse, the constant "bite" of one's conscience, of *Schuldbewusstsein*, the awareness of one's guilt, of a debt (*Schuld* means both) that can never be paid. The distance of several generations from the personages and actions of the Nationalsozialistische Deutsche Arbeiterpartei (or NSDAP, the preferred German shorthand) was no excuse. The fact that at the time considerably more self-avowed neo-Nazis lived in the U.S. state of Idaho than in all of Germany meant nothing. As far as I was concerned, my very presence in the Fatherland as a selective Jew was both a gift to the *Volk* and a stubborn reminder of my people's refusal to be exterminated in our entirety.

So when it came time to sit down and interview the Herrmann daughters, I considered myself a linguistically challenged hybrid of Edward R. Murrow and the Nürnberg interrogators, and my merciless albeit low-syllabic questions took no prisoners—*unlike* the Herrmanns' relatives in 1942, in case they forgot for a *second, vielen Dank*. (Or, for that matter, the Nürnberg interrogators, but this was not a time to think my metaphors all the way through.)

"Do you learn about the Holocaust at school?" I asked Lisette as she yanked her hair into a punishingly tight bun, then resumed scrubbing down the kitchen counter.

"Ja klar," she said. *"Von Anfang bis Ende."* From beginning to end.

"Ende," I said. Interesting. *Interesting.*

"How do you feel about it?"

"Uh," said Lisette. "It was bad. It was really, extremely bad. Obviously."

"Do you know any Jewish people now?" I asked Gisela.

"Nur dich," she said, and then took a slug of room-temperature mineral water straight from the bottle. "Just you."

"Just me," I repeated, scribbling it down dutifully, giving her my best loaded look. Check and mate, Herrmanns.

I may have committed my share of minor infractions in their house, but fuck if I wasn't going to remind them that they were almost certainly the direct descendants of people who had either passively or actively participated in the genocide of the tribe with which I selectively identified when, for example, reminding them of their cultural debt to my people made my behavior as a house-guest appear briefly above reproach. Suddenly snubbing your midday soup and ringing that buzzer in the middle of the night doesn't seem so bad, does it? They didn't need to know that I hadn't set foot in a synagogue since 1986.

In the wake of what I assumed was one of the realest cultural confrontations of the Herrmanns' lives—which they, undoubtedly, viewed as yet another head-scratcher from their poorly groomed exchange student—I was invited to join them on a daylong excursion to the Longest Coffee Table in the World, a food-and-drinks festival where about nine hundred meters of folding furniture was lined up in a field somewhere, and participants partook in the afternoon ritual of coffee and *Apfelkuchen* (a moist apple cake) in the out-of-doors, in what was allegedly the largest mass consumption of such on the planet. Accompanying the main event (to which I referred in my journal as "some sort of bizarre Strudelfest") were various carnival-type booths with raffles and other attractions I did not understand. Indeed, when the Herrmanns invited me to this shindig I had no idea where I was being taken, because they explained:

"We're going to the [something something adjective noun], *willst du mitkommen?*"

And I was so proud of myself for understanding the modal-separable-prefix construction of *willst du mitkommen* ("do you want to come along?") that I smiled and nodded and got in the car. Because if there was anything my hard-hitting interview taught me, it was that it's a good idea to ride to an undisclosed location with a bunch of Germans who vaguely dislike you. For the record, it was a sparklingly blue day, everyone was in a fine mood, and the *Apfelkuchen* was (as *Apfelkuchen* usually is) magnificent, the perfect mixture of tender and doughy, not too sweet, not too tart. And the coffee was terrific: smooth, oily, and strong as hell (not unlike, I imagine, the Aryan weightlifting specimens at the 1936 Olympics).

As is common in outdoor food-and-drinks festivals in Germany and Austria, patrons at the Longest Coffee Table in the World paid a five-mark deposit for their ceramic mugs, which was reclaimable upon said mugs' safe return or, in case the drinker traipsed off with it, effectively cemented a legitimate purchase. Once again, I did not understand any of this at the time, which is why I was both surprised and moved that the Herrmanns pointed to the blue-and-white *Kaffeetasse* I held in my hands, painted admirably literally with a picture of Germans enjoying coffee and cake and the slogan DIE LÄNGSTE KAFFEETAFEL DER WELT, and proclaimed: "This is for you!"

And they say none of us will ever see any reparations.

Aside from that single day of family cake enjoyment, the

primary activity that finally endeared the Herrmanns to me (and vice versa) was my absence. Despite the periodic discomforts of my residency there—no photograph of me, in any state of grooming, would ever grace their mantel—they gamely agreed to look after my gargantuan suitcase and most of my array of questionable synthetic garments during the final month of my trip, which first involved returning to the tour bus—my old friend—for a somber sojourn to the former German Democratic Republic and the Buchenwald concentration camp, and then, at long last, two weeks with my Eurail pass, most of which I planned to spend on a pilgrimage to Prague, where I would walk in Kafka's shadow and visit his corpse, an activity I assumed he was looking forward to as much as I was.

My final destination was Amsterdam, where I had vague plans to meet up with every friend I knew who was currently backpacking in Europe—plans that somehow came to fruition, despite the fact that nobody involved had a cell phone or even access to e-mail, and that almost everybody involved was spectacularly high for most of the time. While in Amsterdam I also partook in several important cultural expeditions, such as waiting outside—and then being turned away from—the Heineken Brewery (tours booked up months in advance), the Van Gogh Museum (closed on Mondays), and the Anne Frank House (you think you can just *walk in* to the Anne Frank House without waiting in line for seven hours? Maybe if you're Gary from Take That you can). The only museum that granted me admittance was the Museum of Sex, which did not have anything in it I could not otherwise learn from one of my many unintentional diversions into the Red Light District, where I was equally shocked to behold both live legal prostitutes and—displayed in the window of a porn shop with all of the pride of a freshly baked baguette—a dildo approximately the size and width of Arnold Schwarzenegger's arm. I also made the excellent decision to blow the last of my travel budget on a "souvenir" from an establishment called Body Manipulations, by which I mean I had my right nostril pierced by a mild-mannered Dutch lesbian who wielded a hollow needle with the grace of a surgeon.

Thus, it was with pupils fully dilated, a new hole in my face, and my clothes and skin oozing with hashish that, on my penultimate day in Europe, I took the short train ride back across the border into Germany to see the Herrmanns one more time and retrieve the balance of my luggage. And, despite the fact that I was newly punctured, clearly intoxicated, and smelled substantially worse than Bath & Body Works raspberry-cassis exfoliating soap (which had run out shortly before I left their house), the Herrmanns answered the door legitimately amused to see me.

"*Hallo*, Rebecca!" said Frau Herrmann, working her lips into an actual smile. "You've stuck something in your nose!"

She then proceeded to feed me a full *Mittagessen*, which I scarfed as I fielded as many questions as I could about my trip. Because it turns out that what makes you savor boiled potatoes in white sauce is two weeks spending your food budget on ice cream, beer, and drugs. And the surest remedy for your remedial German is two weeks trying to get by with your absolute jack-diddley-squat *zero* Czech or Dutch. And the best way to appreciate the uptight strangers who begrudgingly housed you for a month is to spend two weeks sleeping on train-car floors and on the business end of snoring frat guys in grimy twenty-person backpacker hostel rooms. The Herrmanns even schlepped all the way back to the train station in those BMWs with me and my giant suitcase—which was now just a bit heavier due to the addition of my keepsake cup from the Longest Coffee Table on Earth. I brought that mug back with me to college and, for the rest of my student years, assigned it the function of topmost honor in my *Lebensraum*: my ashtray.

4.

Schriftverkehr

n. correspondence, from text *and* intercourse.

ex. The opposite of writerly solitude is *Schriftverkehr*. (And also regular *Verkehr.*)

In the opening scene of *Before Sunrise*—the 1995 film that created outsized expectations in a million heady, angst-ridden college students, or at any rate in one, named me—Ethan Hawke's character Jesse meets Julie Delpy's character Celine when they overhear an Austrian married couple scream at each other on a train. Neither Jesse nor Celine speaks German, so the particulars of the fight (which is about how the husband thinks the wife is an alcoholic) are lost on them. Still, they bond over the public display of acrimony and strike up a conversation that doesn't end until twenty-four hours later—when they part ways as the loves of each other's lives.

I wonder what would have happened to them if, instead, they'd overheard a nineteen-year-old girl with a well-tended head of

American hair shriek at a ticket-taker, "DO YOU SPEAK EN-
GLISH?" Maybe they wouldn't even have noticed each other, because
Ethan Hawke would have boinked the do-you-speak-English girl
instead. I don't know. What I do know is that I witnessed such a
display on a Prague-bound train at the tail end of my first summer in Europe, which also happened to fall some scant half-
year after *Before Sunrise* caused me to assume my future spouse
would manifest himself on one or another form of rail transport.
And, flanked by my new study-abroad friends from Münster,
Layla, Justin, and Freddie, my instinct was to put on hold my
search for a soul mate, roll my cosmopolitan eyes, feel superior,
and eavesdrop.

The ticket-taker, who was a Czech woman with a mullet,
answered the girl in the way all unamused bemulleted Czech
ticket-takers do when asked if they speak English in All-Caps
American: "A *little* bit." That was, of course, far too modest; she
spoke English quite well—had, in fact, just done so to my group
five minutes prior—and had likely deployed this answer to avoid
prolonging this particular conversation. If you wanted to talk to
someone who only spoke *a little bit* of a language, that would
be me; I had attempted to memorize five phrases of Czech, with
wildly incorrect pronunciation, from my *Let's Go* travel guide.
Many well-meaning (but misinformed) friends have assumed at
different points in my life that because Germany and the Czech
Republic are adjacent, German and Czech are similar, or at any rate
speaking German in the Czech Republic will get you understood.
What it will get you is well-deserved nasty looks for reminding the
Czechs of their hundreds of years of Austrian colonization, which
were followed near-on directly by two decades of war and geno-
cidal annexation.

Sure, there was once a thriving Prague German dialect and a substantial German-speaking minority (of which the Kafka family, like most Jews, was a part), but that business was all well in the past by the time I boarded the train during this particular summer, practicing those five Czech phrases with unstartling ineptitude, given that Czech, to the untrained Anglophone ear, is about as intuitive as dolphin noises. But still, the simple fact that I was trying at all—that I had wished the self-same questionably coiffed conductor a *dobrý den* and muttered *děkuje* (or something sort of like it) in thanks after she checked my ticket—made me, I hoped, a different caliber of traveler than that girl at the other end of the car, who I surmised must have learned the All-Caps technique from her parents condescending to their household employees.

"HOW LONG TO PRAGUE?" said the girl, who had not taken the hint that the conductor didn't want to hang out.

"I'm sorry?"

The girl pointed theatrically to her watch. "HOW MANY *HOURS* UNTIL WE GET TO *PRAGUE*?"

We were about eighty kilometers away, and had in fact just crossed the Czech border, enduring the minor excitement of passport control in the days before the European Union, by which I mean fifteen stern-looking Czech police stormed the train (also with mullets, possibly the new country's national haircut). They'd sternly checked our passports, then bestowed them with stern stamps full of strange words with too many consonants and accents on letters I didn't know could have them. To answer the girl's question, it took about an hour to travel eighty kilometers by rail, but on *that* day, the train was subject to a fifteen-minute delay, on account of the fact that Ms. How Many Hours and her colleagues attempted to present the conductor with Eurail passes, which were not valid in the Czech Republic in 1995. The train squealed to a halt, the girls surrounded in an instant by the stern-looking border cops and three more conductors. Now *this* was worth at least a quick scene in the melancholy, atmospheric Linklater rip-off movie I had decided to shoot in my head for the duration of my train travels. Was there an impishly handsome man-boy reading Klaus Kinski's autobiography anywhere on that car, perchance?

I craned my neck as How Many Hours and her friends pooled their cash to see if they had enough money to buy Czech Railways tickets for those final eighty kilometers (I'd purchased a thirty-nine-dollar "Prague Excursion" add-on to my own Eurail pass, which was, given the Czech Railways prices in 1995, an obscene overcharge).

"What about DEUTSCH?" she asked. "Will you take DEUTSCH?"

Across from me, Justin snorted.

"Yes," said the conductor. "We will take deutsche marks."

"THEN MAYBE WE DON'T HAVE TO WASH DISHES!"

I pulled on my cigarette and exhaled dramatically in the girls' general direction.

The small crowd of stern assembled Czechs did not get the dishes joke, because the Czech penalty for not having enough money to pay for a meal probably involved being locked in a dungeon, like Václav Havel.

I removed my Walkman (in which I was enjoying a rare respite from the *Pulp Fiction* soundtrack thanks to Layla's They Might Be Giants tape), now not even pretending to avoid the *Schadenfreude* of watching my countrywomen probably get thrown off a Czech train in the middle of nowhere. Freddie raised his head, clad as ever in the multicolored beret that covered his ponytail (don't judge; every other guy had a ponytail in 1995), and peeked over the row in front of us to get another look.

"That is an *affront against corduroy*," he declared, regarding the How Many Hours girl's wide-wale skirt. I took Freddie's comment as a personal validation of my own sartorial choices, given that I was at that moment also clad in corduroy, namely a pair of cutoffs with an approximately three-inch left-right length disparity, the result of my own recent hasty intervention with a pocket knife in the girls' room at the Münster high school where we took our language classes. Ordinarily I would have doubted the sincerity of Freddie's derision of what was quite clearly an attractive young lady, but he only had eyes for Layla, whose deep-olive complexion, waist-length black hair, gargantuan eyes, and teeny-tinyness made her a dead ringer for Princess Jasmine (albeit one who elected not to shave her legs or armpits).

Freddie and I continued pulling on our respective cigarettes. Ever the astute poseur, when at last my foul pouch of Drum ran out, I had begun alternating between L&M, his own preferred brand, and Gauloises, which came in a chic blue box and were heavily favored by Justin, who was currently doodling a map of Scotland. He was planning to go there at the end of the trip, because that was where, as he'd reminded us for the entire summer, he was possibly ironically and possibly seriously convinced he'd be locating and retrieving Excalibur.

"Justin, I hope before you go looking for your sword, you finally wash your hair," I said. "It would be a shame to be so unkempt when you assume your destiny."

I actually understood Justin's plight better than anyone might have suspected, given that my own motives for going on the

Münster summer program were similarly oblique and destiny-related. Sure, I wanted to goose my language level so that I could actually fulfill the terms of my hastily declared German major upon my glorious return to campus. (And that had clearly gone great.) But again, this was for the sole purpose of dedicating as large a portion of my remaining studies as possible to Franz Kafka, a collection of whose diaries and parables (still, alas, in translation) I was reading reverently while smoking and listening to "Particle Man." I had at that point, thanks to four weeks with the Herrmanns, developed some doubts and insecurities about hanging around Germans. But I was still committed to learning enough of the language that I could read Kafka—who, as every Herrmann took turns to tell me, was *not* German—in the original.

Kafka in translation, I'd decided, was akin to carnal relations impeded by an industrial-strength prophylactic (which happened to be the *only* type of relations in which I had heretofore ever partaken, being a savvy nineties woman. I took the TLC "Ain't Too Proud to Beg" video very seriously). But with him, I wanted an absolutely pure experience of *Schriftverkehr* ("correspondence," but literally "textual intercourse"). I wanted to absorb the words exactly as he wrote them, and I wanted to commune with his spirit. This would only happen via the twofold accomplishment of my learning German (which would, alas, take protracted effort), and my embarking on my own pilgrimage, in that summer of 1995, to the city where my deceased soul mate had spent the overwhelming majority of his life. I would pay homage to his birthplace (or, more accurately, the edifice that stood on its footprint); I would walk the path from his home to his office at the Workers' Accident Insurance Union; I would take long, mournful Kafkan ambles in dark alleys at twilight and be visited by the ghosts that haunted his pages (*Kafkan,* obviously, since *Kafkaesque* was a word that people who'd never read Kafka used to pretend they had, and Kafkan was the word I'd read in the literary journals); I would pay my respects at his gravesite. Prague might not have held any stone-encased weaponry for me to extract, but it held my destiny nonetheless. And that destiny was, at this point, having its style severely cramped by the mere fact that I hailed from the same country as those girls at the other end of the car, who had spent the Germany-side portion of the journey extolling the literary superiority of V. C. Andrews's work of incest-porn, *Flowers in the Attic.*

My patience for what was, in hindsight, a perfectly ordinary group of young women on the train was admittedly already worn thin due to my general American fatigue. Before being sprung to ride the rails of my own volition, I'd been sequestered on another infernal bus for two more weeks of Teutonic tourism amid the rankling homesickness of our Münster group. One socially maladapted Virginian, Wallace, was so distraught about the lack of "real food" in the *Vaterland* that he was almost in tears by the time we pulled into Berlin, our final stop—and, in his distraught state, he came to fisticuffs with the far more diminutive Ephraim, our trip's only other Jewish participant, after referring to our hostel's rudimentary bathing facilities, quite unfunnily, as "gas chamber showers."

By the time my small cohort broke from the ranks of official collegiate tourism, my worldly nineties self had just about *had it* with culturally insensitive American WASPs (despite being half Anglo-Saxon myself). So when, in our last moments in the grimy Berlin-Lichtenberg rail station, which at the time handled all travel to "the East," some unshowered blond backpacker heard us speaking English, I was already on guard. He ambled up and asked, "How do you get to the center of town?"

Ugh. It was *Berlin,* dude, which *anyone* with a functional knowledge of German geography should know had until very recently been *divided by a big-ass wall,* and it had an East "Center," Mitte (which was enormous), *and* a West "Center," the *Bahnhof Zoo.* Did this guy not own any U2 albums?

"Do you mean, like, Unter den Linden and the Brandenburg Gate and such?" Justin had asked.

"Sure," said the guy.

After we directed him to the correct S-Bahn, he asked: "Do you, like, *have* to pay to ride?"

"It's Germany, man," said Justin. "They're pretty anal."

"Ahem," I said. *"Unser Zug fährt ab"* (Our train is leaving). I hoped Mr. I-Don't-Know-Anything-About-Germany-*Schwarzfahrer* might think I didn't speak English.

"Sorry," said Freddie. "We have to go. We're going to Prague."

"Oh really?" asked the guy. "I'm headed there next."

"Ha," said Justin. "Maybe we'll see you there."

"Seriously, you should probably buy an S-Bahn ticket," said Layla.

As we'd boarded the train, Freddie—being all too aware of what had heretofore been my significant residual summer-long mopeage vis à vis a certain Dylan Gellner—gave me an elbow to the ribs. "Send me a postcard when you run into that guy in Prague." Ugh, as *if.* At any rate, as soon as the train got moving, Ms. All Caps and her sorority sisters had started yakking at top volume and I forgot all about that doofus, since I had new *Landsleute* (literally "country-people") to stoke my feelings of intracultural superiority.

The Prague we finally reached that night existed in the fleeting decade between the fall of the Berlin Wall and the emergence of the Czech capital as a tourist destination. Today, the booming vacation rental industry has converted the entirety of Prague's enchanting medieval center into temporary housing for well-to-do vacationers and foreign businesspeople. The Czechs who actually remain in their priced-out metropolis—now so crammed with tourists that it is difficult to see a cobblestone under your feet or hear a word of Czech in the out-of-doors—live in the substantially less postcard-friendly outer districts. These are often the Soviet-constructed *paneláky*, or "panel-housing," veritable forests of cement and cinder-block high-rises, erected in great haste and constructed primarily out of asbestos and frigid resignation.

Prague's metamorphosis since the end of the Cold War has, in many ways, been as visceral and grotesque as Gregor Samsa's. The very qualities that make the place a must-visit have made it all but unrecognizable to its own people. In the "city of a thousand spires"—famous for its buildings dating back to the eleventh century, its stunning castle on a hill, its mist-shrouded bridges and narrow, haunting maze of winding alleys—precisely all of these seductive elements have enticed all manner of overpriced tourist traps into the prime real estate (including but not limited to a TGI Friday's). Many an astute literary theorist has suggested that in *The Metamorphosis*, it's the Samsas' gleeful participation in the dehumanizing capitalism of the industrializing continent that causes Gregor's transformation in the first place—and so it is only fitting that the haunting city of Gregor's creator has itself in recent decades transformed into a monstrous creature of post–Cold War commerce, a shell of its former self, all but uninhabitable by its inhabitants.

This live-action Disney postcard was but a far-off glimmer in the EU's future when Freddie, Justin, Layla, and I finally disembarked at the main train station—in true Prague form, half art nouveau masterpiece and half squat concrete Soviet terror—and bade our corduroy-blaspheming compatriots a silent, glowering farewell (in my case). We had no place to stay. But, despite the incredulous protestations of my friends, I knew we would soon. The tourist trade in what had until only very recently been the iron-curtained-off capital of Czechoslovakia was in its infancy, and as such the youth-hostel scene was largely limited to official Hostelling International setups, complete with curfews, lockouts, sex separation, and, most importantly, an average occupant age of eleven due to the omnipresent school groups (who were always accompanied by mid-forties teachers of each sex, who looked like they were about to die).

While the city's bevy of old-school one- and two-star hotels would have been a boon to a group of functioning adults, our five-dollar-a-day housing budget precluded such luxury, and we were left with Prague's only true bargain hospitality option, an analog precursor to Airbnb that has sadly gone the way of other vestiges of post-Soviet underground commerce. What I mean is, if you were a nineties university student traveling on a shoestring to any recently "opened" jewel of the former Eastern Bloc, you disembarked from your train to find a row of earnest, shabby-looking guys brandishing reasonable command of English and incomprehensible maps, asking if you needed accommodation. *And you said yes,* because this was actually a safe, economical, and culturally appropriate form of lodging. And, after a guy showed you a few generic pictures of a flat all decked out in 1970s-issue Communist finery, and quoted you a price of twenty U.S. dollars per night for quadruple occupancy (*cash only, and please do pay in dollars or deutsche marks; our currency is unstable*), you got into a tiny car *with this complete stranger* and let him drive you through a strange city in the pitch dark until you reached an ancient, crumbling apartment building, and hiked up seven flights of stairs to a flat belonging to a local family, who had sequestered themselves in a few out-of-sight rooms.

Although the stay-with-a-stranger scheme was generally safe, there were still a few ways the Czechs took advantage of Western idiots such as myself. Pickpocketing had not yet reached the celebrated Prague art form it is today, but only because there were already so many other legitimate avenues for ripping off tourists, such as tacking on massive "bread charges" and service fees to restaurant meals of fried cheese and beer (in Czech on the bill, of course), or pricing souvenirs at random. But the exchange rate was so brutally in our favor that getting ripped off in Prague for three days straight still cost less than one meal in Germany, and so, like the tacky Western idiots we were, my friends and I bought up the whole town, crowing all the while about *just how cheap* everything was.

I singlehandedly and with tremendous glee wiped out the entire wares of the Franz Kafka Museum, which at that point was a one-room affair run by two ancient Jewish ladies—probably the two last surviving speakers of the Prague German dialect in the city—whose exhibit consisted in its entirety of German and Czech first editions of *The Metamorphosis,* plus one hairbrush that might or might not have belonged to Him. The whole lot in the souvenir section—five books each in English and German, three posters, one set of postcards—probably cost me less than twenty dollars, and I could not have been more pleased with myself.

I mean, sure, I was as much of a crass Western colonialist as the other backpackers snickering about one-dollar packs of cigarettes and fifty-cent beers, but at least I was colonizing in the name of the greatest writer in history—whose craggy, Gellneresque visage stared out from coffee mugs, T-shirts, posters, magnets; everything *but* books, and I bought them all. I also, of course, bought several books, from every slapped-together shop or kiosk I came across, including a stand-alone version of *Betrachtung,* or *Contemplation,* a collection of parables that was one of the few volumes Kafka published during his lifetime, and which I quoted with the kind of single-minded piety—and dubious hermeneutics—that fundamentalist Christians use to quote Scripture. So yes, the rest of the tourists treated Prague like their own personal bar. But I was obviously superior to them, since I treated the city like my own personal bar *and* my own personal literary shrine, and its most famous author like the boyfriend who could never dump me (because he was dead).

And so, although I was enjoying my imperialistic American adventures with my friends, indulging in selectively upcharged cuisine and cheap smokes, I was also off-track from the true purpose of my pilgrimage: my destined communion with Kafka in the city whose claws he could never escape. All of us were enchanted with the architecture and general atmosphere of Prague, but it went without saying that I was the *most* enchanted. Hence, the furtive entry into my artisanal travel journal wherein I emoted, in what was at the time my adverb-rich prose style of choice: "Sitting on the wall of the Charles Bridge. Prague is truly and undoubtedly the most *amazingly, enchantingly, gracefully, beautifully* haunting place I have ever witnessed on this Earth." And what I needed to consummate my relationship with "my" city ("This city, this city," I helpfully annotated) was to be all by myself, goddammit.

By ten the next morning I got my wish: Freddie, Layla, and

Justin had gone on, the former couple to go have sex in some country that took Eurail passes, and the latter to find his sword. I was five thousand miles away from everyone I knew, in what I had recently decreed to be my favorite place in the entire world, with nowhere I had to be, nobody else's schedule to consider, and nobody to answer to. I had all the thousand spires of the city to myself—just Franz, the shadowy lanes he used to walk, a few million nonplussed Czechs, and me. It was going to be perfect.

Six hours later, I'd become so despondent from not talking to another person all day that I was afraid I'd forgotten how to speak. I was so eager for companionship—so terrified that I had, after half a day, sunk so deep into myself that I had no choice but to regard others, as Kafka had written, "with the gaze of an animal"—that when an old guy (actually a Canadian dad in his early forties) approached me at a café and asked me about my forest-green Waterman fountain pen (you think I wrote in my artisanal journal with a Bic, like some sort of plebe?), it was the undisputed high point of my day. So chilling was my solitude that the next morning, as I shuffled through Old Town Square, I spied Mr. Lichtenberg-Train-Station-Do-You-*Have*-to-Pay, gawking up at the famous astronomical clock—and I walked straight up to him, touched him on the shoulder on purpose, and said: "Hey."

He looked me up and down for a good thirty seconds before he placed me.

"Whoa," he said. "Berlin train station?"

"That's me." The crowd assembled around the clock began to stir.

"So you *do* speak English," he said.

"Yeah," I said. "Sorry about that. I just really like speaking German in Germany."

"It's a terrible-sounding language. Wait, look—I think that clock is doing something weird." Sure enough, out of a minuscule doorway over the elaborate gold-plated face—one that held three interlocking plates marking the places of the celestial bodies using extremely sound fifteenth-century science—shot a bunch of grotesque little dolls who chased each other around on rails for a few minutes before disappearing whence they came.

"I read in my guidebook one of those figurines is supposed to be a medieval caricature of a Jew. Pretty fucked up, huh?"

"I like that you memorized your guidebook," said the train-station guy. The crowd around us dispersed and then it was just us two.

"So," I said, "how'd the whole not-paying-for-the-S-Bahn thing go?"

He ran a hand across his forehead; it was a sweltering day and it seemed as if not a single one of the thousand spires cast a shadow.

"Oh," he said. "I totally got caught. They came right for me. I guess they have cameras by the ticket machines or something."

"Bummer," I said. "How much did they fine you?"

"I got away with it. I just played it really, really dumb."

"That must have been a challenge."

He didn't seem insulted, but largely because his attention had wandered to a giant ticket booth in the middle of the square, advertising an R.E.M. concert.

"Wait," he said. "Is that tonight?"

"It looks like it," I said. "I'm sure it's sold out."

But it wasn't. The show was being held in the 220,000-capacity soccer stadium, and apparently the tour booker had overestimated the post–Velvet-Revolution appetite for mournful nasal ballads. The *Schwarzfahrer* and I each bought a ticket for an extravagant fourteen dollars, and thereby inadvertently agreed to attend in tandem.

"So," he said, "we've got about five hours to kill. We might as well walk around together."

A five-hour-time limit; a stranger with a scraggly mushroom bowl cut, whom I met in the general vicinity of a train. A stunning foreign cityscape; a spaghetti-strap dress over a T-shirt (just like Julie Delpy!). Richard Linklater, I hear you loud and clear.

"Sure," I said. "Why not?"

Tschüss, writerly solitude. *Na shledanou,* quiet introspection, as the Czechs would say (maybe; my five phrases didn't yet make me an expert). But, I countered to myself as the two of us set off toward the winding river that bisects the old city, was this choice to spend the day with a gentleman stranger not *itself* the filling-up of my life with precisely the kind of adventurous, grown-up anecdote that would fill *later* writerly solitudes? (Yes?) As we started across a bridge a few down from the Charles, I looked behind me and noticed the towering brutalist monolith that was the Hotel Inter-Continental. This unsightly concrete-and-glass edifice was once the Communists' prime location to house visiting dignitaries, due to its majestic view of the Vltava River and the gorgeous tile-roofed buildings on the opposite side. But for me, thanks to an edifying paragraph in my *Let's Go* that I had indeed dutifully memorized, the site of the InterContinental held something even *more* important.

"Hey," I said to the train-station guy. "Do you know where we are? Do you know what that is?"

"An ugly building?"

"Yes," I said, "but before that ugly building was built, there used to be some apartment houses there—and guess who lived in one of them? *Franz Kafka* and his family. He lived with his parents until he was almost forty. Before he died, he shacked up with his girlfriend in Berlin for like a year. But other than that, he pretty much never left their house, even though he hated his dad."

"Huh," said the train-station guy.

"And guess what? This bridge that we are walking across *right now* is the bridge that Georg Bendemann jumps off at the end of 'The Judgment'! Can you believe that? I can't believe I'm here."

"I'm not familiar with GAE-org Bendemann." The train-station guy was looking to our left, at the spikes of the cathedral in the middle of the Prague Castle, which sits on top of a giant hill.

Georg Bendemann, I explained, was *only* the protagonist of a terrific—by which I meant horribly disturbing—short story, about a guy who lives with his aging father in an apartment by a river. A story whose entire first page I could now read in the original German, all by myself! Georg and his father get into a very weird argument about Georg being engaged, and then the father insinuates that Georg only loves his fiancée "because she lifted up her skirts"—you know, *for the sex*—and *then,* the story goes fully off the rails when the father goes on a very strange rant that gets deadly serious. "Finally," I explained to the train-station guy, "the father goes: 'You were actually an innocent child, but more actually you are a devilish adult—and now hear this: I sentence you to death by drowning!' And then Georg *actually runs out of the house* and jumps off a bridge."

"Cool," said the train-station guy. "But it wasn't really *this* bridge."

"No, obviously not," I said, "because the story was made up. Although pretty much everything Kafka wrote was about his shitty dad, I guess."

"Wow," said the train-station guy. "Do you have issues with your dad, too?"

"Actually," I said, "my dad and I are best friends."

"Even weirder."

"I didn't even get to the best *part*! The best part is that the story ends, 'Just then an unending stream of traffic went over the bridge.' But in *the German*," I said, having not technically yet read the end of "The Judgment" in *the* German but parroting Prof. James Martin, "the word they use for 'traffic' is *Verkehr*, which literally means 'intercourse.' So the story basically ends by saying just then an 'endless fucking' went over the bridge. And—you'll never believe this—Kafka dedicated the story to his fiancée. '*Eine Geschichte für F. B.*' How fucked up is that?"

I had to stop here, because I was out of breath from walking, talking, and smoking at the same time, and because I was way too overexcited to be not only treading in the footsteps of greatness, but sharing that greatness with a male human my own age, albeit a sweaty one who did not seem angst-ridden or brooding *at all*, and who had a strange rash on his chest, and who felt himself above the act of paying to ride the train. But aside from that, this was pretty much a perfect serendipitous and peripatetic date. I stopped in the middle of the bridge to light another cigarette, and to preserve the moment I assumed we were having.

"I don't really like Kafka," said the train-station guy. "All that German stuff is too cloying in its darkness."

"I'm a German major," I said.

"*Eech*," he said. "Why?"

"I enjoy the cloying darkness, for one thing."

"I only like the Victorians," he said.

I took a swig from my water bottle.

"Hey," he said, "I've been meaning to ask you something. What's your name?"

We'd been walking together for an hour, and neither of us had managed this gesture.

His name, it turned out, was ridiculous. A three-surname WASP conflagration with a roman numeral after it. No name I could fabricate could possibly be as self-parodic as his actual name was. "By the way, I do *not* usually look like this," he said, pointing to his threadbare T-shirt, worn shorts, Tevas, and scraggly, growing-out version of the dread mid-part mushroom, a.k.a. the omnipresent haircut favored by any mid-nineties white guy who didn't have a ponytail. "It's just because I'm trying to fit in while I travel for the summer."

You're *traveling*, are you? You *don't* say.

"I'm from Connecticut," he continued. Of course he was. "But I go to school in England."

"Interesting," I said. That would explain the Victorians. "Where?"

"Uh," he said. "This is going to sound way more impressive than it actually is. But *Cambridge*." He said it with the kind of put-upon mortification that people get when they say they went to college "in the Bay Area" or "near Boston." Oh, for Christ's sake, just say you went to Stanford or Harvard. We're all very impressed.

This train-station guy had some nerve, insinuating he was slumming it with me. Didn't he know *I* was slumming it with *him*? I should have preferred my goddamned writerly solitude to hanging out with some Aryan-Master-Race looking preppy-cum-hippie who only read *Middlemarch*, a work I objected to on principle due to the eight-million-part BBC adaptation that had aired on PBS and caused Sharon Schuman, Ph.D., to monopolize the family

television for all of 1994. I should have—I knew I should have—
stuck to my café glowering and my artisanal travel journal, but my
dirtiest secret turned out to be that I could only stand my own
company for half a day.

As the heat of the afternoon finally abated—Prague's latitude
meant the sun wouldn't set until damn near midnight—the train-
station guy and I returned to Old Town Square to find that the
R.E.M. poster now had CANCELED scrawled over it. "What happened?" the train-station guy asked.

"Drummer get brain aneurysm," said the ticket-seller.

"Holy shit," I said. "Is he dead?"

"No, is fine. But concert cancel."

"Can we have our money back?" I asked.

The ticket-seller—who had himself sold me the very ticket I
held in my hand—feigned a look at the serial number on the side.
"I am sorry," he said, "but you did not buy here." *So* Prague.

Now we didn't even have the pretense of "needing" to kill time
together—and yet, the train-station guy looked at me, at my Julie
Delpy dress still stuck to my back with the day's sweat, and said:
"Want to go grab something to eat?"

We went to a pub where I did my very best phonetic attempt at
the question *máte vegetariánské jídlo* ("do you have vegetarian
food") and received an excellent plate of butter-drenched potatoes,
which I washed down with a fifty-cent Pilsner Urquell. As I was
meticulously cutting my fourth potato with my knife and fork (if
only the Herrmanns could see me now), the train-station guy took
a slug of his beer, set it down on the bare table (I'd already stolen
his coaster to add to my collection), and asked: "Have you ever,
like, just hooked up with a person you had no intention of being
in a relationship with?"

"I guess," I said. I changed the subject and asked him how he ended up at Cambridge in the first place. "Are you, like, a Rhodes scholar or something?"

"Hardly," he said. "I went there for my junior year abroad on an exchange program, and then just sort of asked if I could stay, and they said yes. So, through the back door, effectively."

By the time we finished dinner, it was after nine and the sky was finally beginning its fade from blue to that sort of nebulous blue-gray after the day and before the dusk. Old Town Square had all but cleared out for the day, and as we walked over the cobble-stones, the train-station guy looked at me, and then around him, and said:

"Is this such a *Before Sunrise* moment, or what?"

And the thing is, it was. Technically, I was being handed every-thing I'd prayed that the Eurail gods would deliver, minus a few middling specifics that might have gotten lost in the cosmos. So why did I feel so weird? Really, *Middlemarch* fan and Kafka-underappreciator or not, did I have anything better to do at this moment? Were the voices in my head really going to be better to hang out with?

"Ha," I said. "I guess it is."

We decamped onto the steps of the monument to proto-Protestant martyr Jan Hus, at which point I realized that accord-ing to the Linklater-film playbook it was time to escalate matters by doing something intimate. In *Before Sunrise,* Jesse and Celine just up and start sucking face on Vienna's iconic Riesenrad Ferris wheel, but I had something even more intimate in mind. I would let the three-named, Roman-numeraled train-station guy where no man (or woman) had heretofore been: deep into the pages of my artisanal travel journal. I flipped to the entry I'd written during my brief but nevertheless monumentally important moment of writerly solitude the day before. The passage I wanted was a short-story fragment I'd jotted down in emulation of all my favorite writers, who allegedly mixed in their fiction attempts with banal records of their social calls and their shopping lists. My completely original future Nobel-Prize-in-literature contender was about a nameless narrator who enters a mysterious and shadowy house, where (need it even be said) everyone already knows him and nobody likes him. I hoped it would evoke the proper response of mingled awe and trepidation.

Instead, the train-station guy gave a little laugh and said: "Ugh. That is *so* Kafkaesque."

My forehead crumpled under my terrible bleached bangs, and my lower lip did the thing it does when my feelings get hurt, jutting out about a foot. How *dare* he? Sure, what he said was 100 percent true. My precious fountain-pen offerings—the veritable spewing-forth of my innermost writing-guts—were shallowly mimetic drivel, but still, I wasn't expecting the opinion of some mouth-breathing preppy to cut so deep. Especially someone who used "Kafkaesque" as an *insult*. In *Before Sunrise,* a Viennese fortune-teller approaches Celine while she and Jesse are enjoying their fourteenth coffee in a courtyard. (I once did the math, and given Vienna prices, they spent about seventy-five dollars each just on coffee alone—and yet they "had" to walk around together all night, because Jesse "couldn't afford" a hotel. Weak pretense, Linklater!) And then Jesse has the nerve to condescend to Celine and go, "I hope you don't take that any more *seriously* than some horoscope in a daily syndicated *newspaper,*" as if Celine, a *graduate of the Sorbonne,* cannot compartmentalize mysticism. Yes, my prose was immature, vague, and too heavily influenced by one writer

I probably liked too much. Yes, Celine probably enjoyed the fact that the fortune-teller told her she would become "a great woman" and that's why she didn't mind getting fleeced. But so what? Let us be us. Why can't we be imperfect without reproach from guys who are also imperfect? *What is it,* I thought as I glowered, *about young men and their need to police the expressions of the women they are trying to impress?*

After about two minutes of feminist silence, the train-station guy said, "Aw, I feel bad. I'm sorry. Kafka has some really good stories, you know. Although I've only read *The Metamorphosis,*" he said.

"*Pfft,*" I said. "That's *beginner* Kafka."

"Touché."

Then the train-station guy slid a clammy arm around my shoulder, and not only did I let him, but I emitted a minor shudder, the kind usually reserved for the acknowledgment of an electric current of attraction.

As the dusk deepened from voluptuous to near-orgasmic, we ambled down to the river for a view of the castle, now lit up gloriously against the violet sky.

"Hold on," I said. "I have to write about this sky so I remember it."

"Ew, don't *ever* write about the *sky,*" cautioned the train-station guy. "It's so *trite.*"

"Shhh," I said. "I'm not writing it for *you.*"

Our location was so impossibly romantic that it made *Before Sunrise* look like *Schindler's List.* The scene was set; the lighting was exquisite—it was a first-kiss moment to make any director proud, and all it lacked was a sincere feeling of romance. Instead, I was just confused: though he didn't appreciate my art, the train-station guy was a perfectly nice person, actually very smart, and not *un*cute underneath his affected layer of grime. And, despite his denigration of my taste in literature both received and created, he seemed pretty interested in me. That was what I *wanted,* right? I would probably never have a moment like this again—young, free, and stupid on the bank of the Vltava River during sunset, with a guy who clearly wanted to kiss me. I basically had no choice but to realize it fully. So we kissed.

And it was monumentally gross.

I had by no means been expecting a great frenching session like Celine and Jesse's epic spit-swap on that Ferris wheel, but the train-station guy's unfortunate combination of stale nicotine saliva and mealy-mouthed lapping technique was lacking enough in physical chemistry that even the perfectly curated romantic moment couldn't save it. And yet. Have you ever gotten to the point in an ill-conceived venture when you decided, for whatever reason, that you'd sunk enough time and effort into it that you might as well see it through? (See also: obtaining a literature Ph.D. But I digress.) So, I agreed to wipe the following day clean of plans (I'd intended to venture out to the suburbs to visit Kafka's grave for the first time, *alone,* an activity I'd been putting off largely due to my fear of the Prague metro map) and meet up with the train-station guy in the morning. At that point, we would ditch our respective Hostelling International accommodations and, as the kids say, "get a room" together. It was, to this day, the firmest advance commitment to *Verkehr* that I have ever made.

While the relentless staging of the previous evening had all but coerced me into making out, the next day's ordeal gave me ample time to think over my decision and back out of it. And yet, as we were turned away from one after another hastily erected tourist-accommodations office because nothing in our budget was available, my determination to see the day's events through wore on—nay, *strengthened,* on par with the train-station guy's increasing perspiration. This despite the fact that I assumed that the attendants *everywhere* we inquired knew instinctively that we were seeking a spot for a tryst, and heartily disapproved.

"No, idiots," I imagined them saying to themselves in Czech, "I will not furnish lodgings for your hasty, ill-advised sex-plans."

After four hours sweating around the city with my "small" secondary suitcase in tow, we finally found ourselves back at the grimy main train station, where the rail-side accommodations office catering to the truly desperate (desperate *to have sex,* I assumed they assumed) made a reservation for us and armed us with a map and extensive metro directions to what appeared to be an abandoned hospital deep in the boonies (where obvious havers of poorly thought-out sex should well be banished).

"Are you sure this is it?" he asked as we approached a sad concrete building so brutal that even the term *brutalism* didn't do its architecture justice.

"Look," I said, pointing to a small cardboard sign scrawled with HOTEL that someone had stuck in a window diagonally. The receptionist spoke no English, but she did speak about as much German as me, and that was the only way we were able to check in.

"Still think it's a terrible language?" I asked, as we used our huge old-fashioned key to unlock a pocket-sized, whitewashed room with a twin bed flush against each wall, presumably unmoved since the tuberculosis patients, or unmedicated schizophrenics, or Soviet political prisoners slept there last.

"Well," he said, "for twelve dollars I don't think it's all that bad."

"Oh holy shit," I said. "It's our own bathroom. With a *bath*!" I'd only been enjoying youth-hostel bathing facilities for a few weeks, but that was long enough that I couldn't believe this place had seen fit to give us our very own cardboard-stiff washcloth that posed as a towel *and* a bar of soap. Sure, that soap was so desiccated it almost certainly predated the Velvet Revolution, but at my normal caliber of lodgings, if you didn't bring it on your person, you couldn't use it to clean your person.

"Um . . ." said the train-station guy, reaching out for me expectantly as instead I raced to the tub and filled it, both to kill time and to model excellent bathing-behavior. "Okay," he said. "Okay." I shut the door behind me.

When at last I emerged and sat, with hesitation, on one of the tiny beds, he squeezed himself in next to me (still, alas, unbathed), and said:

"This is the *slowest* hookup *ever.*"

"Christ," I said, "it's two in the afternoon, and we're already bunked down ten miles from anything. What's your hurry?"

"I just figured," he said, "that when you wanted to get a room, you really wanted to get a room."

"Well," I said, "maybe I just wanted to *hang out.*"

"Obviously that's fine, too," he said, nineties guy that he was. "But are you, like, *sure* you don't want to do anything?"

"First things first," I said. "Where are your condoms?"

"Uh," he said. "I didn't bring any." (Never mind. Worst nineties guy ever.)

I sent him out for a box, and while he was gone I made a list.

Pro: My first one-night stand! How grown-up and cosmopolitan and European and glamorous!

Con: I wasn't sure I liked this guy enough to have sex with him.

Pro: BUT, this guy liked *me* enough to have sex with *me*!

Con: Isn't that threshold really low?

Pro: *Praha*, the Czech name for Prague, also means "threshold"! And wouldn't that be a beautiful name for a baby girl?

Con: Jesus H. Christ, Schuman, concentrate for one second. Do you want to have the sex with this stranger out of some sort of misplaced *Before Sunrise* longing or no? You can back out and he's not going to be mad.

Pro: Dylan Gellner didn't like me anymore, but this guy did. How would I be sure another guy would ever like me again? This could be it!

Con: You have some serious problems with self-esteem, did you know that?

Pro: You came to Europe for adventure, and this is an adventure, so do it. Do it! *Do it.*

I stared around the room, which was bereft of all décor save for a single pot of artificial flowers on the tiny table in the corner. I paused in my stare-fest to scribble, with immense seriousness, in my artisanal journal: "I cannot believe what I am about to do."

The door opened.

"Got 'em. The guy at the cigarette kiosk *winked* at me, I'll have you know."

The consummation that ensued was epic in its badness, due, I am sure, to both parties' inexperience. At that point I boasted a full history of three sexual partners, thus making me the undisputed Wilt Chamberlain of the encounter: the train-station guy revealed to me that he'd only had sex with one other person, and only one *time*. This in and of itself is nothing to be ashamed of— except, in my wizened old age, I now know that when a guy tells you he's "only done it once," what that means is that he is too ashamed to admit to full virginity. In the end it was academic whether he was an actual virgin or just mostly a virgin—the result was an encounter that felt orchestrated by a seven-year-old who thinks he knows how sex works holding forth on the playground.

"Did you, uh . . . ?" I asked, when, after about fifty seconds, the train-station guy's herky-jerky force continued but his tumescence did not.

"Yeah," he said. "I was trying to again."

"Um," I said, gently pushing down on his back to bring the motion to a merciful halt, and grabbing with terror at the base of the condom. "That's not how it works. Did they not have sex education in Connecticut? You could get me *pregnant* that way."

Why, why, *why* did I even *think* that thing about naming a baby girl Praha? Schuman women are notoriously fertile! Shit shit *shit*.

The train-station guy rolled off me, and I grabbed my dress to mop his sweat off my stomach. "That was . . ."

I pretended to be extremely busy procuring a glass of water.

"It was like we were two ill-prepared dancers using different music," he said.

Excuse me? All *I'd* done was try my level best to respond to his paroxysms in a manner that might allow me to experience any pleasure—an attempt, by the way, that failed. To top it off, critical or not, the train-station guy had become flooded with postorgasmic bonding hormones, and I had not.

"You know," he said, "it wouldn't be impossible for us to continue a thing. You know, travel on together, and then maybe visit at Christmas and breaks and such. Write letters. I love correspondence. It's a lost art."

"What happened to *have you ever just hooked up with someone*?"

"Have you ever just looked at your forearm?" he asked. "It's a beautiful forearm. I'm going to draw a snail on it."

"Must you?"

"Yes." The ball point pen tickled and the snail looked ridiculous.

"Do you know what?" he asked.

"I definitely do not."

"I just want to sleep."

Hallelujah. "Oh God!" I said. "Me, too. Those youth hostel beds—"

"No," he said, "I wasn't done. What I wanted to say was: I just want to sleep *with you in my arms.*"

"Uh," I said. "Aren't these beds a little small for that? I mean, it's so *hot.*"

I barricaded my twin bed against its own wall, and as the train-station guy drifted mercifully off, I simultaneously congratulated and chastised myself for my triumphant new turn as a femme fatale, one who possessed simultaneously excellent and self-destructive decision-making skills. We both woke up from our sweaty, poorly timed naps around eleven. I faked sleep while the train-station guy ate a snack and flipped through one of his Victorian masterpieces for a few hours.

The next morning, the train-station guy and I were at an impasse: he was supremely wounded that I would not even *consider* altering my plans to accompany him on to Budapest, where, he said, we could have a sensual time at "the baths." (This repulsed me, but I did not know that Hungarian baths are typically congested with senior citizens and sex-segregated.) I, in turn, was supremely insulted that *he* did not understand that I had come to Prague almost entirely to visit Kafka's grave, and would not be leaving without doing so, *alone*. Finally, he decided that the extent of my inconsiderateness could only be expressed in overly earnest song. Had I ever heard "Don't Think Twice, It's All Right?"

"Uh," I said. "Uh," I said again, in an effort to force anything, anything at all, into my mind that I could say out loud in order to dissuade this gentleman from breaking into song. "No?" I finally lied. "But did you know that everyone thinks Kafka is buried in the *Old* Jewish Cemetery, but he's actually—"

"It's by Bob Dylan," said the train-station guy, who would clearly not be waylaid with fun facts about exactly where the sharply dressed but nonetheless fully decomposed corpse of Franz Kafka was currently hanging out. "Man," he said, "I wish I had my guitar."

Yeah," I said, "it's too bad you don't! Anyway, the *New* Jewish—"

"It really sums up how I feel right now," he said, "and it goes like this."

He began to sing Bob Dylan's breakup anthem unto me a cappella, and ruin what is arguably a great song forever. The serenade did, however, make me feel less guilty about *kind of wasting his precious time*, and after a clammy farewell kiss on a crowded metro back into the hub, my suitcase and I, now twice-liberated from company I didn't want but sought out anyway, procured yet another bed at a hastily thrown-together hostel (this one consisted of twenty cots shoved into a high-school gymnasium), and I finally—*and* in requisite writerly solitude—made my way to Kafka's grave.

Because—and no matter what the train-station guy thought, this is a very interesting fact, goddammit—Kafka died in 1924, thus qualifying him as "old," many visitors to Prague incorrectly assume that he's buried in the Old Jewish Cemetery. What they don't know is that by "old" the Czechs mean older *than G-d Himself*—the most recent grave in that hot mess of jumbled abutting headstones is from about 1600. No, Kafka is buried in the New Jewish Cemetery—which, like the city's "New Town," is still older than the oldest part of the United States. The Jewish organization that runs the operation is fully aware of the *telos* of most of its foreign visitors, and thus several signs point the way to its most famous inhabitant (using, of course, the honorific warranted by his law degree: DR FRANZ KAFKA). He lies underneath its most famous marker, a striking Cubist masterpiece of light gray marble that sticks out from its staid neighbors. The obelisk-shaped headstone widens as it emerges from the earth, giving the illusion that it is a jewel whose pointing tip is piercing down into the coffin below. It also looks ever so slightly unstable, even though it's of course quite solid—not unlike the trees in one of Kafka's little parables, which "seem to lie sleekly, and a little push should be enough to set them rolling. But no," Kafka's narrator writes with an almost-audible sigh, "it can't be done, for they are firmly wedded to the ground. But see, even that," he twists back at us, with the winking instability that undergirds so much of what Kafka wrote, "is only appearance."

There would be no solitude for me here, it turned out. To my right sat two convivial guys from Spain pulling on a massive joint. And to my left sat a pale, slightly scruffy guy about my age, with dark hair, dark eyes and glasses, and a look of sincere, pensive focus, scribbling with a fountain pen in what appeared to be a well-worn journal. I eyed this young man surreptitiously. I did not walk up to him or touch his shoulder. I did not say "Hey." I did not attempt to curate or direct. I was tired. I sighed, and I scrawled a heartfelt elegy to Kafka in my terrible German, which I ripped out of my artisanal travel journal and stuck under a rock below his head-stone, where it joined a few dozen just like it. The guy eventually got up and left. We never so much as made eye contact.

The next morning, as I rumbled my suitcase over the cobble-stones in Old Town Square on my way to the train station one last time, I heard the dulcet tones of all-caps American English. Sure enough, right there in my path was the How Many Hours girl from the train, brown corduroy skirt as fetching as ever, hair once again an immaculate cascade of corkscrew curls just grazing the small of her back. She was deep in conversation with a coterie of cute slack-jawed British guys, explaining to them what a "serious dive" her hotel was. I couldn't help but think that I'd have been better off spending the past few days hanging out with her, skimming her British-guy castoffs, none of whom would dismiss my prose as *Kafkaesque* (because none of them would give two shits about my artisanal travel journal, or know what that word meant), and all of whom probably knew how sex worked.

Four months later, back at college, I got a curious postcard with a UK stamp. On it was a deftly detailed, Victorian-style narration of an encounter with a prodigious street violinist. The music, the train-station guy wrote, was so enchanting because it "swirled about the unsayable." I thought twice, but I didn't answer, and the textual intercourse ended there.

5.

Ostalgie

n. *longing for the good old days of the German Democratic Republic, from* east *and* nostalgia.

ex. All the *Ostalgie* in the world is no match for a sink-shower combo.

When I returned from my summer abroad in 1995, I had somehow managed to become a bit more conversant in German, though still, for some reason, not magically fluent. Still functionally illiterate in the language of my new college major, that meant there were no more compact-dictionary achievement awards for me. In fact, sophomore year every other German major got one *except* me, because my achievements had been terrible, and as a first-semester junior they only got worse. The remaining faculty in the German department, it seemed, did not have the reverence for my intellect that Professor Martin did. Either that, or they were justifiably annoyed that I refused to make the effort required to read things like E. T. A. Hoffmann's "Der Sandmann," a story about a sexy lady-robot who walks around going *Ach, Ach* (and possibly some other things; all I understood was *Ach, Ach* and the word *Automat*). But didn't these profs understand that it would be useless to make all that effort when I was going to spend the second half of my junior year in Berlin? And this time it would be different. I would make German friends. I would get a German boyfriend! (For linguistic purposes, *natürlich*.) I'd come home fluent without trying, ready to write my trenchant senior thesis on Kafka, also, I assumed, with minimal trying—so why did everyone insist I keep trying all the time? It was exhausting. Who was it who said that if your work feels like "work" you have the wrong job? I didn't know (as looking it up would have required work), but that person was wise as hell. I chose Kafka because I *loved* him. Like most twenty-year-olds, I was fairly certain that real love didn't take work. I chose a German major because I had a gift for language learning, and *gifts* meant you didn't have to do anything. Right? Why hadn't all these functional adults around me figured that out?

I packed for my six-month trip at my parents' house back in Oregon while watching *Shallow Grave,* the movie where a baby-faced Ewan McGregor and his two flatmates find a briefcase full of cash under macabre circumstances and end up trying (sometimes with success) to kill and dismember each other. It was my favorite film at the time, not because of its Chaucerian cautionary tale about money (I hadn't done well in my Chaucer seminar), nor even because it exemplified the psychopathic self-interest inherent in all young adults, but simply because I had a blinding crush on Ewan McGregor's underweight, pasty, track-marked character from *Trainspotting,* Mark Renton. I was far too chickenshit to try heroin, but my *spirit* was, I insisted to myself, properly Rentonian, as I sat folding clothes into my gargantuan suitcase with an uncharacteristic amount of patience and care, hopped up on four Tylenol-3 tablets, the kind with codeine.

Some of my more earnest college friends had turned me on to Tim O'Brien's *The Things They Carried*, and since to me embarking upon six months as an exchange student in Berlin was pretty much the same thing as going to Vietnam, the significance of what I chose to take with me weighed heavily on my addled mind as I compiled the following essentials for my journey:

Black outfits: this included my certified "on-the-prowl" shirt, a skintight half-zip blouse made of stretch nylon that resembled a wetsuit without any of its attendant practicalities, paired with the ubiquitous and quintessential "night-on-the-town" bottom-half of 1996 (i.e., black stretch flare pants, so snug and shoddily made that they had already split once down the rear end).

Guitar: On which I could play the five chords of "Wonderwall" and nothing else.

Discman: top-of-the-line model at the time, with ultrasophisticated anti-skip technology.

Beauty products: In a case that was larger than the entirety of what I now bring on month-long trips, dedicated solely to a palette of glitter finishes, which I applied daily with complete disregard to (or in full

ignorance of) every cosmetician's directive to emphasize one feature and one feature only.

My *Time Out Berlin*, already memorized, cross-
referenced, and annotated according to a one-to-
three-star system of priority.

Condoms: A twelve-pack, which I thought struck
exactly the appropriate balance between caution and
overconfidence.

Yes, I did engage in some low-level high-risk behavior (mild
opiate abuse; wearing sunscreen with an SPF of less than 30), but
when it came to the big things—pregnancy and STDs, arriving on
time for international flights—I was the clear precursor to my current self, who uses a turn signal in empty parking lots. So that is
how I found myself, in mid-February 1997, in the international de-
partures lounge of JFK, four hours early but looking like an extra
from a low-budget rave movie. As I reapplied my rings of black
glitter eyeliner, my classmate Laurel's dad wondered if I had de-
signs on the pilot. (*Maybe!*) But seriously, this was Berlin; I had an
image to maintain, even on the plane.

The meticulous cultivation of my image had actually begun
several months prior, when I filled out the worksheet that would
match me with the appropriate host family for my initial one-month
homestay. Living with a German family would, once again, serve
as simultaneous language and cultural immersion before I moved
into my more permanent home in the Freie Universität dormito-
ries, which were populated entirely by English-speaking international students and located deep in the bucolic woods of the village

of Dahlem, which is barely even in Berlin proper. The homestay might have been my only chance to experience the actual city I had chosen specifically because its sheer size, very recent history, large immigrant communities, and legendary nightlife had made it the least-German of all the German cities that offered study-abroad programs. Berlin was a place where I could soak up the language by way of staying out until 10:00 A.M. at an impromptu art-club, not sitting through another awkward *Kaffeeklatsch* with a bunch of uptight, statuesque blondes who disapproved of me—so, my experience in Münster still smarting, I wanted any future Herrmanns to know what they were in for.

When it came time to let my new German *Mutter* and *Vater* learn about me, my policy was unflinching aggression about the unabashed me-ness I was *not* going to compromise for *anyone*, thank you very much.

"I am a *strict* vegetarian," I explained. "This means that I *do not eat meat, ever.* This *includes* chicken, which Germans generally view as a variety of potato, but I do not. This also *includes* meat stock, which I can *taste,* so there is *no point* in trying to sneak it in." This last bit, by the way, was a lie; I had eaten plenty of meat stock on my last trip, much of it unnoticed. "I wear my hair *very* short and dye it bright, unnatural colors with great frequency." This was included specifically to avert any Kelly-esque bait-and-switch disappointment. "I am a *moderate* smoker and would like to be able to smoke *in my room.*" "I am *Jewish* and would hope that what-ever family houses me treats my religion with the *appropriate amount of cultural sensitivity,* given the context."

What the beleaguered program directors managed to come up with was a compromise, one that ended up making me the envy of all of my program friends (until, that is, they saw my bathing setup): I was offered a sublet in an apartment with a "host mom" who was another student, four years older than me. And the apartment, I found out to my breathless delight, was located in Prenzlauer Berg.

Back in 1995, when Herr Neudorf's tour bus had finally pulled in to Berlin, I'd asked him in total earnestness: "Where do all the *punks* hang out?"

Without missing a beat, this seventy-year-old German man had answered: "Prenzlauer Berg!" (and then threatened to tell my *muzzah* where I was going and what I was up to). After a mere seventy-five-minute ride on the S-Bahn, Justin, Freddie, Anneke, Layla, and I had been treated to the single coolest tableau of outdoor cafés and pubs we had ever seen. All the buildings were unpainted stone and concrete, pockmarked with the craters of what I assumed was actual World War II damage (it was just from age, but allow me my historical fantasies). Every centimeter of side-walk was covered in tables, and every table was full of young people, all of whom were drinking beer at noon and had more holes in their bodies than they were born with. The neighborhood, at the time still so freshly colonized by the postreunification youth that it didn't quite know what to do with itself, was a six-square-mile clubhouse of people too cool to go to school or have jobs.

"Prenzlauer *Berg?*" I therefore squeaked on the frigid day we all met our host families, in the hesitant, overpronounced German of a college student who's rarely had to use the language in the wild. "Prenzlauer *Berg!*" I was already excited enough that while every-one else was making awkward, bad-German conversation with middle-aged uptight people, I was making awkward, bad-German conversation with a bona fide real-life German young adult: Gertrud, twenty-four, a student of Anglo-American literature at the Humboldt-Universität, who had grown up in Chemnitz, a town in the former GDR that until quite recently was actually called *Karl-Marx-Stadt*.

She had blond hair down to her chin, as angular and unadorned as East German architecture. She smoked cheap cigarettes, wore no makeup, and her voice was low and sultry, like Marlene Dietrich's. She had several handsome suitors, all of whom knew about each other. And she lived, on her own, in *Prenzlauer Berg*. "But that is the very best quadrant within the city!"

"Don't get too excited," she warned. "I don't live in 'cool' Prenzlauer Berg. I live in *far* Prenzlauer Berg. I live in the East."

"That is so *perfect*," I said. "I love the East. I love everything about it."

I had just decided this fact on the spot. Yes, I thought, *I love the East*. I mean, it made perfect sense. I hated Ronald Reagan, after all. It turns out that the Germans have a word for the feeling I was affecting: *Ostalgie*. It's a portmanteau used to describe selective longing for the "good old days" of the GDR—and it's big business. Today, *Ost*-themed clubs and parties charge patrons hard-earned euros for the opportunity to dress in drab eighties outfits and sit around drinking intentionally bad beer, and an unironically (or perhaps meta-ironically) materialist fervor exists for the products of the GDR. Starting as early as 1992, there was a rush on: furniture in the relentless mustards and oranges that comprised many a socialist realist film set; giant bleep-bloopy electronics (some of them designed to facilitate spying on one's nearest and dearest); housewares and packaged foods; and, finally and especially, the Trabant car (or Trabi), whose iconic shape— like a 1955 Buick washed and dried on the super-hot cycle— reappeared in the form of planters, sculptures, or in rare cases still sputtering down the road. (I'm sure Erich Honecker's ghost is very proud.) As far as trend affectations go, *Ostalgie* is probably one of the least understandable to outsiders from the West, given that for most of us, especially in my generation, East Germany was a punch line, best signified in a 1988 women's Olympic gymnastics team sporting identical feathered men's haircuts and painfully obvious signs of steroid abuse. And after all, what would be the American equivalent of nostalgia for one of the most universally disliked political eras of the past? A Red Scare prom? But, I say with either pride or shame (I haven't decided yet), some of us *totally* got *Ostalgie*.

My wholehearted adoption of East German identity was especially impressive given that I'd had a particularly apolitical few years since my attempt with Dylan Gellner to turn AP Civics into the Sixth International (or at least Sweden). Sure, I'd voted for the first time, for Bill Clinton, in the 1996 presidential election. But the Internet wasn't a thing yet, and the only television I watched was *Melrose Place* once a week in the Main House smoking common room, so I was a far cry from the bleating social justice warrior I am today. Indeed, my choice to declare a near-immediate allegiance to all things *Ost* upon my arrival in a city whose dividing wall had only recently been dismantled was 100 percent based on which subset of Germans I perceived as being slightly less prone to yelling at me all the time. I guess the personal really is political, Monsieur Foucault.

"You'll find out just how much you love the East when you see your room," said Gertrud with a near-imperceptible smirk, which is German for laughing your ass off. "Come on. We have a long way to go."

Gertrud wasn't kidding. For our orientation, the study-abroad program had put us up at a youth hostel in the same pastoral western outer district, Dahlem, where the university was located, so the first leg of our journey took place on the S-Bahn, which ran from those leafy outer neighborhoods to the main transit hubs of the central districts such as Mitte (which means "center"). I watched out the window as the sky turned from silver to purple, trying not to topple over while I kept one hand on my boulder-sized suitcase and the other on my guitar. The buildings of Dahlem, Steglitz, and Schöneberg whizzed by, with their innocuous mixture of fake-old, real-old, and IKEA-chic. Slowly the gentility gave way to graffiti, and I thought of the Iggy Pop song "The Passenger," which legend has it he wrote while riding the S-Bahn in the late seventies. As the train vibrated under my feet and I watched the buildings get grimier, Iggy's lyrics started to make perfect sense—here I was, the passenger, *under glass,* both a part of this immense, sprawling city that seemed almost like a living organism, and alienated from everyone who actually belonged there. These, I realized, were *the city's ripped backsides*! This was the *bright and hollow sky*! Too bad that song's killer riff was comprised of three chords that weren't in "Wonderwall."

Then, in the distance, what looked like the dismembered skeleton of a mammoth extraterrestrial robot-dinosaur came into view against the sunset.

"Was ist das?" I whispered.

"Das sind Kräne," said Gertrud. "Cranes. The biggest continuous construction site in all of Europe."

It was Potsdamer Platz, whose endless panorama of just-started building sites would be the defining silhouette of Berlin's skyline for years. The prewar *Platz,* or square, was once the nightlife and traffic epicenter of the German capital, its spirit immortalized in a jubilant expressionist painting by Ernst Ludwig Kirchner—two chic women, one in black and the other teal, whoosh along in a blur of grand hotels and foot traffic. Potsdamer Platz was blown to kingdom come during the war, but its real demise came when it was split in two, with much of its former glory paved over in favor of the "death strip" between the Berlin Walls. For the Berlin Wall was actually two parallel walls, the western one covered in graffiti, the eastern one pristine; between them was a wide expanse pocked with gentle methods of interloper discouragement (trenches, beds of nails)—and, lest those not be discouraging enough, patrolled by armed East German guards in towers. But now, with the Wall and the death strip gone, workers at the largest construction site in Europe were busily erecting a sleek, *supermodernen* corporate park, whose defining decorative features would be the mammoth logos of Sony and Daimler.

"Come on," said Gertrud. "We get off here."

Somehow a full working S-Bahn station was in place amid the endless scaffolding and no doubt heavily managed chaos, so we dragged my suitcase a frigid kilometer through the rubble until we got to a bus stop. Gertrud looked at her watch. "Should be here in three minutes," she said. And it was. Exactly.

As the cranes of Potsdamer Platz faded, I noticed yet another bizarre silhouette. This time it looked like the Death Star impaled on a chopstick. It was the *Fernsehturm,* the Alexanderplatz TV tower, unofficial symbol of East Berlin. I craned my neck as we grew closer. It was immense. *"Riesig,"* said Gertrud. "Huge, right? Some people say it was supposed to look like an eye that could see you everywhere."

"It looks like an evil disco ball."

"A little bit, yes."

The bus turned a corner and two fearsome apartment high-rises greeted us. They looked like wedding cakes made out of cinder blocks and bombs. (The technical name for their style, pride and joy of the German Democratic Republic, was "Socialist Classicism.") The street was different, too—wider, starker, not a tall tree or cobblestone in sight. "What's this street called?"

"Karl-Marx-Allee," said Gertrud.

"*Nein.*"

"*Doch.* And *that's* the name they changed it to after the Reunification."

"What was it before?"

"Stalinallee."

"*Nein.*"

"*Komm schon.* We're getting out here."

"You *live* on Stalinallee?"

"Don't be silly. This is where we walk to get the tram. We still have twenty minutes to go." Jesus H. Christ, Berlin was huge.

Finally, after a near-two-hour tour through architectural and political history, I reached my new home, and I learned what Gertrud meant about "far Prenzlauer Berg." Our street, Rudi-Arndt-Straße (named in honor of a Nazi-turned-Social Democrat), was a good twenty-five-minute walk from the sprawling cool-kids' fort I'd fallen in love with a few years before. The sole establishments on our corner were a bakery that only seemed to be open from six to eight in the morning and a store that sold back braces and orthotics.

As I took in my new neighborhood, the biting February wind bounced off the expansive, treeless Soviet boulevard that served as our cross street, ricocheted off our block's row of squat, mean-looking, cinder-block apartment buildings, and careened directly down the back of the vintage faux-fur jacket that I'd chosen, with severe incompetence, as my winter coat. I camouflaged my chill by taking a lengthy pull on my Gauloise before stomping on it, as Gertrud led me into our building's unheated, unpainted, dank concrete foyer.

"This door never locks; nobody ever commits any robbery in this neighborhood."

She punched a button on the wall, which illuminated the staircase for thirty-five seconds—which was, I would soon learn, exactly enough time to get two-thirds of the way up the stairs to our apartment. The building clearly hadn't been renovated since its days as assigned housing in the very early GDR (or perhaps since the First World War), and thus, as a selectively eager German Studies student, I could not be more thrilled to be *living* the melding of the two Germanies. (Who needs reading when you have living? Suck it, *reading*.) My compatriots in their well-appointed family abodes in the stately Western districts of Charlottenburg, Schöneberg, and Wilmersdorf were going to be *so jealous*.

I was awed at getting to live in total independence in an apartment that cost less than three hundred dollars a month (Germany was in its final years of the deutsche mark, which was currently getting creamed by the U.S. dollar). I would have my own room, tiny and stark, outfitted with a twin mattress and limp little polyester duvet, both of which I suspected had been stolen outright from a youth hostel by Callie, the girl who was subletting out the room while she and her boyfriend traveled through Turkey for a month. The only piece of furniture other than the bed—and a coffee can filled with cigarette butts labeled ICH BIN DER ASCHENBECHER DER REVOLUTION (I Am the Ashtray of the Revolution!)—was a massive coal-burning oven, which served as the room's sole source of heat.

"Here's how you work it," said Gertrud, as she listened to the messages on her answering machine, all of which were from suitors, each of whom sounded very angry but wasn't. "You take a lump of paraffin, then ball up some newspaper around it, and then light it on fire and throw it in with the coals, like so."

That seemed easy enough.

"But make sure this little door is shut exactly right."

"Why?"

"Because otherwise you'll get carbon monoxide poisoning and die."

The kitchen was the apartment's only communal space, and so small it barely fit a tiny, wobbly table and two mismatched chairs. "Here's the *Kaffeemaschine*," she said, pointing me to a three-part coffee gizmo, whose three parts were clearly different sizes, brands, and vintages. "I basically just put together things people give me so that I don't have to spend any money." Why hadn't I thought of that? Gertrud was so cool. Maybe if I put together my own coffee maker and smoked cheaper cigarettes, I'd have multiple suitors, too.

The "bathroom," meanwhile, was two-part: in the tiny kitchen, directly next to the sink that doubled as a vanity (by virtue of having a five-inch shard of broken mirror glass affixed to the wall above it), was a much larger sink, ringed by a curtain and connected to a small contraption that looked like R2-D2 in his larval state.

"This is the *Wasserheizer*," Gertrud explained, a teeny-tiny hot water heater, which, when turned up to its maximum for the better part of an hour, would then and only then produce exactly ten minutes of hot water.

"But try not to use the whole tank, it's expensive."

Bathing required either a supreme comfort with in-apartment nudity (which most Germans have) or being the only one home, as the sole possible way into this shower was to saunter across the unheated kitchen naked, then climb, limberly and *quite* immodestly, into the basin, before assuming a trembling sit-squat that served both to tone the thighs while I bathed and force me—through inability to hold the position—not to use the whole tank of hot water.

"Please tell me the toilet's not in the kitchen, too."

"It's on the landing a flight of stairs down," said Gertrud, as she weighed which of her three boyfriends to call back first. "Now feel free to unpack and get settled. I have to go to the doctor to find out why I'm getting so fat."

"But you're not fat!" I said. This was true. Gertrud was athletic and healthy-looking, rosy-cheeked and outdoorsy, and probably an American size eight on a bloated day, which was two sizes smaller than me. I wonder how fat she thought *I* was?

"You Americans," she said, "always telling each other you're not fat. I was at my cousin's yesterday and she said, *'Mensch, du bist wirklich dick geworden! Was ist los?'*" ("Man, you've gotten really fat! What's up with that?")

"That's awful!"

"No, it isn't," she said. "It's *true*. She's right. And now I'm going to go find out why. Maybe it's a thyroid condition."

"Well, I think you look nice." I excused myself to mountaineer down to the commode.

Unlike the building, the door to the toilet-room—moist, pitch-dark, unpainted, with a greased-over window and a scratchy roll of *Klopapier*—absolutely *did* lock. This last fact was impressed upon me particularly acutely at seven thirty-five on my third morning in the place, when, tampon groggily placed into the hand where the double-ended key usually was (one for the toilet, the other for the apartment, which locked automatically behind me), I arrived at the decrepit water-closet only to realize that while tampons are indeed miracles of modernity, they do not open doors.

I hot-footed it back upstairs—in my plaid flannel pajamas, my unmet biological needs now transitioning from pressing to emergency—and buzzed the apartment's doorbell for five straight minutes, until a severely perturbed-looking Gertrud answered, roused as she was from either slumber or intimacy with Sebastian, the hunky ponytailed thirty-five-year-old who was the current favorite of her three suitors. As soon as I told her what happened, however, she burst out laughing.

"Ein Tampax statt 'nes Schlüssels!" she yelled. "A tampon instead of a key!" "Who *does* that?"

Because, of course, forgetting a key is just the kind of thing that Germans simply do not do. It would be like an exchange student in the United States setting his bed on fire and then explaining, chagrined, that that sort of thing happens back home all the time.

While Gertrud definitely possessed her genetic allotment of efficiency—she was punctual everywhere she went; she never ran out of or misplaced anything; she traveled everywhere by bicycle, even in the dead of winter, and knew how to maneuver through traffic with a deft mixture of caution and aggression—her four-week tenure as my mentor, cultural ambassador, and only German friend led me to the greatest epiphany about the Germans of my short life: It wasn't that Germans didn't like me. It was that *West* Germans didn't like me. East Germans (*Ossis*) like her were patiently curious about the way I did certain things—walked around barefoot, answered the phone "Hello?" instead of barking my last name into it, failed to stand up and move toward the train door a full stop before I was due to exit the U-Bahn—whereas West Germans (what we would now consider "Germans") could be mortally offended if I kissed them on the cheek hello the wrong number of times, or changed from my outdoor-shoes to my indoor-shoes (*Hausschuhe*) five minutes too late for their liking. According to Gertrud, this was not because, as I had assumed before, I was a patently offensive person—it was because *Wessis* were spoiled pains in the ass, who outright assumed they were better and more cultured than their Eastern counterparts just because they'd had uninterrupted access to Coca-Cola for the last half-century.

Gertrud, born in 1972, was part of the second generation of native *Ossis* who actually grew up in the GDR, with the Berlin Wall falling only in their late adolescence or early adulthood. They'd grown up in the Pioniere, the East German scout troops, singing chipper Socialist anthems and staying for weekends in their state-allotted cabins. They'd played games in apartments provided by the state and ridden to school on Soviet-installed streetcars. Sometimes they'd been enlisted by the Stasi, the secret police, to spy on their parents—and sometimes their parents had been enlisted to spy on them.

These snippets of GDR culture have, along with the state-appointed vacation cabin, disappeared, and are available today only in ironic form via *Ostalgie*-themed hotels, stores, and parties— and that's kind of a shame. Look, I've seen *Good-Bye Lenin!* and *The Lives of Others* more times than I can count. I've taken a tour of the Hohenschönhausen Stasi prison led by a former inmate, who described in excruciating detail the time she was made to sit in the water-torture machine for seventeen straight hours. I am fully aware that the division of Berlin ripped families apart and sometimes even killed people. I know the Stasi were among the most brutal surveillance forces ever to exist (and they did it through the admirably low-tech methods of medieval torture and coercing one out of every two people to spy on each other). But I'm just saying: there were things about the *Ossi* mentality that I very much preferred—and in 2009, 57 percent of former East Germans agreed with me, answering in the affirmative a survey in *Der Spiegel* about whether the GDR had "more good sides than bad." Of course, for me it had less to do with guaranteed employment and lack of toxic late-capitalist morality than people being way less uptight about all of the things I did wrong, such as eat Nutella after 11:00 A.M. or drink water from the tap.

I was, however, also a huge hypocrite. Because of the threat of carbon monoxide poisoning, I never made a concerted effort to light my bedroom's coal oven, so I was miserable and freezing all the time and dreamt only of cozy quarters with modern radiators and scalding showers. Gertrud worked her own *Kohlenofen* spectacularly, but the mile-thick cinder-block walls in the apartment meant that I could not leech off her ambient warmth, and so I lived the end of that biting winter sleeping on the floor of an unheated concrete room. Once, when I caught a cold, in order to stop shivering for long enough to fall asleep, I had to put on every article of clothing I owned.

There was also the matter of the shower.

"Hey, Rebecca," said my classmate Diane on my tenth day at Gertrud's, as we awaited a lesson on another suspect set of German idioms in preparation for the TestDaF, the German-for-foreigners language exam we were supposed to take before classes began in earnest in March. "Did you straighten your hair?" Diane was an old-school labor-rights Catholic from Philadelphia who went to Columbia and took zero shit whatsoever. I was glad that for whatever reason she seemed to want to be my friend, because otherwise she would have scared me.

"Is that, perhaps," I asked, "your polite way of asking me why I'm so dirty right now?"

"I didn't think it was that polite," she said, taking out her homework, which was, as always, perfectly completed. She glanced at my own half-filled worksheet, which had both a coffee and a wine stain on it. I had been quite erroneously put into the "advanced" group for language immersion, because the placement test was written, and I wrote several measures better than I talked (and talked several measures better than I read).

"My *hair*," I said to Diane, "is dirty all the time because I rarely bathe, because the bath in my *Wohnung* is a sink the size of a milk crate, and to use it I have to wait until my *Mitbewohnerin* is out with one of her gentlemen callers so that I don't inadvertently spread-eagle her while I'm climbing in or out. But don't worry," I said, "I have a system."

"I don't know if smoking so many cigarettes that you can't smell anything counts as a 'system' per se," she said.

"Here's how it works," I said. "If my clothes are clean but *I'm* dirty, then I put on my clean clothes and *my clothes* clean *me*. But if I've taken a shower, then *I* clean my clothes."

"This system sounds infallible."

"You live with *Wessis* in Wilmersdorf, so you wouldn't understand." I surreptitiously sniffed my armpits, then cried quietly inside while I daydreamed of saunas and hot springs.

It wasn't until later that week, however, that I hit peak fake-*Ossi* hypocrisy: I went home with a British tourist I met on the U-Bahn, almost entirely because he was staying at a posh hotel—in

Charlottenburg, a bourgeois enclave I affected to despise—and therefore in possession of central heat, a massive bathtub, and thick down bedding. Peter—I never learned his last name—was a restaurant manager from Bristol who had recently expatriated to Prague to run a chain of golf courses. (This was the first I'd heard of anyone golfing in Prague, and it depressed me.) He was in town for a golf-course-management trade show, and was out to sample Berlin's legendary nightlife alone. He accosted me when he heard me speaking English on the U-Bahn with my friends and demanded I help him locate a club called Delicious Donuts Research. His hobbies, I would soon learn, included ripped jeans and women of all ages with "eyebrows that go up," whatever that meant (my own eyebrows have a distinctive peak, so I guess I qualified). He proclaimed that, judging by my clothes (a gunmetal shift dress from the Gap that was meant to evoke Shirley Manson from Garbage, but for tepid suburbanites), makeup (the usual), and demeanor (the affected worldliness of an unworldly twenty-year-old), I could have been anywhere from eighteen to thirty. He was twenty-nine, and as the U-Bahn slid into the stop I helped him locate, he said, "I think it's only fair that you should escort me to this club."

I got out with him and was halfway down a dark alley before I thought to ask: "Any plans to kill and dismember me?"

"Not that I can think of."

The club had a velvet rope and a furious-looking woman working the door.

"*Bist du auf der Liste?*" she asked. ("Are you on the guest list?") Never one for confrontations and always the rule-follower, I prepared to turn around.

"I'm sorry," said Peter. "We don't speak German. And we've come *all* the way from *London* just to come to this club."

"All right," she said in English. "But only because you're from England. I thought you sounded *American* walking up." Her face looked like she'd swallowed a hedgehog.

I clamped my mouth shut as we scuttled in.

"So you're a poor student then," Peter declared as I winced at the subsequent ten-mark door charge, as that would effectively use up my two-falafel food budget for the following day—a day when, it merits mentioning, I was due at 8:00 A.M. sharp to tour the old Stasi headquarters with the study-abroad program.

"I'll buy your drinks," Peter offered, improving the evening immediately. "Do you like Jack Daniel's?"

I did not, because Jack Daniel's is vile, but I accepted one with Coke nonetheless. This is because I could normally never afford a cocktail, or a *Longdrink* as it was known in German, one of those great expressions, like *das Handy* for mobile phone or *ein Messie* for a hoarder, that is nominally English but succumbed to the charming German tendency toward literalism in the translation process. Anyway, *Longdrinks* at a club cost upward of fifteen marks apiece, which was usually more than I spent in an entire day. I managed to get two free glasses of Jack to burn their way down my gullet before Peter suggested, with more English politeness than I have ever heard, that I might like to accompany him back to his hotel.

"But that *wouldn't* necessarily preclude sexual activity," he cautioned.

"I would not want to preclude sexual activity," I assured him, trying my best not to let my visible excitement show—excitement, mind you, partly at approximating my latest idealized movie tryst (Mark Renton and sexually liberated schoolgirl Diane in *Trainspotting*), but just as much at adjourning to a place I was pretty sure was not currently freezing and possessed a shower I could stand in. We left immediately.

"So," he said, once I'd made my way past the disapproving gaze of the front desk clerk, "what do you like? Sexually?"

"Well," I said—and then he opened the door to his room. "Holy shit, is that a *down* duvet?"

"Obviously," he said. "Now, as far as oral sex, I find it blinding, and I can't get enough. Do you share a similar proclivity?"

"I'm sorry," I said, "but can I just get under that comforter for a second while we talk? Wait," I said, peeking into the bathroom. I saw a stand-up shower, presumably connected to a giant hotel-sized hot-water tank. "I'll be out in forty to forty-five minutes."

I remember very little about the sexual activity that was not precluded that evening (although I'm pretty sure the ludicrous ripped state of my tights was remarked upon with glee as they were dispatched), although I certainly don't remember it being bad. But I mostly remember this: it was with sincere pangs of longing—perhaps even *love*—that, at the precipitously arriving hour of seven in the morning, I wrested myself from the embrace of the bourgeois down comforter, back into my gunmetal dress (which, alas, reeked of the Jack Daniel's that had emanated from my pores) and faux-fur outerwear, and out into yet another razor-sharp late winter day. I showed up to the Stasi tour half an hour late, to see firsthand the various bleep-bloopy devices and medieval torture techniques favored by the very people I claimed to prefer over the uptight assholes who dared to furnish Charlottenburg hotels with luxury bedding.

It turns out I wasn't the only one suffering from early-onset *Ostalgie* that might have come from a disingenuous place, or at any rate an unsavory one. In this I was joined by a rather sizable demographic—one that has, alas, all but disappeared in the intervening decades. This disappearance is not, as you might think, the natural result of twenty-first-century German capitalism's sensible-suited dominance, but rather it owes to the relentless whims of Mother Nature herself. I speak here of the venerable extinct creature known as the East Berlin *Oma,* or granny: violet of hair, slow of gait, thick of dialect, crotchety of disposition. If, in the late 1990s, you happened upon a purple-coiffed *Dame* of Friedrichshain, Prenzlauer Berg, Treptow, or Lichtenberg and asked her about reunification, chances are she would tell you without hesitation she preferred things the way they were before.

I had the pleasure of making the acquaintance of just this sort of lady—her name was Frau Helga—during my third week in Berlin, after losing yet more of my personal effects on German public transit. This time it was the S-Bahn, on my way home from language class one Friday afternoon, when I got distracted by the East Berliner *Oma*'s diametric opposite, the *Wessi* pensioner with nothing better to do than inform complete strangers exactly how wrongly they are doing everything. She had been yelling at me for speaking too loudly to Diane. *"Ruhe!"* she cried across the train car. *"Sie sind nicht auf der Bühne!"* ("Shut up! You're not onstage!")

Despite the indisputable fact that I definitely could have taken that old broad, I found this incident rattling enough that I lost my bearings and skedaddled without my purse, sacrificing yet another handbag to the uptight, towheaded gods of German transit. When I returned to Gertrud's that Friday afternoon with the irate West-German octogenarian surely in hot pursuit—my apartment key having mercifully been stashed in the pocket of my faux-fur jacket—and realized what I'd done, I nearly knocked myself unconscious smacking my own forehead. For in that purse, along with several extravagant MAC lipsticks, directions to the TestDaF I was definitely going to flunk that coming Monday, and an entire week's budget in cold hard deutsche marks, I'd also been carrying my U.S. passport.

Even under the best of circumstances, it is never advisable to lose track of an important document in Germany—not because it's particularly dangerous (although a genuine U.S. passport would, in 1997, have fetched a good price), but because Germans really lack empathy about this sort of thing. Germans simply do not misplace their stuff, like, *ever*, so the sneering superiority they display when an American admits to having done so is nigh on intolerable. Sure, we won the war, and the war before that, and the Cold War, too, but at least they never lose their goddamned car keys. I had only recently learned this when, just a few nights before I lost my purse, after dancing all night at the Metropol club, I reached into the pocket of my omnipresent black stretch trousers, only to find that my coat-check ticket had been sacrificed to the gods of the dance, or possibly dropped in the toilet. When I explained this to the coat-check woman, she looked at me like I was a cannibal.

"Verloren?" She snorted. *"Wie ist das nur möglich?"* ("Lost? How is that even possible?")

"Well," I said, "I had it, and now I don't."

"Gibt's doch gar nicht," she said, which means "I can't believe it," but literally means "That doesn't exist at all." The Metropol club literally did not have a protocol for lost coat-check tickets, because literally nobody had ever done it before in the history of the Metropol club.

The ideal situation would have been simply not to tell any Germans what had happened, go straight to the U.S. embassy, and wait for four hours to get a replacement passport, with nobody to see my transgression but a fellow American witness (to swear under oath about my citizenship), and a giant smiling portrait of Bill Clinton. But that wasn't possible, because German offices— even the American embassy—go dead to the world beginning about 2:00 P.M. on Fridays (and on every made-up-sounding holiday in the Gregorian calendar). I had no way of rectifying the situation until at least Monday—when, of course, I would be required to present said passport as identification at the DaF exam I wouldn't be able to find and would certainly not pass. For the entire weekend, I was a stateless person, dependent upon the kindness of strangers, or at any rate having to borrow money from a bemused Gertrud, as soon as she was able to wrap her mind conceptually around such a bizarre and unthinkable act as the one I had committed.

"What do you mean you *lost* your passport?" she asked.

"Well," I said, "curiously, what I mean is that *I had it, and now I don't.*"

"*Gibt's doch gar nicht.*"

On Monday, I showed up to language class ready to beg someone to come spend the day with me at the embassy (and lend me two hundred marks)—only to find a genuine Deutsche Post snail-mail letter addressed to me, care of the study-abroad office, in German handwriting:

> *Esteemed Frau Schuman*
> *On the night of 25 February 1997 you left your hand-*
> *bag on the S3 train. I recovered it and brought it home.*
> *You may telephone me and set up an appointment to*

*come retrieve it between the hours of three and five in
the afternoon on Tuesday or Wednesday.*

Regards
Fr Helga Haider

Although exceptions certainly exist, when a German finds
something that doesn't belong to him—even if that something is a
wallet, with credit cards and a passport and cash—he methodically and calmly tracks down the original owner and returns it,
cash included. That's not to say that Americans are inveterate
found-wallet thieves—I once managed to drop my wallet onto the
New York City subway tracks, and it was recovered by an MTA
worker who dutifully went through every business card in it until
he found someone who could call me. But when I finally shuffled
to the Union Square police station to recover my possessions, the
forty dollars or so in cash was understandably gone, and I didn't
even care, because any cash in a found wallet is due reward for the
finder. It's the American way.

What blew my pomade-crusted little head off about the whole
debacle was how unsurprised every German I told about it was.
"Of course someone found it," they all said. "Of course she's
returning it to you." *Natürlich!*

"It was *very* stupid of you to leave your purse on the train like
that," said Frau Helga, when I finally worked up enough courage
to telephone her. "Very, very, *very* stupid."

"*Danke schön,*" I said.

"You really shouldn't have done that. You're lucky I found it. *It's
a purse,* I told myself when I saw it. *A purse! Who leaves a purse
sitting around? What a stupid thing to do.*"

"*Jawohl,*" I said. "*Danke schön.*"

"And then I saw that you were an American exchange student, of all things! Do Americans often just leave their purses on the train?"

"*Danke,*" I said. "*Vielen, vielen Dank.*"

Frau Helga eventually gave me directions to her apartment and implored me to come recover my possessions as soon as possible, and I obeyed. Her building was a sooty concrete number in an even more distant part-of Prenzlauer Berg than Gertrud's. The place was substantially larger than ours, with an actual living room and an actual sofa, upon which the plump, mercifully slow-talking Helga welcomed me to sit, and upon which my purse waited for me—with, unsurprisingly, all of its contents, down to the pfennig. Everything in the apartment kind of matched my vintage purse, since it had easily been there since 1962. The furniture, the tchotchkes, even (especially) the tin of wafer cookies Helga graciously served me were aged; I didn't nibble on them so much as gnaw. It occurred to me that Helga, living alone as she did, probably didn't entertain much, and I wondered with a bit of sadness how long that tin of cookies had been waiting for company.

"*So,*" Helga said, "*was machen Sie hier?*"

"I have come in order to pick up my purse," I said.

"No," she said, "I mean here in Berlin?"

"I am a student of German literature at the FU."

"That's nice," said Helga. "I don't like to read."

"*Ja,*" I said, because I didn't know what else to say.

"Your German is very good," she said. Aw. I liked her.

I studied her face as she sipped her coffee out of a tiny, delicate cup. She was ruddy and small-eyed, not graceful but definitely resolute. I looked down as I sipped my own coffee, then realized she was studying me, too.

"Sie sind so schön," she said. ("You're so beautiful.")

I ventured an awkward *Danke* and clawed my coffee cup in one hand and the Lucite handle of the purse in the other.

"When you're beautiful, life is easier for you," she mused, which brought another underwhelming *Ja* from me.

"I was never beautiful," she said, "and I had a hard life."

I wanted to know: *How hard, and why? Hard in what way?* I thought it would be rude to ask, though—and I also didn't know how to say "in what way" yet. So instead I just looked at the nicely framed picture of a teenage girl that Helga had placed on her mantel.

"Meine Tochter," she said, following my eyes. ("My daughter.") "She wasn't beautiful, either."

This also wasn't a lie—Gertrud was right about Germans' bluntness, and I really could have asked Helga about the difficulty of her life and she wouldn't have found it offensive—but I just couldn't bring myself to say to this sweet old lady, *Yes, your daughter is really unattractive.* Even though I guess it was true, at least in that photo, which showed a young woman, about eighteen or nineteen, with squinty eyes, a bulbous nose, squishy cheeks, and an unfortunately prominent snaggletooth. As I mulled the linguistic nuance that would have enabled me to say something palliative (she had, for example, very nice hair), I realized that Helga had used the past tense about her daughter. *Meine Tochter war nicht schön.* My daughter *wasn't* beautiful.

Only then did I start to notice that gazing at me from every available surface in the apartment was the same picture of the girl, which looked like a standard-issue class portrait, likely from her last year of school. It dawned on me, as Helga talked and I understood about a third of what she said, that when there is a framed picture of a girl on the mantel and that same picture embroidered on a pillow, and indeed all the pictures of that girl stop at a certain age, that girl is dead. And she was. And it was awful.

"An accident," Helga explained. The daughter, with the homely face and the hard life, had been killed in the early eighties. Helga didn't have any other children. As I did my best to chew her wafers and gulp down her coffee, she looked at me like she wanted to swallow me whole, a grief-stricken witch to my poorly comprehending Gretel. I don't know if I would have been able to say the right thing to her even if I'd been a native speaker of German. In my present state it was hopeless. I looked at her and nodded solemnly with a mouthful of wafer.

"But you," she said. "You're so beautiful and you're still so young."

"Danke," I said, because I couldn't say anything else.

Eventually the conversation turned to something that didn't make me want to hurtle myself face-first into a river of my own tears: *die Mauer,* the Wall, as in, nostalgia for. The veritable ease of life for the beautiful, and whether or not I belonged to that demographic, and the anguish of grieving one's own child—those would have been beyond my meager, self-absorbed little skill set even if I'd been able to sustain a conversation. But the relentless encroachment of crass Western capitalism into the helpless Eastern districts, and its veritable steamrolling of the elderly population, which was just minding its own damn business—*this* I could get behind. I perked up immediately. "Everything's so different now," Helga said, "with the *Mauer* gone."

Nod.

"Worse."

Another vigorous nod.

And then: "There's black people everywhere now."

Oh boy.

I froze and one of those infernal wafer cookies, never making good progress to begin with, lodged itself in the back of my mouth. Not particularly loquacious before, I was now rendered 100 percent mute. My experience with blatant American racists (as opposed to the passive-aggressive or dog-whistle kind we all know and probably don't love) was limited to my maternal grandfather, who used the n-word in front of me once before my mom read him the riot act. And my German acquaintances were limited to progressive-minded younger people. What I would soon find out from my program directors upon relating this anecdote, though, was that the Frau Helgas of the former East were not anomalous, and their sentiments unfortunately extended to some of their grandchildren, who had taken up with neo-Nazis. For several years after reunification, in fact, the Berlin guide books warned Jews and people of color to avoid the more remote eastern districts altogether, for fear of violence against "foreigners."

All of my insistence about the superiority of the East was suddenly threatened: They might not be keen on yelling at me for walking in the wrong direction on the sidewalk, but were they *racist*? Because even someone as self-absorbed as I was knew that was worse. One of the many unfortunate side effects of the Eastern Bloc's isolation was a near-total lack of immigration from any noncommunist country. The West, on the other hand, had instituted a "guest worker" program after the war, which had brought in a massive influx of cheap labor from Turkey and North Africa. This program was, of course, exploitative—but at least it meant that folks in Düsseldorf, Cologne, West Berlin, Frankfurt, and Munich had at least *seen* a person of color before 1990.

In 1997, despite the confusion of my Jewish grandpa—himself the son of a man who'd escaped from pogroms on foot at the age of eight, bribing the guards at the Polish border to fire their guns into the air and deliberately miss (basically the Jewish emigration tariff of 1884)—as to why I'd want to devote my undergraduate years to German Studies and set foot in the Fatherland to begin with, and indeed, despite my own selectively Jewish righteousness and insistence that everyone around me feel guilty all the time, there were still more neo-Nazis in my own Fatherland than there were in Germany. But what neo-Nazis there were lived in my precious East Berlin and fed off the xenophobia and fear engendered by five decades of communism, fomenting the very resistance to reunification that I had found it so charming to adopt.

I finally managed to swallow my wafer cookie, washed down with the last of the now-tepid coffee. "Once again," I said, cradling my purse safe in my lap like a little baby, "I thank you so much. But now I must be going."

"Of course," said Helga. "But be careful out there. It's dark now, and this neighborhood—it's terrible. You'll walk an entire block without seeing a German anywhere." (Including, of course, myself.)

I took one last glance at the needlepoint pillow of Helga's daughter and let the heavy door of her apartment shut behind me. I heard three locks click as I shuffled down the pitch-black hallway, fumbling for the thirty-second-long light switch I knew was somewhere.

6.

Wohngemeinschaft

n. *apartment share, abbr.* WG, *from* dwelling *and* community.

ex. Triangular room in *WG* for illegal sublet, DM 300. Near transportation and entertainment. Electricity, hot water, ceiling-swing, some cigarettes, cultural metamorphosis, unlimited petty tyranny incl.

Boooooop. Booooooop. Boooooop. Booooooop. Booooooop.

The German landline issued its disconcerting monotone beep as I held my breath on the other end of the receiver. It was my worst exchange-student nightmare: calling a German stranger unsolicited; failing to be understood—or, worse, being sure that the German stranger was silently deriding my language abilities. *Please don't pick up, please don't pick up, please don't pick up.* A rather counterproductive prayer, to be sure, as one doesn't find a new place to live by letting the phone ring, hanging up, and then talking to nobody. On the fifth or six *boooooop*, a sharp voice answered.

Come on, Schuman, I told myself. Sei tapfer! *Be brave!* There was no way I was getting stuck out in the Freie Universität dorms, twenty-five miles from anything interesting, with only a bunch of dorko international students to keep me company in my dingy complex that was basically prison with beer. What the fuck was I going to do out there? *Study?* All the cool kids in my program had taken our possibly misguided directors' offer to refund our dorm fees and search for housing independently in correspondingly cool Berlin WGs (*Wohngemeinschaften,* literally "living communities," the German name for an apartment shared with someone who isn't one's family). And since I already lived in a WG with Gertrud, I couldn't be expected to stop now and be subjected to such indignities as rules and not being cool. What the fuck use was living in the coolest city in the world, at its second-coolest time in its history (after Weimar, *natürlich*), if I wasn't going to be cool? This was a potential tragedy. Too bad the only way to find a WG was to step directly into the gaping Nietzschean abyss of terror that was subjecting random potential roommates to my halting, phlegm-filled telephone Deutsch. This I did by answering ads placed in the *Zweite Hand,* a free weekly that was like Craigslist, but in print and with slightly fewer dick pics.

"*Hallo? Halloooooooo?*" repeated the voice on the other end, perturbed at my twenty seconds of heavy-breathing silence. My throat had once again coated itself as an immediate reaction to any attempt to speak German with anyone. I finally managed to croak out the single sentence that I'd been practicing under my breath all day: "*Ist das Zimmer noch frei?*" ("Is the room still available?")

The voice at the other end paused, but not because he didn't understand what I said.

"*Äh . . . nein. Nicht mehr. Tut mir leid.*" ("No. Not anymore. Sorry.")

I assumed he paused because he was attempting to process someone being so terrifically rude. Germans are in some situations a direct people: as Gertrud was so kind to point out, they will think nothing of telling you that you have gained weight. But in other situations, they have ironclad laws of politeness. One of these is that when telephoning a stranger, you are expected to give your entire curriculum vitae as your initial greeting. This I learned the hard way, after Gertrud overheard me have one of my doomed conversations and set me straight. The sole acceptable manner in which to announce myself on the other end of a telephone when answering an advertisement for a vacant room from the *Zweite Hand* rivaled a passage out of Robert Musil's two-thousand-page novel *The Man Without Qualities*: *Hallo, guten Tag. Mein Name ist Rebecca Schuman, und ich bin Austauschstudentin aus den USA. Ich habe Ihre Anzeige in der Zweiten Hand gelesen, und ich wollte wissen, ob das Zimmer noch frei ist.* I wrote it out and practiced it two hundred times in front of the mirror.

For my troubles, I managed to book exactly two viewings of available rooms within my monthly rent budget of three hundred deutsche marks (the rough equivalent, at the time, of $175), a price point at which the pickings were slim to none, and Slim had just walked out the *Tür*. Furthermore, any place that was available to the likes of me was nightmarish, such as the austere room (with yet another coal oven) in Friedrichshain, where the proprietor was a mopey schlub in his late thirties who insisted that anyone who moved in had to hang out with him.

"So," I said, when he wouldn't stop staring at me, "what do you do?"

"Ich bin Arbeitslos," he said. ("I'm unemployed.") *"Und was machst du denn in Berlin?"* he asked. ("What do you do in Berlin, anyway?")

I told him I was a student of German literature at the FU, which at this point was almost true—language class was over, the FU semester was imminent, and I was even mildly excited to choose between a course on Bertolt Brecht and one on Weimar modernism. Brecht plays were morally instructive and short (bonus), but Weimar modernism included the excellent paintings of Otto Dix, who specialized in the *Neue Sachlichkeit,* New Objectivity, in which Dix deliberately made pretty people ugly and grotesque, when he wasn't drawing worms crawling out of the skulls littering the battle sites of the First World War. Another substantial selling point of Dix's paintings was that I didn't have to look any words up to read them.

"*Ach so,*" said Herr Sad-Sack. "What authors do you like?"

"I am a great admirer of Franz Kafka," I said.

"*Er war kein Deutscher.*" Did every German in the world have direct orders from the ghost of Johann Wolfgang von Goethe himself to disown Franz Kafka? They were the ones with the imperialistic language that colonized half the damn continent with their *Lebensraum.* Maybe they were just jealous that Kafka was so good and *Faust II* was bat-shit crazy.

"Well," I said, "I *also* enjoy the poems of Gottfried Benn." I'd just discovered them, and because they were short and used small words, Benn had officially become my second-favorite author. Also because he was dark and disturbing: much of the verse was set in a Berlin morgue around 1912, because Benn was a medical examiner by *Brotberuf,* which literally means "bread-career" but is German for "day job." My *Lieblingsgedicht,* or favorite poem, I told the guy, was a particularly graphic piece of expressionism called "*Schöne Jugend,*" or "A Fine Childhood," about a family of rats discovered inside the decomposing body of a young prostitute.

At the end, the mortician drowns them in a bucket. "Oh, how the little snouts squeaked!" Excellent dinner-party fodder, I found. "Have you heard it?" I asked my potential new roommate, who finally found occasion to stop staring at me.

Directly after that, I schlepped out to the desolate nether regions of the eastern district of Treptow, populated only by neo-Nazis, their racist grannies, and Hans and Effi, the two incredulous roommates who were attempting to rent out a windowless closet, one that might have been able to accommodate a twin mattress on the floor if it were placed diagonally. "It's yours if you want it," said Hans. I kept the Gottfried Benn quotes to myself and tried not to weep openly until I'd made it halfway back to the U-Bahn.

In the depths of my housing despair, Gertrud persuaded me to see a movie, the highly anticipated feature-length version of *Kleiner Arschloch* (*Little Asshole*), a proto–*South Park* cartoon starring a gleefully obscene little boy. I only understood about a fifth of it, and I was too deeply ensconced within my own personal storm cloud to laugh at anything I did understand, with the sole exception of the titular Asshole's grandpa—voiced by legendary German comedian Helge Schneider—who insisted that he was a tithe-paying worshipper at the Church of the Holy Vagina. After the film ended, I very much wanted to harrumph my way home and feel sorry for myself within the confines of my own frigid four walls while I still had them, but Gertrud cajoled me into going out with her and Paul, a very tall and floppy-haired friend from Chemnitz who was now a computer science student at the FU. "Look, I'll even *invite* you," she said, meaning she'd pay.

Unable to pass up free beer, I moped my way to the bar and then fretted in silence. I had had it with Berlin—it was fucking freezing, everything had meat in it, there were racist grannies everywhere, and nobody would let me live with them. And, worst of all, I definitely wasn't cool.

The good news is that if you are in an uncool mood and don't feel like talking to anyone, going out drinking with a bunch of Germans is exactly the right thing to do with yourself, as you will not have to utter a single syllable. There's an old joke related by Walter Benjamin (another legendary German comedian), about three authors who are out at a pub. After fifteen minutes of silence, one of them says: "It's hot today." After another fifteen minutes of silence, the second says, "No wind, either." And the third one, after another fifteen minutes, goes: "I came here to *drink,* not to talk!" The joke was supposed to be making fun of the Swiss (Germans are always picking on the Swiss), but I have instead found it to be a nonfictional account of almost every night out I have ever spent with German-speakers of any nationality. These are people who do not engage in small talk. If you ask a German-speaker *wie geht's* (how they are), you'd better be prepared to hear some details about irritable bowel syndrome or some such, because that motherfucker assumes your query is sincere. Germans either talk about real topics or they don't talk at all. If you don't know the person well, or are not intimately familiar with either German football rivalries or the ninety-thousand political parties, you can expect to sit there in silence.

The bar Gertrud and Paul chose was near pitch-black inside, which saved the proprietor the trouble of decorating, save for a row of sticky semicircular booths. Paul disappeared and reappeared with three beers. The three of us drank in silence, lit cigarettes, smoked them, put them out, lit more. After the requisite hours of staring, Gertrud became the evening's abject blabbermouth.

"*Na du,*" she said to Paul, who was hunched over one of the same cheap cigarettes Gertrud preferred. "Rebecca's looking for a place to live."

At that, Paul shot up to his full height, and his small round glasses almost flew off his pale visage. "We have one for you!" he said. "Wait, how much can you pay?"

"Three hundred."

"That's exactly what it will cost!"

"Oh, you'll like their place," said Gertrud. "It's in Kreuzberg. And it's not really a flat per se . . . it's a *Fabriketage.*"

I had gotten mildly better at admitting I did not know every German word in existence since my time in Münster as failed *Ersatz*-Kelly, so I believe I actually asked what a *Fabriketage* was, since its literal translation, "factory story," didn't conjure up any sort of human dwelling. "I don't know the English word," said Gertrud, and Paul just shrugged—I would soon learn that Paul, like a proper East German child, had learned Russian as his foreign language. "A *Fabriketage* is a . . . you know, a *Fabriketage*. It's like a big space that takes up the whole floor."

"Oh," I said. "A loft."

"*Ja genau!*" said Paul. ("Yes, exactly!") "A loft."

Was he serious? Had I just been offered, sight unseen and purely because of my excellent ability to materialize three hundred deutsche marks per month, a room in *a super cool loft in Kreuzberg*? Was I about to stop being polite and start getting real?

Not necessarily. The place went by the official moniker *Loftschloss,* or "loft-castle," which was a play on the word *Luftschloss,* which literally translates as "air castle" but is the German word for "daydream." And it was the stuff of daydreams, if you daydreamed about living in a midcareer David Bowie video, which I obviously did. It took up an entire story of a building not zoned for residence, just above a ground-floor tire shop and below a third-floor Turkish mosque. It was located near the Görlitzer Bahnhof train station, which had once held political significance as the final stop on the U1 line before the Wall. Correspondingly, Kreuzberg had been the grungiest district of West Berlin, its property values plummeting when the Wall bisected many of its streets (and a few of its actual buildings, for good measure). A lot of its apartment houses were simply abandoned, and then reoccupied by members of the counterculture who elected not to pay rent in exchange for living without electricity or heat. A mere seven years after the Wall fell, Kreuzberg had gentrified only slightly, home to a vibrant community of Turkish immigrants and the working poor, some of the city's most legendary dive bars, and most of its few remaining actual squats. It was undisputedly Berlin's most interesting neighborhood, and not just because its main thoroughfare, Oranienstraße, boasted one otherworldly watering hole after the next, so many that I once tried to order one beer at each of them and only made it halfway down one block before I ran out of money and lost the ability to see straight.

There was Milchbar, whose jaunty underwater murals— complete with a 3-D shark eating a surfer—were in stark contrast to its rough-and-tumble clientele, which allegedly included the members of Die Toten Hosen, Germany's most famous punk band. There was Schnabelbar, another pitch-black affair with spiky postmodern sculptures jutting out of the wall. There was a place just called Z, which I am pretty sure was a cover for an illicit massage parlor in the back. There were the legendary rock clubs Trash and

SO36, both of which were so grimy you had to make sure you were wearing something you could throw away afterward, in case you had to sit down somewhere inside.

So yes, technically the Loftschloss was indeed a fabulous loft right in the middle of the most interesting neighborhood in the best city in Germany. However, one *kleines Problem*: Paul didn't have the authority to offer me a room in it, and furthermore, what I hadn't really been offered wasn't actually a room. What I hadn't been offered was actually a corner of the living room partitioned off by a heavy black curtain. And what I didn't realize was that there was actually another partition in the loft: between inhabitants, some of whom wanted another roommate and her three hundred deutsche marks to offset the rent—and, it turned out, the costs of a substantial and probably illegal DIY renovation—and some of whom wanted the living room to retain all four of its corners.

This was, however, not properly communicated to me (or, at any rate, I didn't understand it if it was), so when Paul invited me out to "meet the rest of them," I labored under the deluded assumption that the subsequent three hours of silent glowering was but a fun, informal get-to-know-you event. What it was, however, was an audition—specifically, an audition for Leonie, a formidable urban-planning student and eco-warrior with a crew cut and a permanent scowl, who I quickly gathered was the Loftboss.

I was to meet the Loftschloss group at a pop-up bar in the basement of an apartment building in Mitte, the kind of place so endemic in postreunification Berlin that it was impossible for the order-loving authorities to keep track. To find it, I had to sneak into a locked courtyard behind some residents, then follow the noise until I found an unmarked door to the *Kellerbar,* where bottled Beck's was served through a hole bashed through a wall. It was kind of hard to see, on account of the shoulder-to-shoulder tall people wearing scarves indoors and the cement-thick smoke. If I hadn't dragged Gertrud with me for moral support, I would have just turned around and run home.

"Oh, don't be a coward," she said. "Go. Look, Paul is *right* there. He likes you. The others might not, but Leonie doesn't like anyone."

As soon as Paul saw us he disappeared in the direction of the hole in the wall and, true to form, rematerialized with a beer, which he placed into my claws after kissing me briefly on the cheek. (This is a charming affectation in a culture that otherwise abhors physical contact. To this day I'm not sure how most Germans reproduce. I assume it has something to do with very orderly machinery.) "*Du*, I'll introduce you to everyone," he said, and by "introduce" he meant point at them, mumble a name, and not expect them to acknowledge my presence or even look up from their loud arguments about the environmental impact of open-toed sandals.

The friendliest of the bunch was Johannes, with a shock of bright blond hair that stuck out in electrified curls about six inches in all directions, a broken front tooth, delicate cheekbones, and skintight jeans covered in multicolored patches, in the manner of early-season *Punky Brewster*. His primary act of friendliness was that he made eye contact when he nodded at me wordlessly, and he thrust his open pack of Lucky Strikes in my general direction. Detlef, from Hamburg, baby face clashing with his black leather jacket, even managed an actual handshake, and his subsequent lack of conversation was of the distinctly benign and classically German variety. Then, however, there was Rolf, petite and handsome, but dark and dour, a *Sprockets* character come to life who actively sneered when Paul brought me over. "It's nothing personal," he said, "but I really don't want another flatmate. Especially not in the living room." Nice to meet you, too, man.

And then the cluster of Loftschlossers parted to reveal the infamous Leonie. "It *might* be personal," she said, before coughing theatrically and making a face at my cigarette. Leonie was from Munich, and her apparent iron-fisted rule of her household presented a rather distorted view of the Bavarian character, which is generally regarded as among Germany's most laid-back. Over the ear-splitting electronic music, she explained that she refused to travel internationally because of the environmental damage, therefore implicitly disapproving of my presence in Germany to begin with.

"And what are you doing here, anyway?" she asked. "Studying literature?"

"*Ja.* My most favorite author is Franz Kafka."

"What a cliché." To her credit, she didn't go out of her way to tell me Kafka wasn't German.

"I also like the Bertolt Brecht," I said, which was even true, given that I'd just chosen the Brecht seminar and purchased a full stack of his plays.

"I prefer the writings of Judith Butler."

"Never heard of her," I said.

Leonie laughed out loud, and then asked me if, since Paul had described me as Jewish, I was a Zionist. Since I'd never heard the German pronunciation (*TSEE*-on-*IST*), I didn't know what she was talking about, and she laughed even harder. I excused myself to go find what passed for a ladies' room at this establishment, got lost for twenty-five minutes, and possibly ended up relieving myself in the facilities of someone's private residence, whose door was inauspiciously left unlocked. (Well, auspicious for me. Inauspi-

cious for the poor schmoes who lived there.) My only other conversation with anyone for the entire evening wasn't even with a
Loftschlosser. It was with a really weird friend of Detlef's, Moritz,
who had spent a year of high school in Connecticut and spoke
a disturbingly perfect WASP English that made him resemble a
spiky-haired Patrick Bateman in leather pants. This was going
great.

After Rolf's disconcertingly schoolmarmy girlfriend showed
up to spirit him away, and Moritz and Detlef peeled off to go to
another party (I hoped no women were dismembered as a result),
Paul, Johannes, and Leonie huddled in what appeared to be an
intensive confab. One of Gertrud's gentlemen had also shown up,
and they were off canoodling somewhere, so that left me, alone
and staring through the smoke at these perplexing strangers, only
one of whom seemed even mildly enthusiastic about my joining
their "living community," and the rest of whom seemed at best
indifferent and at worst openly hostile. After about fifteen minutes of kibitzing, everyone gathered their coats and packed up
their cigarettes and slugged back the last of their beers, and just as
they were about to leave, Paul turned to me and gave a quick jerk
of his chin in the direction of the door—which, to be fair, is German for "definitive invitation to accompany us to the next questionable guerrilla drinking establishment, and the one after that,
and the one after that, too."

That evening Paul was wearing a fluorescent turquoise jean
jacket, and as I waddled on my short legs behind these considerably taller people, I would sometimes nearly lose sight of them in
the muddled dark of Berlin's rogue tangle of half-constructed
streets, if not for the fortunate beacon of Paul's blinding garment.
Four increasingly illegal bars later (one of which, in lieu of a

restroom, had a toilet shoved in the janitor's closet), it was nearing five in the morning, and I was no closer to knowing whether or not I'd be allowed to join the Loftschloss. Paul simply kissed me on each cheek and told me to *mach's gut* as I dragged myself onto a night bus, freezing and dejected. I was almost too dejected to notice the stark, austere beauty of those Stalinesque wedding-cake buildings looming in the dull-blue darkness, the menacing disco twinkle of the *Fernsehturm* as my bus glided by. And I was definitely too dejected to care when a cute guy who looked to be my age bummed a cigarette after I disembarked near Gertrud's, and also too dejected to enjoy the small victory of telling him I lived *gleich um die Ecke,* the idiom for "right around the corner" I'd been practicing all week. What good was having all of these adventures if five German strangers I wasn't sure I liked were ambivalent about letting me squat in their living room? I slept until two the following afternoon.

But halfway through my first pouty coffee, Paul called Gertrud's place and instructed me to come by the Loftschloss, drop off as much of my stuff as I could carry, pick up my new keys, and would I please bring the three hundred deutsche marks in cash? Apparently they had all proclaimed me cool enough to live with them based solely upon whatever they had gleaned from ignoring me. This, I would soon learn, was an excellent demonstration of a near-universal national telepathy: Germans are able to gather all pertinent information about each other from glowering silently in each other's general direction at bars. Somehow at the end of the night a lot of them pair off, then move in together, have kids without being married, take their full year's parental leaves, and live happily ever after.

"It's in the second *Hinterhof* behind the Sanders Tires sign," said Paul.

Hinterhof literally means "courtyard behind," and it refers to the building at the rear of the courtyard that almost all German apartment houses have—in many cases, court*yards,* plural, as the Loftschloss was technically in the courtyard *behind* the courtyard behind.

I nervously *Guten Tag*'d the blue overall-clad auto workers as they very loudly dislodged some hubcaps. I even-more-nervously buzzed the button marked LOFTSCHLOSS 1. ETAGE (in Germany, the ground floor is "floor zero," which causes some confusion among Americans and not a small amount of yelling from perturbed neighbors). As soon as Paul let me in and I entered the vestibule of my new home for the first time, I was awash in the smell of concrete and plaster and something faintly sweet, which I would soon learn is a smell oddly common in Kreuzberg loft buildings, and which to this day, if I catch a whiff of it, makes me so nostalgic I start reaching for my pack of Lucky Strikes, even though I haven't smoked in a decade and a half.

The Loftschloss was not, as Gertrud had warned me, one giant room. It was *two* giant rooms, plus an actual freestanding, wall-enclosed bathroom with its own stand-up shower and central water heating and everything. I'd barely had a chance to peer around the vast, definitely-industrial-looking space—pipes visible everywhere, unfinished walls, and not a residential fixture in sight—before Paul thrust into my hand the most curious set of keys I'd ever seen. There was a regular-sized one for the door of the loft and a bizarre, giant, cartoon-looking thing wider in circumference than a number-two pencil, with no method of affixing it to any sort of chain. This, Paul explained, was for the outer door, whose lock hadn't been updated since before the war. You operated it by sticking one end of the key into the keyhole, turning it around until it caught, then swinging the door open, walking through, and pulling the key out the other side of the door. You had to unlock the door from the inside to get out, as well as from the outside to get in. This seemed to me rather terrifying, but perhaps just as the Germans assumed nobody would be forgetful enough to lose their coat-check ticket at the club, so did they assume nobody would be careless enough to set a fire.

"The others are all out," Paul said. He grabbed my suitcase, wheeled it across the industrial carpet, and lifted a thick black curtain that had been suspended on a rod balanced between two giant pipes that ran across the ceiling.

"But what's this?" I asked. There was an actual bed there, with a white metal frame that looked like life-sized dollhouse furniture.

"Oh, we put it together for you," said Paul. "That was actually Leonie's childhood bed in Munich."

"Look how close it is to the radiator!" I said.

Paul looked concerned. "Are you going to be too hot? We can move you."

"Nein!" I assured him, and was then left to unpack my Urban Decay nail polishes and traveler's checks and giant plastic travel speakers alone, before I collapsed for a luxuriant nap, which I took with my *bare feet* poking out from under the blanket. I awoke to the sound of glasses clinking and the smell of smoke; someone seemed to be having a party at the small round table that sat some nine feet away from my room's partition. Was I invited by default, just by living in the party room? What if they all ignored me—like, not German-ignored me benignly, but ignored-ignored me meanly?

On my first day? I cowered under my covers, thumbing through my copy of *The Threepenny Opera*. Was the name Mackie Messer supposed to strike fear into my heart? I couldn't tell. But at least I could put the opening number to the music in my head. I would have no such luck for *Die Heilige Johanna der Schlachthöfe*. Even though the plays required, you know, effort, they were actually pretty interesting. *Perhaps I should be too scared to enter my own living room more often,* I thought. Eventually, though, my bladder's demands became unignorable, and I had no choice but to peek my head out from behind my wall-curtain.

"*Ach*, Rebecca," said Paul, who was flanked by Johannes and two people I'd never seen before, a beautiful girl with glowing skin and her boyfriend, a genial-looking guy with red hair and a beard. "You're alive! *Komm schon*, join us for an amaretto! You're not the *Hausmaus!*"

The girl was Anke, the guy Andreas, and they were yet more friends from Chemnitz. Those *Ossis* were really tight. Paul poured a shot of liquor into what I would later learn was an egg cup, and I pounded it back before I noticed that my companions were sipping theirs daintily—especially Anke, who only had about half a sip's worth to begin with.

"We're celebrating," explained Andreas. "*Anke bekommt ein Kind.*" This expression, *ein Kind bekommen*, literally means "to get a child." *From where?* I wondered—and then I figured it out. She was *pregnant*. That must have been why her skin was so luminous. But wasn't this terrible news, as a pregnancy would be to myself and literally anyone I knew? Weren't they too young? (They were twenty-four, and they didn't seem upset.) *But she was drinking!* Paul watched my eyes rest on Anke's tiny glass of amaretto before I composed myself and said, "Wow! That's wonderful! Congratulations!"

"Don't be such an American," he said. "A little sip of amaretto is *fine*."

I blushed and grabbed a cigarette, then looked at Anke guiltily. *"Kein Problem,"* she said. I'd just lit up and blown a satisfying cloud into to the sexy darkness of the living room when I heard the door unlatch and then yelling, of which I only understood the phrase *es ist zum Kotzen,* which literally means "it is to the vomiting," but is slang for "it's absolutely sickening." Paul excused himself and walked across the cavernous room, bare but for the table and my curtained-off corner, to talk to an obviously irate Leonie. All I could make out was "[something something] knew [something something] smoking [something something] living here!"

Leonie, I soon found out, claimed severe allergies to many common irritants, including cigarette smoke (except, funnily enough, when she was out at any bar, Kaffeehaus, or club), which she also happened to loathe (100 percent correctly, of course). But for some reason, in the Loftschloss she'd been outvoted by Paul, Johannes, and now me (implicitly; it was clear that I would not be getting a full Loftschloss vote anytime soon). Thereafter, despite her vomit-related protestations, a cloud of airborne nicotine hovered at all times near our twelve-foot ceilings. The smoke snuck into the far corners of the oddly sunny "west wing" (*Westflügel*), which was currently one massive Pergo-floored room, but would soon house all five of the other Loftschlossers in quasi-separate dwellings they built themselves. It permeated the dark-blue industrial carpeting that covered the "east wing" (*Ostflügel*), the half of the loft designated as the living room, and peeked beyond the thick black fabric that served as my wall.

That first night in the Castle, after what sounded to me like a German Edward Albee play, Leonie and Paul seemed to reconcile (the détente involved "[something something] window [something]"), and Andreas, Anke, and their tipsy fetus were loosed into the Berlin night, with assistance from Paul and his giant cartoon key. I crawled back into my toasty corner and smiled myself to sleep at how quickly your life can change, if you just follow the right jean jackets through the streets in the middle of the night. I was going to be *so cool* for living there.

The next morning, however, was no time to be cool. It was, instead, time for manual labor, which I quickly realized came with the terms of my nonexistent lease. The task ahead, of questionable legality, was the self-administered renovation of the west wing, which was to be divided into a kitchen and three bedrooms: one *Einzelzimmer* (single room) each for Detlef and Rolf—who, I learned near-immediately, were never home—and a massive triple at the wing's far end, which Johannes, Paul, and Leonie would share. That wing had been in a state of mid-division the very day I moved in, so my true introduction to the loft and its inhabitants— and to speaking German all day long and finally slipping uncomfortably into fluency—coincided with a crash course in interior renovations.

"*Rebecca!*" Leonie yelled at me from atop a ladder I was steadying, after definitely not enough coffee. "*Gib' mir den Akkubohrer!*"

"The what?"

"*Akku . . . bohrer.*"

I held up a hammer. "*Das?*"

"*Nein. AKKU. BOHRER.*"

I held up a bucket of half-mixed plaster. "*Das?*"

Finally, Leonie clambered down from the ladder I'd been holding up with not a small amount of brute force, stomped around me, grabbed a cordless screwdriver, muttered "*Nutzlos,*" and then huffed her way back up the ladder. *Akku* means "rechargeable battery"; *Bohrer* means, literally, "screwer" (heh). Not a word that had been on my vocab lists in German 102, 202, or 310, but I certainly knew it now.

Ludwig Wittgenstein uses a construction site as an example of language learning in the *Philosophical Investigations*—the boss says, "Bring me a board!" and the analphabetic assistant learns what a board is through petty tyranny. Wittgenstein castigates us for believing, wrongly, that this method of language learning ("ostension") is how we learn our native tongue (because, he points out, in order to understand the gesture for "this is a board," we have to understand what "this is" means, and thus in order to learn language we *already* have to understand how language works). But it is, he admits, a working (albeit clunky) method of *second* language learning, and it is basically how I functioned as building apprentice at the Loftschloss, learning the words for *crossbeam, nail gun,* and *socket wrench* by being prompted to do things with them, and then accordingly shamed until I figured out what word I'd never heard before went with what object I had never used before.

As a second-language teacher, Leonie left a bit to be desired.

"Your German, *übrigens*—which means 'by the way,'" she told me a few mornings into my apprenticeship (switching into barely accented English for "by the way"), as I held a wall panel in place while she stuffed old copies of the *Zweite Hand* into it as insulation— "is even worse today than usual."

Leonie was always, in fact, the first to point out a misconjugated verb, a misgendered noun, a trailing off midsentence because my language was too simple to express a complicated opinion.

"I really can't emphasize enough," she continued, "how bad you are at German." There is a certain kind of German who truly believes she is "helping" the second-language learner by quickly pointing out all of her mistakes before she can finish an utterance—the *Sprachpolizei*, the language police—and what they really "help" me do is become abjectly terrified to say a single goddamned word, for fear that if I do, it will be my incorrectness, rather than the content of what I am trying to say, that is communicated.

"It doesn't matter what I say to Leonie," I said that night to Diane, over one-mark shots of watered-down tequila, at a café about two hundred paces away from the *Schloss* that ran a special Thursday-night promotion on watered-down tequila. "All she hears—all I feel like anyone hears—is *ich bin fremd*. I am foreign. *Ich bin fremd, ich bin fremd, ich bin fremd*."

"Why don't you just tell her to *Verpiss dich*?" she asked. "That means 'fuck off,' and she'll be impressed with your fluency."

The worst thing about being an intermediate second-language speaker around critical people is that when they criticize your language abilities, it feels like they are also criticizing your intellect; in mocking your clunky construction of a thought, they seem to believe that you really think that way all the time.

"You must have had terrible grades in German class in school," Leonie said about a week into the renovation, as both of us began smearing plaster on the wall of what would soon be Detlef's room. "Your teachers must have been *very* frustrated with you."

"Well," I said, glooping my plaster around in a figure-eight, "they didn't have a chance. I didn't study German in school."

"*Wie bitte?*"

"I did Spanish in school," I said. "*And* I was the best in the class, actually." Finally, a moment when my host country's tendency toward bluntness would pay off. "I began German at the start of university," I said. "Which was"—I stopped to count—"two and a half years ago."

Leonie stopped mid-dunk into the plaster bucket.

"Really?" she asked. "*Well*, then."

She'd assumed that American children, like German children, begin foreign languages—*plural!*—in about the third grade. She'd assumed that we are a nation of monolingual idiots because we are impervious to our years of instruction, when we are, on the contrary, a nation of monolingual idiots because of institutionalized ethnocentricity and xenophobia, and near-total lack of instruction altogether.

"For two and a half years," she said, "you're actually not so terrible."

Although that was high praise, my general sensitivity toward criticism of any sort, combined with my specific antipathy toward Leonie herself, meant that I spent my first month in the Loftschloss attempting to prove that I was smart, while simultaneously saying as little as possible. Contrary to the way I have spent every other minute of my life, hours went by when I uttered nothing at all, as I helped convert the loft from an industrial space into a residence—for which, mind you, it was not even close to properly zoned (they had a "corporation" running out of it, something to do with Johannes and Paul's computer work). As Leonie reminded me every single day, were the landlady, Frau Richter-Schmitt, to do a pop-by unannounced, at no point was I to admit that I lived there and paid rent. This also meant that in no way was I allowed to *anmelden,* or register my address with the police, which meant, in turn, that I would be unable to obtain the student visa that I had been strictly instructed to get. Not only was I living in an illegal residence, I was also living there illegally. (Back then, however, there was a loophole in the law—as long as you left the *Bundesrepublik* before your three-month tourist visa ran out, you could just come right back in for another ninety days. All that mattered was that little passport stamp from the Czech Republic or Poland, both of which were a few hours away by train.)

I'm not being fair to Leonie here, by the way. She wasn't a villain. She actually felt pretty neutral about me, and simply enjoyed giving me grief, which the Germans describe using the unsavory word *verarschen,* which literally means "to assify (someone)." She was also just *really* German. (A real *Wessi,* I would have said about six weeks earlier.) What I would call, in my wishy-washy American way, different *preferences* for how to do something inconsequential—knotting a scarf, opening a window, plunging a French press, eating cheese—many of the Germans I've met would recognize as grievous misdeeds against humanity, requiring the swift performance of a public service, namely both noticing the transgression and bringing it emphatically to my attention. If I protested that their constant criticism (they would call it "help") hurt my feelings, Germans would respond that the ridiculous delicacy of those feelings is simply another fault that needs to be addressed immediately.

Once when Leonie thought I was either asleep or gone, I overheard her talking to Paul at the table. "Rebecca's so *quiet,*" she said.

"No, she's not," he said. "She's just afraid of you."

"Nonsense," she said.

I waited until she'd left to tiptoe out into the living room, where I saw that she'd doodled in her notebook, in huge letters, the following directive:

ICH VERBIETE REBECCA, MICH ZU FÜRCHTEN.
(I forbid Rebecca to be afraid of me.)

To be fair to all other Germans, plenty of them are substantially more laid-back about the way other people do things than Leonie was, and not just *Ossis* such as Paul, who was so lackadaisical about washing dishes that he protested when Leonie reminded him to rinse, a rare moment in which she and I were aligned. ("Bah!" he'd said. "It's not necessary!") By far the most easygoing resident of the Loftschloss was Johannes, he of the *Punky Brewster* jeans, busted front tooth, Lucky Strikes, and giant wild mane. He and Leonie were best friends, which only made sense, because they were polar opposites, and if you averaged them out, you got a normal person. He was skinny as a two-by-four and she was curvaceous (though a far, far measure from *dick,* or "fat," which is how her flatmates inexplicably described her). His hair inhabited its own zip code; her head was shaved (possibly in homage to Judith Butler). He was vegetarian like me—yes, German vegetarians exist—and she ate like a regular person. And where her personality was as rough as the sandpapery toilet tissue in every restroom in the Federal Republic, his was as soft and gentle as a tiny baby lamb. And that is why, when Leonie declared to the rest of the house that erecting slightly more permanent walls in the corner of the living room, to make the sixth bedroom (*my* room) into an actual room, was "lowest possible priority"—while looking me right in the eyes—Johannes insisted we raise those walls as soon as Detlef's plaster was dry. He was protecting me from her. And so obviously I fell in love with him immediately.

The nascent stages of our relationship were kept ambiguous through a clever switch-out of German dative prepositions, which every beginning German student knows are the easiest to remember because they can be sung to the tune of the "Blue Danube" waltz. The night after he and Paul finally hung my walls up (as Leonie popped bubble wrap passive-aggressively in the other room), we went out to Milchbar to celebrate. I drank a few glasses of Aventinus, a special beer that wasn't easy to find and was famous because it had the same alcohol content as wine. As it did every night at Milchbar, Iggy Pop's "The Passenger" came on the stereo, and, as transpired every night at Milchbar, every single German in attendance broke from their silent smoking (or impassioned debates about the Green Party) to sing along full voice with Iggy and David Bowie during that chorus of *La*s.

"Come on," Johannes said to me as I was midway through my final Aventinus slug. And out we went under the bright and hollow sky. As we rounded the corner of Oranienstraße, I knew the moment was right. (At any rate, I'd had enough beer.) I grabbed Johannes by his skintight yellow trousers (he called them his *Wertherhose,* after the outfit Werther wears in Goethe's novella for the lovelorn). I pinned him against the grimy wall of a crumbling building and stared up at his frizzy blond halo.

"You're beautiful," he said in English (he'd attended an American school in Korea and spoke fluently). "Don't do all that makeup shit."

This was highly debatable: I was at the time sporting a bleached-white buzz cut, the result of boredom, Leonie's clippers, and very strong German box dye, and it made me look like the spitting image of Mike D from the Beastie Boys. Nevertheless, I humored Johannes and wiped off my Chanel Metallic Vamp lipstick and we kissed, a study-abroad cliché come to glorious life, illuminated by the streetlights, jolted through with the buzz of a not-insubstantial amount of alcohol and the frenetic city around us. *OPERATION FIND GERMAN BOYFRIEND: CHECK! Hooray!* Now I'd get fluent in the language for *sure*.

Our coupling was hastened when we came home to find an immovable passed-out rando in Johannes's bed—somebody was always crashing at the Loftschloss on no notice—and Johannes had no choice but to traverse back to the east wing and bunk with me. The next morning, after our relationship had been consummated (and during which I learned that *Gummi,* the German slang for "condom," is disturbingly similar to *Kaugummi,* "chewing gum"), Johannes took it upon himself to read Leonie the riot act about the bed-interloper.

"You can't just let *anyone* stay *anywhere!*" he said. "I came home and I couldn't even sleep in my own fucking bed."

"Oh *please,* your *Schulfreund* Klaus was here for two weeks and I didn't say anything."

"That's because I didn't put him in your *bed.*"

"Wait, where did you sleep, anyway?" Leonie asked, eyebrow arched.

"Ich hab' bei Rebecca geschlafen," he answered with a shrug, which technically means "I slept with Rebecca," but uses the dative preposition *bei,* which means "with" as in *at someone's house.* When you sleep *bei* someone, that usually means you're crashing on the couch or the floor. What he didn't say was what had actually happened: *Ich habe mit Rebecca geschlafen,* which means exactly what you think it means, and which would have been indelicate to say outright, even for a culture that so cherishes its bluntness.

Our relationship eventually became unambiguous, a development that three out of the four other Loftschlossers found insignificant (it is possible that Detlef and Rolf never even realized it, given that they were never home). I can't really blame Leonie, though—she and Johannes were best friends, and my swift ascendance as his girlfriend, which resulted in us being cleaved together for days at a time, provoked seething jealousy in me anytime the two of them wanted to hang out alone, or disagreed with me about anything, or—an altercation of which I am not particularly proud—decided to prepare a meal of fried fish together even though Johannes was supposed to be my co-vegetarian. Most of the time, though, Johannes acted as a giant-haired human shield, sheltering me from the more-inane instances of Leonie-related pedantry while still including me in the everyday household activities, which involved *Run Lola Run*–levels of improbability, minus the petty crime and time travel—so, primarily a lot of questionable hairstyles and techno music.

I wouldn't say, however, that this was a period of assimilation into the late-nineties Berlin milieu. This is because *assimilation* is not a strong enough word. It was a time of full-scale metamorphosis into monstrous Eurotrash. I started dressing differently, trading my black garments for clashing bright separates—which I accessorized, at all times, with one or more scarves, no matter the weather, as per Eurotrash bylaw. At Johannes's request, and because it clashed with my clothes, I neglected my extensive, expensive, and lovingly curated makeup collection in favor of four days' worth of facial oil. (It probably goes without saying that, in accordance with the local mores, I lessened my showers to twice or thrice weekly.)

I started acting differently, turning up to study-abroad functions with at least one Loftschlosser in tow, or blowing them off to hang out at home, which—having been furnished with a functioning stage (including microphone and amps), three dismembered mannequins, and a rope swing hanging from the ceiling, was now officially cooler than most local establishments. I started eating differently, finally learning how to butter my bread correctly—methodically and in a perfect even layer, out to the exact edge of every piece—and correspondingly embraced the tradition of the ninety-minute Berlin breakfast, undertaken with alarming propriety even by squatters who lived in rubble. (I also started putting Bailey's in my morning coffee instead of cream, though this was an entirely individual affectation.) I started speaking differently—in, at long last, fluent German, albeit a slang-heavy and grammatically suspect dialect of my own devising that was my earnest adoption of Johannes's single rule about second-language acquisition: *Just don't give a shit.*

But even after all this, I wasn't truly considered a Loftschlosser until I developed the ability to stop being shocked when my roommates did something so bizarre that, until they did it, I never would have even considered in the repertoire of human action. One afternoon, for example, Paul came home with a used television, a thirteen-inch model that had most definitely broadcast the fall of the Wall live. He and Johannes immediately set about sawing a rectangular hole through the living room wall, creating the world's first flat-screen by shoving the set into that hole so that its backside hung directly over the toilet in the bathroom on the other side.

Another morning—by which I mean noon—I awoke to the urgent demand from Leonie and Paul that I come downstairs to participate in the Gay Pride Parade *immediately.*

"*Los,* Rebecca!" Leonie said. "*Heute ist* Christopher Street Day!"

"But I'm wearing my *Schlafanzug!*" I said, pointing to my green-and-black oversized flannel pajamas from the Gap.

"I know!" she said. "You're dressed perfectly."

I ended up going out dressed like that to a fairly snobby restaurant for lunch.

It was my official rule never to turn down an invitation by a Loftschlosser, because each one took me to a weirder place than the last, deeper into the Berlin that my *Time Out* guidebook had never seen. One night, it was a tire-fire party in the backyard of a squat, whose residents performed their toilette in a full-sized bathtub placed on top of two adjacent stoves. At some point I told some of them that I could play "Wonderwall," so, in between excoriating my country's imperialist foreign policy and correcting my grammar, the "occupiers" (the literal German for squat is *besetztes Haus,* or "occupied house") thrust an out-of-tune acoustic guitar into my hands.

"Oasis spielen!" they cried. "Oasis! Oasis! Oasis!" They pronounced it Oh-*AH*-sis.

The next week, it was onto the handlebars of Johannes's bicycle with me, as he careened through the deserted streets of Mitte at four in the morning, en route to a bar called *Dienstagsbar* because it wasn't a bar so much as a random gathering of people with cool hair in a gravel-covered vacant lot, and it only happened on Tuesdays. As we rode, we screamed the lyrics to a Jürgen von der Lippe song, whose comedic nuances I did not understand but whose spirit nevertheless seemed right:

> *Feet in the fire, nose in the wind*
> *Men will be men, men will be men*

The next week, it was a pop-up art show by one of Leonie's friends, comprised entirely of stuffed-panty-hose sculptures, that took place inside a filthy abandoned bunker. Sometimes I felt like my roommates just woke up, combined a bunch of random nouns and verbs, and then decided to go do whatever that was.

In the late spring, we threw what was supposed to be a rent party, but on which, I am fairly certain, we lost money. At a series of increasingly heated planning meetings, Leonie and Paul almost came to fisticuffs over whether or not we should serve homemade fries, which she insisted could be prepared in bulk on our fifth-hand stove and the rest of us viewed as a mild-to-moderate grease-fire hazard that paired especially unsavorily with the fact that technically our building was always locked from the outside. The party was almost called off entirely due to these creative differences, until Johannes came through the door one day wielding a contraption from the mid-1970s that looked like a Barbie Dream West German Nuclear Fallout Shelter.

"Ach du Scheiße!" said Leonie. "Where did you find that?"

"Zweite Hand," said Johannes. "The party snacks are solved!"

Everyone let out a cheer except for me, who had no idea what the fuck the thing was.

"What's wrong, Rebecca?" asked Leonie. "Haven't you ever seen a sandwich maker before?"

"Not one like that," I said, believing, rube that I was, that a *sandwich maker* was a pair of hands and a knife.

It was essential that this party be perfect for me, because I'd invited all of my study-abroad classmates and it was imperative they see firsthand exactly how cool my life was. And I think that when the magical day arrived—sturdy milk-crates full of Hefeweizen procured, peculiar elder-flower punch mixed, sandwich menu curated (Nutella DM 2,50; Cheese DM 3)—they had a good time. But it was hard for me to tell, because for most of the party I was stuck on "key duty," which meant I was responsible for using my giant Disney *Schlüssel* to let some partygoers in and others out, at random and somewhat indeterminate intervals made ever more complicated by the fact that nobody had a mobile phone yet.

Our guests stayed so late into the wee hours—dancing; swinging from the ceiling; staring at each other wordlessly and then pairing off into life partners; eating sandwiches—that Paul had to blow his saxophone directly into their drunken ears to get them to stumble out into the *Hinterhof.* When I finally trod into my corner of the living room at eleven the next morning, I found a strange guy sleeping in my bed.

"*Hallo,*" I said. "I live here."

"Huh," he said, and puffed languidly on the cigarette whose ashes were falling onto my sheets. "Is this yours?" He held up a haunting-looking children's book, *The Three Golden Keys,* by Peter Sís. "It's wonderful. Just wonderful. I can't believe these illustrations."

I'd never seen the book before and didn't know how it got into my room, but it looked like the guy needed some more time alone with it, so I slunk back into the kitchen and grabbed one of the few remaining bottles of beer. I popped off the cap using one of the four cigarette lighters that lived permanently on the kitchen table, then used the same lighter to ignite a Lucky Strike from one of Johannes's half-open packs.

As I took a slug, Paul shuffled in with his hair sticking straight up and his shirt on backward. He nodded, grabbed a bottle for himself, and handed it to me to open, since I already had a lighter in my hand.

After about fifteen minutes of sipping and staring out the window through a smoke cloud, he said: "You're up early."

I nodded.

After about five more minutes, he said: "It might be cold today."

I looked vaguely in the direction of the living room, ashed my cigarette, yawned. We were, after all, there to drink, not to talk.

7.

Liebeskummer

n. heartbreak, from love *and* grief.

ex. On account of your *Liebeskummer,* I will forgive you that supper of Jägermeister.

For the next eight years, the closest I would get to Berlin would be my unpaid, uncredited (and correspondingly untrained and unqualified) work as a dramaturge, dialect coach, and prop master for an off-off-off-off-off-Broadway play called *Berlin,* which went up at the Tribeca Playhouse in the fall of 2001, in the shadow of the World Trade Center wreckage. Despite being an "equity showcase" put on by a bunch of then-amateurs, *Berlin* had a sold-out run. It was an awful, somber, unmoored time to be in New York, and people related to the beautifully written story, which itself took place amid rubble.

It was an improbable but redemptive romance between Heike, an aging ex-Nazi screen idol, and Bill, an American GI. And despite my substantial failure to coach the lead actress, Renata (whom you may recognize as different characters on about ninety-four episodes of *Law & Order*), to sound less like Madeline Kahn in *Blazing Saddles*, and despite my lackluster attention to replenishing the fake stage-whiskey, and despite the fact that it didn't get me anywhere near actual Berlin, *Berlin* was also a rousing success for me personally. This was not just because I got the script changed when the playwright wanted the two leads to travel to a hotel "a couple hundred miles east" of Berlin, which is Poland. It was also due to the improbable and redemptive romance between the hot twenty-two-year-old prodigy who played the American GI and yours motherfucking truly.

In addition to being the unpaid and uncredited dramaturge, dialect coach, and prop-master, I was also the play's sign-in manager on the day we auditioned for the male lead, Bill, a wide-eyed teenager who loves *The Great Gatsby* and is several measures out of his depth in the occupied, decimated German capital. We had Renata already, Madeline Kahn accent dialed all the way up, and I watched as Bill after Bill—all comely, overeager waiter-actors in their mid-to-late twenties—ambled onto the stage in the rented rehearsal space to read with her. They were all fine—you know, for actors. They read their lines with commitment; they made "choices" about the character (as they say in showbiz). But they were all still clearly acting, trapped in a mimetic performance (as they say in the academic biz).

"All right," said Mark, the director, when yet another earnest but mediocre Bill left the stage. "That was great. We'll call you." He turned to me. "Anyone else?"

There was one more person on my list, but he was nowhere to be found. Maybe he'd heard Renata's accent and skedaddled? I sprang up from my folding chair in the back and did my best self-important theatrical scamper out into the hall, where, sure enough, there was a guy with giant blue eyes, filthy blond hair, and almost impossibly delicate cheekbones, slumped down in one chair while his propped-up feet rested on another, headphones turned so high I could hear every word of what he was listening to, which was "Heart-Shaped Box" by Nirvana. From the looks of him, when that record came out he was in utero himself. He wasn't handsome in the tanned, muscled, hairless, simultaneously-oversexed-and-sexless *She's All That* teenybopper manner that was currently the rage in Hollywood—but he was arresting to look at. I touched him gently on the shoulder and he jumped. "Oh, sorry!" he said. "Am I up?"

I led him into the theater and he loped onto the stage. He sat down next to Renata and before he said a single word, everyone in the room could feel a palpable, yearning, profound sexual tension between them. In that moment I wanted nothing more than for someone to want me in the way this guy wanted that woman. What he did wasn't acting. He just *was*.

Goethe's most trusted colleague was a fellow named Friedrich Schiller, who idolized his friend so much that after Goethe's demise, he kept the writer's skull as a souvenir and used it as a paperweight. (Or, at any rate, what he *believed* was Goethe's skull; most Germans were buried in mass graves back then, and Schiller simply chose the largest of the skulls in Goethe's cohort, because obviously Goethe had been the smartest of whatever lot he was interred with.) Schiller was a wonderful writer in his own right, of tumultuous Sturm und Drang plays and the lofty works of "Weimar Classicism" (basically, he and Goethe imitating the ancient Greeks and Romans). But one of his most famous writings is an essay called "On Naïve and Sentimental Poetry."

Schiller's theory was that most poets are what he called

"sentimental"—he didn't use that word in the way we use it now, but rather to denote the clear act of labor present in most writing. Sentimental poets might be technically perfect, and even great—but they were always clearly trying, often really hard. Naïve poets, on the other hand—by which he meant his buddy Goethe—didn't have to imitate nature, because they just *were* nature. They were possessed by beauty, by the creative *Dämon*, who took hold of them and guided their hands. Their work could be messy (although Goethe's wasn't); it could be rough, but it was, in Schiller's conception, genius. Genius was hard to describe—although Schiller certainly did his best, and had a helpful exemplar in his skull, I mean friend—but you knew it when you were in its presence. And that October 2001 day in fake-Berlin, in real New York, with the smoldering World Trade Center leaking noxious smoke into every corner of Manhattan, there was genius on that stage.

"Great," said Mark when the scene was finished, and I realized I'd been gripping the sides of my chair so tightly they made my knuckles white. "We'll call you."

The play had its second lead—and, more important, Rebecca Schuman was interested, despite the fact that he was three and a half years her junior and seemed to have a shaky relationship with shampoo.

During production, as I futzed with the genius's props and gave him a crash course on the grisly and desolate occupation of Germany (itself the result of my own crash course at the New York Public Library), I teased some personal details out. He was from Connecticut, had gotten his first TV role as a high-school senior, then acquired an agent and a manager and skipped college to move straight to the city and book jobs.

"So is this what you do all the time?" he asked before tech rehearsal, as I rushed in with some dubious bodega vegetables so that Mark, the goddamned visionary auteur, could have real fucking food onstage during a meal scene.

"No," I said. "I work as a Web editor at a nonprofit, down in, you know, the financial district." I pointed in what I thought was the general direction of my day-job's office on Broad Street, which was a twenty-minute walk away. "But now I'm just part-time there, because . . ."

"Got it."

"I started out as an editorial assistant for a book publisher."

"Cool," he said. "I love to read."

"Mostly I got coffee and made Xeroxes," I said. "But every once in a while I got to do something interesting. Like, once my boss was trying to woo P. Diddy to write an autobiography, and I got to shuttle him up a freight elevator. He was called Puff Daddy then."

The genius didn't look as impressed as he should have.

"It was just him and me and his son and this giant bodyguard. He drives a completely silver Mercedes."

"Is that what you want to do with your life?" he asked. "Like, edit? Or assist editors? Ferry P. Diddy up the elevator?"

"I guess," I said. "At one point I think I wanted to be a writer. I write things for the Internet sometimes. I realize that doesn't really count."

"I'm always trying to write things, but I never get past the first paragraph. I have no discipline."

"Oh!" I said. "Once this really intense dude from the Church of Scientology was mad about how he'd been portrayed in one of my boss's books, and he showed up at the office and, like, wouldn't leave."

"Now *that*'s fucking cool," he said. I smiled and cleared my throat as Mark blew in and glared at me for fraternizing with the talent.

The genius did love to read. He was currently midway through *No Logo* by Naomi Klein, and had as a result duct-taped over what few corporate logos remained on his threadbare clothes. (He was also in the process of watching every Kurosawa film ever made, in chronological order, and planned to move on to Sergio Leone next. Autodidacticism was, by the way, *such* a Schillerian-genius quality.) We exchanged books—he gave me Garth Ennis's brilliant *Preacher* graphic novels, and I, at this point having looped all the way around to self-parody, brought him Kafka's *Complete Stories*.

"I had a pretty tough time getting through the 'Penal Colony' one," he confessed. Not because it was too violent, though. Because it was "kind of boring."

"How can you say that? That story is gripping from the first word to the last."

The first time we ever socialized away from backstage was the wrap party, where we ignored everyone else and afterward shared a cab to our respective homes—mine a studio near Lincoln Center whose four walls I could touch at once, his a one-bedroom on the East Side, whose rent was financed by his acting jobs: a Lifetime movie; a tiny role in an upcoming film where Harrison Ford was the Russian captain of a submarine and for authenticity spoke English in a thick Russian accent; an episode, need it even be said, of *Law & Order*. Everyone in the cast and crew of *Berlin* saw us get into a cab together and assumed certain things—but, in fact, what was happening was an actual, multifaceted, honest friendship.

All right, this was primarily because the genius hadn't been interested in me romantically. Instead, he was trying to date the girl who'd played his sister in the Lifetime movie, but she had a boyfriend, and it was all very John Hughes (whose films I much preferred to Kurosawa's). She was sleekly coiffed and lithe as a gazelle, and had been nominated for a Golden Globe; I was a stumpy-legged fake dramaturge with a haircut I gave myself. She was in magazines and on the side of buses; I read magazines and *took* the bus. I was perfectly aware that Molly Ringwald ends up with Blaine, and Duckie is forever doomed to staring sexlessly in the mirror at his own awesome hat. But you know what? I'm here to tell you that sometimes Duckie *does* get Molly Ringwald, even if Duckie is a thick-stemmed twenty-five-year-old female dramaturge and Molly Ringwald is a much better-looking male actor on television. For as it happened, one night, as we splayed on his futon (as friends), stuffed full of gummi frogs we'd procured from the bodega next door (as friends), after spending the earlier part of the evening smoking weak New York pot (as friends) through an apple bong (which we'd carved as friends), he grabbed my head and planted one right on me. "Say something German," he said. "Anything."

"Uh," I said. "*Warum? Was soll ich sagen? Ich weiß nicht, was du willst.*"

"God, that's so fucking sexy," he said.

"Uh," I continued, paragon of articulate bilingualism that I was, "I just told you I, like, didn't know what you wanted."

"Who the fuck cares?" he said. "It sounds hot. Say something else."

Two weeks later, the lease on my miniature studio was up and my career as an unpaid dramaturge meant I lacked the means to afford its rent anymore. He suggested I move in, and we lived together for half of George W. Bush's first term and a good portion of his second.

My new actor boyfriend took great pleasure in introducing me to his friends as "a German-speaking writer." And, in the spirit of Kafka's *Trial* and the endless hermeneutics of "Before the Law," that was both true and false at the same time. I certainly spoke German better than, say, someone who doesn't speak it at all, and I certainly put pen to paper on a regular basis (or, at any rate, finger to keyboard, enough to develop carpal tunnel syndrome), but in the years following my B.A., I didn't get much published (except on the Internet, which barely counted), and my German weakened and then atrophied like the leg muscles of someone who's been in traction for a year.

Sure, when I first moved to New York after graduation in 1998, I'd attempted to keep up my fluency in creative ways. At that editorial-assistant job, for example, I took it upon myself to compose a fax in German to Leni Riefenstahl. Not at random, mind you; she'd published a photo book with my boss, a notoriously mercurial editor with an impressive Rolodex. When he wasn't directing me to type out correspondence to Johnny Rotten, however, he was yelling at me in a way even Germans had never prepared me for. He was so legendary for intemperance, in fact, that I started journaling my various indignities (sort of like how the philosopher G. E. Moore kept a diary specifically dedicated to the different ways in which Ludwig Wittgenstein hurt his feelings). Anyway, Leni Riefenstahl never faxed back, and until *Berlin,* I went about systematically forgetting my German as I purged my wardrobe of its jubilant Eurotrash brights.

The closest I came to interacting with the German canon was the tattoo I'd gotten at a dingy parlor by the Lorimer Street L train

LIEBESKUMMER 181

station in Williamsburg, after moving there in 1999 in a desperate flight from a terrible relationship with a manipulative dick I met two weeks after graduating from college, whose eighteen months of manipulative dickishness does not merit description. To celebrate my exit, I wanted an indelible marker. In the manner of Kafka's very not-boring "Penal Colony," I wanted the truth of it not simply to be understood with words. I wanted to *feel it,* as the Officer says to the Explorer in Kafka's story, *with my wounds.* This desire culminated in the procurement of a single, two-inch-high tattoo on what seemed at the time the unusual and sensual location of my middle-lower back. It was so small that the visibly annoyed artist—who scoffed *No* when I asked if he wanted to know the significance behind the design, which I created myself by Xeroxing a page out of *The Castle* at 1,000 percent—could only charge the shop minimum of fifty dollars. It took three-quarters of an episode of *The Simpsons* to complete, and hurt slightly more than an aggressive teeth cleaning. It consisted only of a single letter and a single piece of punctuation, made to look as if it had been stamped on with a dirty typewriter key: к. It would be the closest I'd come to thinking seriously about German literature until several years (and a much better boyfriend) later.

Never once did I think about keeping up with my German—language, literature, anything—in graduate school, because graduate school had never been part of my plan—well, *real* graduate school. As another measure of post-relationship-with-the-dickish-guy independence, and primarily because he had "forbidden" me to do something so stupid, I laid out many thousands of borrowed dollars to get an M.F.A. in fiction writing, occupying two evenings a week for two years feeling deeply misunderstood as a group of my peers indulgently discussed my thinly veiled autobiography.

Then, after *Berlin* wrapped and I was shacking up with the kind, generous, and blessedly not emotionally abusive actor, I'd even parlayed that M.F.A. into a quick and depressing semester teaching Business Communications (a.k.a. remedial composition) at an unaccredited secretarial school in New Jersey. But four months spent grading on the PATH train and collapsing every night at nine thirty was enough of a detour into the hallowed halls of academe for me. My parents, two disgruntled English Ph.D.s, certainly agreed.

"Just get famous doing something and get an honorary doctorate," scoffed Sharon Schuman when I told her I'd absconded from the secretarial school. "It worked for Dan Quayle."

"Well," I said, "I'm going to take this job I just got offered at *Dance Teacher* magazine, otherwise known as a surefire route to fame, so I guess you must be very proud."

In college, I had openly mocked friends who wasted a perfectly good Saturday of hungover pizza to sit for the GRE on purpose. I didn't need *grad school*. I'd be doing just fine in the *real world* of *Dance Teacher* magazine, thank you very much—where, it turned out, all anyone wanted to talk about was carbohydrates, and I was abjectly miserable.

Thanks to my actor boyfriend, at least, I'd managed a convenient financial workaround to the incommensurability of twenty-eight-thousand-dollar salaries with a culture where that is how much people spend for their nanny's Pilates instruction—that is, he allowed me to live rent-free, after landing a lead role in a very funny (and underappreciated) movie I'll call *Four Dipshits Go Abroad*. And he also worked in an all-expense-paid trip to visit him on the set—which was in Prague, which according to my 1995 artisanal travel journal was *my very favorite place in the world*.

I hadn't yet earned my annual one-week vacation at *Dance Teacher,* but I talked my boss into letting me go anyway under the pretense that it was a networking trip for the magazine.

"I'll see if any of the stars were dancers. Maybe we can get a cover," I lied.

When I arrived, I got a ride to the set in a chauffeured town car. That day, they were shooting in an abandoned Soviet army barracks outside of town that had been made to look even shittier to fill in for Bratislava (actually a lovely city, but hey). I shared the car with my boyfriend's seventeen-year-old costar, who had been a professional actress since the age of four, was currently known worldwide for playing the younger sister of a famous, let's say, zombie killer, and who, I learned in short order, hated the ethereally beautiful city's cobblestones, spires, and mist-haunted alleys, gave exactly no shits about medieval, baroque, *or* Jugendstil architecture, and who had never heard of Franz Kafka. "I heard you *love Prague,*" she said by way of greeting.

"I *do!*" I said.

"Hmm," she said, wrinkling her telegenic nose. "Can I ask why?"

I had never heard of anyone not liking Prague before, and I had also never had a conversation in a town car with someone famous before, so I went momentarily blank.

"Well," I said, "it's a wonderful city if you, um, like architecture. And literature. And art."

"And cobblestones," she said.

"Yes, and cobblestones."

"I hate cobblestones," she said. "My Jimmy Choos always get stuck in them."

I looked down at my own shoes, grimy silver no-name flats from Urban Outfitters that had a hole in one of the soles.

"I miss L.A. *so* much," she said, as she opened an envelope that contained the script for her next project and inhaled deeply. "Ah," she said, "it still *smells* like L.A.!" This was meant as a compliment.

By the time I'd arrived in the Golden City—my boyfriend's setup was a plush apartment at the InterContinental with twenty-four-hour room service and five-star gym access, so pretty much *in* Kafka's old house—this teenager had established herself as the alpha of the set. But, lack of appreciation for medieval city planning aside, I thought she was sweet—plus, especially for her age, she was eerily prescient. For example, as we took turns bowling atrociously at a cast-and-crew party, she took me by the head and said: "You're so *pretty*!" Granted, this was definitely said in a *be nice to the nonthreatening fat girl* sort of way. I was the heaviest I have ever been (when not also housing another human being), after many weeks working late into the night on deadline at *Dance Teacher*, shoving down potato-chip-crusted mac and cheese from Vynl diner at my desk. But still. A celebrity says you're pretty and you say, "Thank you!"

Then she looked at me very seriously. "What do you want to *do* with your life?"

I reminded her that I was already an adult, and already doing things with my life. "I'm the associate editor of *Dance Teacher* magazine."

She batted the words away as soon as they left my mouth. "No," she said. "What do you *really* want to do?" I was left speechless by a child star who hated everything I loved (including, I suspected, my boyfriend).

On the plane back to the States, I got to thinking that she had a point. What *was* I doing with my life? When I wasn't getting fat at *Dance Teacher* and piggybacking onto my boyfriend's comparatively high-rolling lifestyle, I was moonlighting for an ad-reporting company, writing inane trivia questions about *One Tree Hill* to trick bored housewives into giving away their valuable demographic information. (By the way, I love *One Tree Hill*.) I'd finished my M.F.A. and was putting it to excellent use working seventy hours a week pummeling my mind into numbness.

The child star who said "literally" a lot was right, goddammit. I needed to make a change. After twenty-six years of insisting to anyone who would listen (and many who wouldn't) that I was above studying and trying—that my natural "gifts," whatever those were, required no effort-based bolstering—in preparation for my trip to the Prague set of *Dipshits,* I'd recently decided to start thumbing back through my German copies of Kafka for fun. To my shock, despite the fact that I hadn't had a real German conversation in nearly a decade, I could more or less understand "Das Urteil" ("The Judgment") in its entirety, from the first description of the spring day to the gross naked dad jumping up on the bed to last macabre quasi joke about "endless intercourse."

This time, with a little help from my yellowing compact Freshman Achievement Award dictionary, I didn't just understand the story; I *saw* it. I saw Georg Bendemann's blithe face as he finished a letter to his friend in Russia and went to check on his dad, totally unaware that this conversation would be his last on earth. I smelled the mustiness of Herr Bendemann's room. I felt the sting (metaphorical though it was) of a father calling his son an "evil human being," and then "sentencing" him to death. Sure, it hurt my noggin a little bit to squint through Kafka's sometimes-endless sentence construction, where you have no idea what things are really about until, after what seem like endless clauses and commas, a verb is finally reached. But every time I read a passage, it was like I got . . . *better* at reading the one after it. Like, smarter or something. And it was challenging, sure—but that challenge was *enjoyable*. Wait, was I a book dork? I *was* a book dork. And I needed to own my book-dorkdom and do something befitting it. Something like, maybe, reading "Das Urteil" in a more institutional setting.

So I started researching graduate programs in the New York area—but most of them required the GRE. And I mean, math? I don't want to be one of those *I'm a woman and I'm bad at math* women, because I was excellent at math in high school, but I hadn't so much as thought about math since Dylan Gellner "helped" me with physics in high school (an excuse to go into his bedroom on school nights). But one graduate program in New York, a terminal M.A. in "Humanities and Social Thought" at NYU, merely "recommended" the GRE (*Nein danke!*), and the students seemed to be able to take any course they wanted across the entire university and call it a program. This program also—surprise of surprises—didn't offer any financial aid. I said, *Sign me up! More school! More student loans, please! They will be inconsequential, because my boyfriend is famous now and he will go from comparatively rich to rich-rich and pay everything off, because he is just that nice of a guy! I need more time with "Das Urteil," and I need it now!* I didn't really know what people did with terminal M.A. degrees in Humanities and Social Thought, but I figured I'd sort it all out later when I was many thousands of dollars poorer, but a better humanist and social thinker.

I celebrated my acceptance to the program by quitting *Dance Teacher* and upping my hours as a professional TV watcher to near full-time. That way I'd have more time during the day to study, and to concentrate on taking the next step: applying for Ph.D. programs. What better way to cement the choice to go back to school than to make another choice to go to many, many more years of school? I mean, why not, right? (Besides the fact that I would, at last, have to take that fucking GRE.) Sure, it would mean an infinite amount of years outside of the workforce. But I had a plan. Even if my boyfriend didn't pay off my student loans as a Flag Day present, I would surely regain solvency when my screenplay/novel/ one-woman show/general creative-genius-whatever "hit." I mean, sure, I wasn't working on any of those things, but once I was free of the tyranny and vacuity of carbs conversations, it was only a matter of time.

I also applied to Ph.D. programs because of my favorite M.A. professor, Professor Singh, who taught a Theories of Citizenship course in which I had become acquainted with the political philosophy of a bunch of Germans: Kant, Hegel, Walter Benjamin, even Carl Schmitt, whose "paradox of sovereignty" so resembled the Bush Doctrine that the obscure philosopher, whose works were at the time largely unavailable in English, was enjoying a brief vogue. (This would result in a highly unfortunate crop of dissertations that would be irrelevant by the time they were defended in 2013, as opposed to most other dissertations, which are of utmost relevance.) Because of my recent adventures in Kafka reimmersion, I knew the original language all these Germans wrote in. And so, I figured that a Ph.D. in German was just the kind of obscure credential that would give a quirky future screenwriter/ playwright/novelist/person-who-had-done-none-of-these-things just the kind of heady credentials she needed to distinguish herself from the hordes of other dubious hyphenates in a profession that I hadn't invented yet. My knowledge of German, plus my legitimate interest in Walter Benjamin, G. W. F. Hegel, Jürgen Habermas, *und so fort,* made me an immediate favorite of Professor Singh, who heartily encouraged me to apply for real graduate school.

"You absolutely *must* go for a Ph.D.," he said at his office hours one day, as I talked him into letting me write a paper about Walter Benjamin and "Before the Law" (I had impressed everyone in my class by being able to read this in the original). "You are made for this. *Made* for it."

Nobody had ever said that about me before in relation to anything.

But five (or more) years of school—I couldn't imagine how much that would cost.

"What do you mean, cost?" asked Professor Singh. "Ph.D.s are fully funded."

Wait, five (or more) years where someone else would pay *me* to read Kafka all day?

"I mean, it's not very much money," Singh continued. "Pathetic pittance, really. And you have to teach a class."

Wait, five (or more) *years,* where someone else would pay me to talk about Kafka all day with *impressionable young people*? Done and done.

What came after those five years I neither knew nor cared, because like most twenty-eight-year-olds living in New York and trying to be "creative," I did not have a long-range plan, and indeed viewed anyone who did as a soul-munching Wall Street automaton with one foot in the grave and the other on his godforsaken lawn in Westchester. I would figure it out when I had to, obviously. Even as I applied, the idea of being a German professor as a permanent career—which, by the way, is the sole career for which one is preparing by getting a doctorate in German—barely crossed my mind. I had liked my college German professors fine. But I certainly didn't want to be them, what with having to read Theodor Fontane on purpose (he's the world's most boring "realist," so I guess the best one?), actually know how relative pronouns work, and live somewhere boring and gross. I would apply to exactly five Ph.D. programs, none of which were located somewhere boring and gross: NYU, Columbia, and then three in or near Los Angeles, as my boyfriend had just been cast in a pilot and was gearing up to move there.

Unfortunately, NYU and Columbia were both unimpressed. The only universities that wanted anything to do with me were in California, and they both flew me out on all-expenses-paid campus visits. Wooing is, indeed, standard practice in graduate school recruitment, which makes the prospective future Ph.D.'s heart soar on the wings of the mighty eagle Intellect and her brain think, *Isn't this amazing! Everyone is being so solicitous and treating me like I'm so smart; academia is the best!!! Anyone who says otherwise is just jealous because they're not smart enough! Unlike me! I AM SMART! I BELONG HERE! I WAS MADE FOR IT!* All the professors I met acted as if turning into one of them—a tenured scholar at a well-ranked research university in a desirable area—were a foregone conclusion, obscuring the truth: They were *really* like chronic lifelong smokers who never got cancer. They were the *Titanic* passengers who made it onto the lifeboats. But who had time to question anyone's motives, when I was on an all-expenses-paid trip just for *me*? Yes, I'd been feted and fussed over as a sidekick to the talented boyfriend in whose slender shadow I perpetually and rather happily lived—but still, now it was my turn. And it was just so warm in California. I remember drinking coffee on the UC-Irvine campus with Til, the professor who would end up being my dissertation advisor. I was dressed in a thin blazer in the middle of February, breathing in the balm in long draws, and he assured me: "This is considered cold here."

Later, the department chair handed over a manila envelope that contained my funding package. It totaled over one hundred thousand dollars. For me! *To go to school!* Where there was no winter! How could I not want to do this? I mean, sure, I was suspicious of Los Angeles (having been there exactly once, for the premiere of *Four Dipshits*). But once I moved, it'd be pretty sweet, I imagined absurdly, with no idea what an actual Ph.D. entails (not to mention the traffic on the godforsaken 405 freeway): I'd be living (rent-free, *natürlich*) in Silver Lake or Los Feliz, dividing my time between red-carpet shindigs and seminars, between my boyfriend's vapid Hollywood friends and the enchanting miseries of the (mostly) dead Germans I actually enjoyed reading now, between paging through my boyfriend's scripts and my students' exams. My boyfriend would earn twice as much per episode as my yearly graduate stipend, and we'd laugh about it together and watch *Freaks and Geeks* and drift off to sleep.

The return flight from California landed in a rare snowstorm with lightning. The roads from JFK back to the city were so bad that even if I'd had fare for a cab, I wouldn't have been able to find one. When the subway for which I'd spent forty-five minutes waiting in my California-thin Chuck Taylors finally lurched to a stop about ten blocks away from my apartment, and I trudged home in calf-deep drifts, I thought to myself: *How bad could California be?* I accepted UC-Irvine's offer almost immediately. Two months later, my boyfriend's pilot didn't get picked up and he informed me he'd be staying in New York. Three weeks after that, he broke up with me.

It was as if I'd been clocked in the head by an anvil, albeit one that felt really bad about being dropped from a window I didn't realize was open above me. Why? Why? Why was this happening? There was no other woman—for that, he'd have had to leave the apartment and/or develop some social skills. I hadn't done anything wrong. ("Is it because I got fat while you were filming *Four Dipshits Go Abroad*?" No, he insisted, it was not.) Nothing was really wrong. He was just . . . done. In effect, he did me a favor saving us the indignity of a long-distance relationship. I knew it was the right choice for everyone involved. But being single again—especially being dumped for the first time since Dylan Gellner (but who's counting?)—felt like an anvil, and *then* a swift kick to the kidney, followed by the expert severing of one of my limbs. It's not merely that I didn't know what to do with myself, although I didn't. It was like I'd forgotten how to walk to the corner and cross the street. Not that my boyfriend had been pushing me around in a stroller or anything—it was just that three years had turned me into *someone in a long-term relationship.*

Yea, verily, it had been a near-eternity: I'd entered the relationship in my mid-twenties, and I exited in my *late* twenties. When we got together, there was no such thing as an iPod, and by the time we broke up, everyone had an iPod, including me. And, as if on cue, my iPod gave up the ghost the very day of my dumpage, as I was attempting to get it to play a nonstop Elliott Smith megamix and it grew overwhelmed with triteness. Not to be deterred, I bought a new one (a "breakup gift" to myself despite my lack of an iPod-sufficient income)—and then I marched to the nearest bodega and procured an eleven-dollar pack of Gauloises, even though I hadn't smoked in years. Rather than change my spanking-new Friendster profile's relationship status to "single," I deleted it *in toto* (which, as we now know, turned out not to matter much).

The bad news, then, was that I had somehow committed to move across the country to California and begin my Ph.D. alone, $14,500 yearly stipend and all. The good news, on the other hand, was that I would have a fresh start in this Ph.D. program, where at least *somebody* thought I was worth hanging around with. Of course, those somebodies were also under the impression that I still spoke excellent German—or, rather, that I had ever spoken excellent German, instead of the dubious five-dialect mishmash of curse words and cigarette-based vocabulary I'd finally managed to pick up back in the Loftschloss days. That was the best my spoken German had ever gotten—and it had been almost eight years since then. Graduate students and other academics often talk about something called Impostor Syndrome, which is where you are *sure* everyone else knows exactly what they're doing while you're the lone goon who is nodding along to a lecture on "performativity" without actually knowing what that means. But actually everyone is a goon and nobody really knows what *performativity* means. Except in this case, I actually was an impostor.

It was of tremendous importance that I fix my German before everyone found out I was full of it. With the last of the student loans I had ill-advisedly taken out to fund the thesis semester of the M.A. I was just finishing, I booked an off-season ticket to Germany and a month of eight-hour-a-day instruction at a private language school in Berlin, whose name I remembered from clever ads on the hour-long U-Bahn ride from the Loftschloss to the Freie Universität. "You wear British clothes, cook Italian food, kiss in French, and dance Latin," they said. "But when it comes down to it, do you only understand 'train station'?" That last bit, *Verstehen Sie nur "Bahnhof,"* is an idiom in Germany that basically chastises Germans for being so bad at other languages that all they can do in the countries they visit is ask where the train station is. (Appropriately enough, the only German sentence most of my non-German-speaking friends know is *Wo ist der Bahnhof?*) As a fan of both train stations and chastisement for jingoism, I had always enjoyed those ads, and now, eight years later, I was going to follow through. Yes, sure, I was heartbroken and terrified at a future I was facing both unqualified and alone. But at least I was, finally, going back to Berlin. It would be impossible to stay miserable when I was busy laughing my ass off over *helles Hefeweizen* at the Ankerklause, a pub located inside a docked boat on a canal in Kreuzberg. *Take, that Heartbreak McDipshit,* I thought. I was going somewhere it was physically impossible *not* to have an adventure. *And nobody will be there to protest about how I'm not keeping him company through his alphabetical Kurosawa marathon, you weird motherfucker.*

My first stop off the plane was the non-loft apartment of none other than Johannes and Paul, who were still roommates (the rest of the Loftschloss had absconded to other Teutonic parts unknown years before). They still lived on the U1 line in Kreuzberg. It had been eight years since Johannes and I broke up, precisely one month into my senior year of college, when I realized that my study-abroad self did not necessarily transcend Berlin's borders—and yet he and Paul welcomed me, shoved a bottle of pilsner into my hand, and reinstigated staring-based nonconversation as if I'd never left. Our first stop was a *Grillparty* in a park hosted by Paul's old friends Anke and Andreas, who had "received a child" just after I returned to college; the baby—whose fetal existence amid four drops of amaretto scandalized me so—was now seven, had two younger siblings, and was the ringleader of a rough-and-tumble game of pickup soccer.

But Paul and Johannes didn't really begin their evening until midnight, when I once again hopped onto the handlebars of Johannes's bike and allowed myself to be spirited through backstreets of neighborhoods I didn't recognize (our old haunts in Kreuzberg and Mitte, they explained, were now full of yuppies). We first downed several giant bottles of Beck's, "served" at a chichi members-only establishment whose gimmick was that it had vending machines instead of staff. *I'll just drink away my jet lag*, I thought helpfully to myself, as we then moved on to a tiny, encouragingly dingier club, where Paul shoved yet more Beck's into my mitts and we listened to a band called Die Schlümpfe (The Smurfs, because of course) sing a blistering cover of the Pixies' "Where Is My Mind?"

And it was at that precise moment, hearing that song—which my erstwhile boyfriend had once played some seventy thousand times during a month-long cross-country road trip ("Let's just bring ten CDs and get to know them really well!")—that my evening swerved from euphoric-drunk, to drunk-drunk, and directly on to very-sad-drunk. I spent the rest of the wee hours chainsmoking Paul's cigarettes and crying to Marlene, Johannes's empathetic and messy-haired girlfriend. Silver lining: after eight years barely speaking a *Wort* of *Deutsch*, I managed an entire conversation, about difficult and wrenching emotions—*and* I learned an important new vocabulary addition: *Liebeskummer*. Loosely translated it means "heartbreak," but literally it means "love grief." "How long will it be until I feel better?" I asked her. "A month? Two? Five? Never?"

She just shook her head before looking at the time and declaring that since it was almost four in the morning, they'd better start their night in earnest. The legendary techno club Tresor was about to close its doors for good, and they wanted to make sure they arrived during peak hours. I demurred and took Paul's keys so that I could stare mournfully into space on the night bus and then crash on their couch to grieve my love in peace. "I don't understand why you're paying all that money to stay with a host family!" Johannes said before I left the next morning. "You could have just stayed with us."

"For a month?" I asked. "I don't want to impose."

"Don't be stupid," he said. "I'm insulted that you didn't want to."

That's the thing about Germans. You don't talk to them for eight years, and then you go out to drinks, and they spend the whole time ignoring you while they argue with someone else about football—but then they nonchalantly invite you to freeload for weeks on end.

The next afternoon, I dragged my backpack down to the district of Schöneberg, where my new host family lived: Frau Blodau and her two grown daughters. Rather than not-impose on my old friends, I wanted a do-over of the Herrmann family shit-show I'd created in 1995. I was a grown-up now. I knew enough German to know what the fuck was going on in the house. I was ready to keep track of my keys, to stay off the landline, to take my shoes off at the door and then put on a different pair of identical shoes that weren't allowed out of the house. My showers would be so short they wouldn't even exist. I would be home for lunch, *Mittagessen* (and, why the fuck not, *Abendessen* later on, too), ready to immerse and converse. *Bring's jetzt!*

I was buzzed up into a spacious, high-ceilinged flat, with innumerable mysterious locked rooms off the *Flur*, or foyer, that is the centerpiece of every German apartment. "Welcome, hello!" gushed Frau Blodau, my new landlady . . . in English. I greeted her back in the most accent-perfect German I could, following my own rules for *establishing the relationship in the learned language* and hoping she'd get the hint. She led me into the kitchen and invited me to sit down with her. "I just drink a little wine," she explained—in English. It was 9:00 A.M. It turned out that she was partaking of the hair of the dog, thanks to her monumental *Kater,* which literally means *tomcat* but actually means *hangover.*

"Oh," I said, "were you celebrating?"

"In a way," she said. "It was my best friend's funeral. She committed suicide this week."

Oh boy.

"Did you sign up for full board?" she asked.

"*Ja,*" I answered. "*Und ich freue mich sehr darauf.*"

"You look forward to it, yes, good," she continued in German-syntax English. "But normally we're not eating together. Petra is many nights at her boyfriend, and Elise is forever at the work." She pointed me to some sad packaged bread and a few abused-looking jars of preserves, and the coffee machine (*Gott sei Dank!*), and then showed me to my bedroom, which was furnished top to bottom in what I recognized as the very cheapest versions of everything IKEA makes.

"The bed is in order, yes?" she asked, as I plopped down onto what had to be a two-inch futon.

"*Ja, klar!*" I said. I was going to be Frau Blodau's Kelly, by *Gott,* and no dead friends, English, sad breakfasts, dearth of all other meals, or dubious sleeping arrangements would stop me.

After waking up at four the next morning and passing the time until my pitiful solo breakfast doing sun salutations in my room (a *NEW ME!* habit which lasted precisely the duration of my jet lag), I hopped on the U-Bahn and rode to the genteel district of

Wilmersdorf to begin my reeducation. I'd be attending group class in the morning and then have two hours with a private tutor in the afternoon. "*Ach,* Wilmersdorf," Marlene had scoffed about the language school's location. "You'll learn lots of important bourgeois words like *Sahnetorte.*"

"I already know that word," I'd said. (I'd never actually heard it before, given that cream cakes hadn't been a regular offering at the Loftschloss, but I figured it out through context.)

Wilmersdorf did appear stately when I arrived after a train ride that was, to the second—as the school promised in my registration materials—exactly seven minutes long. There weren't going to be any beers served through holes in a wall (or *Automaten-Bars,* for that matter), here among the nineteenth-century apartment buildings and mellow corner bakeries. I took my place in line to register for my first day of classes and tried not to be proud when I was placed in *Oberstufe,* the most advanced level of German they taught, given that I myself would be entrusted to *teach* beginning German some thirteen months in the future.

At the school, located in one of the nineteenth-century apartment buildings, which had been renovated into a hodgepodge of classrooms and a small café, I tiptoed through a dizzying maze of courtyards and hallways until I found the *Oberstufe* classroom, where about ten adults were conversing in rapid-fire German, each with an accent and set of understandable grammatical errors that gave away not only his or her background, but also, in short order, his or her reason for plopping down 150 euros a week for German class. Katja, from Serbia, was about to enter graduate school at the FU and needed to pass the good old TestDaF in order to secure funding. Being a Slav, she would always use the genitive case when discussing plurals of objects larger than four in number, but never use it when constructing a possessive. Mu-Yuan was a nineteen-year-old from a tiny, provincial village in mainland China, who matter-of-factly informed the class that she had been permanently disowned by her family for marrying a forty-five-year-old German. She was upping her already-excellent fluency so that she could work as an office manager and spend less time cleaning up after the forty-five-year-old's kids, some of whom were older than she was.

Hsu was a Taiwanese guy who normally lived in Paris, a graduate student in translation, and a stellar product of the old-school Asian system of language-learning, which involves a lot of grammar work and almost no conversation. It took him about ten minutes to get out a sentence, but that sentence was always perfect. Goran was another Serb, a pompous medical student on vacation who "collected" languages as "hobbies," as he put it, pompously. Zoë was from the French-speaking part of Switzerland, sent to improve her German by the wealthy family for whom she worked as an au pair. She spoke perfectly already, but put all her empha-SES on the wrong sylla-BLES. And then there were three other Americans: first, John, a retiree who had just moved to Berlin with his boyfriend. His German-language skills seemed based entirely on repeated viewings of Wagner's *Ring* cycle, and he brought the word *Nibelungen* into more conversations than you'd think was relevant. Finally, there were two undergraduates on a study-abroad program. My fellow *Landsleute* didn't have to identify themselves as such; I recognized the same flat vowels, forced umlauts, softened *r*s, and misplaced verbs that plagued my own conversations and gave me away. *Wie lange bist du hier?* ("How long have you been here?" or, literally, "How long are you here?") *Für zwei Monate.* ("For two months," a construction Germans do not use. They just say "two months," or sometimes "since two months.") As the class settled down, I plunked myself between the two Serbs.

"Du siehst genau wie eine Porzellanpuppe aus!"

("You look just like a porcelain doll!")

This was the teacher's way of acknowledging me as a new student, before she handed out one of the most brutal grammar worksheets I'd ever seen. We were to decline compound-adjectival phrases cold:

"I saw a three-weeks-overdue, out-in-the-rain-left-until-it-got-soggy library book."

"I should have gone to the cinema with my didn't-attend-school-so-he-doesn't-know-how-to-read cousin from Hamburg."

After school let out for the day, the undergrads and I reverted to our native ways to learn more about each other.

"Hey!" I said. "Does either of you want to come with me on a sort of nostalgia tour through whatever's left of dirty Kreuzberg?"

My hopes were particularly high for Declan, a lanky twenty-three-year-old senior, also from Oregon (a plus), who had the same haircut as Richard Ashcroft from the band the Verve (a double-plus).

"I'd love to!" he said. "Only thing is, I'm straight-edge and I don't drink."

His friend Callista could pencil in some free time in approximately two and a half weeks, but until then she was way too busy with her studies. *Studies?* In Berlin? Teetotaling? IN BERLIN? Motherfuck. The Serbs were no better—the one only hung out at her lesbian commune, and I couldn't risk asking the other to do anything social, because he would immediately assume I was sexually interested in him, and I could just tell he would absolutely relish rejecting me. (I was not sexually interested in him *in the least,* because he was a pompous asshole.) Mu-Yuan was always busy with her vile-sounding forty-five-year-old husband, and I was too impatient to try to have a full conversation with Hsu. Johannes and Paul, meanwhile, my alleged Berlin crew, had founded some sort of legitimate computer business in their living room a few years back; they now had legitimate offices, employees, and clients and were, as Johannes put it, *eh immer bei der Arbeit,* which is the German expression my new host mom had translated literally to mean "always at work."

Thus, after what turned out to be a misleadingly exciting first few days, I spent most evenings in Berlin sitting at Frau Blodau's kitchen table while she drank and cried, nudging the conversation into German by never uttering a word of English no matter what she said or did, and drinking straight from a bottle of Jägermeister I bought at the grocery store, which I used to wash down my *Abendessen* of fifteen cigarettes, two bags of *Erdnussflips,* and a chocolate baton. My landlady loved dubbed episodes of *Friends,* and who was I to begrudge a grieving woman her Central Perk? I never got any potatoes with béchamel sauce, but I did learn that the German for *How YOU doin'?* is *Na . . . wie GEHT's denn so?* Where was the Berlin I needed, to debauch away the loneliness that threatened to claw me to strips? What a waste of money my new artisanal travel journal was, given that all it contained was a note about a new vocabulary word I learned: *Lebensgefährtin,* which means "life partner." *It is,* I'd scrawled wryly, no doubt distracted by German Monica and Ross in the background, *near-identical to the word* Lebensgefahr, *which means "mortal danger." Ha ha ha ha ha.*

Luckily the unseasonably chilly May had finally given way to a weekend of hot weather, and on cue all of Berlin—which spends its pitch-dark 3:00 P.M. winter afternoons in helpful illustration of the vocabulary word *trübselig,* which means "cheerless," but literally translates to "blessed with drear"—had exploded onto the sidewalks and into the parks. There was but one word that stood between me and some desperately needed mirth: *Picknick.* A German *Picknick* is different from its gingham-blanketed, letter-*k*-bereft, Stepford-inflected American counterpart in several ways. First, the provisions. While a well-stocked American basket might contain a stack of ham sandwiches and a thermos of lemonade, Germans (and expatriates in an *Oberstufe* class) will descend upon a *Picknick* as if it were a potluck during the apocalypse, with foodstuffs piled higher than the Berlin Wall (most of which requires a real metal knife and fork to consume, which of course they also bring)—and, of course, alcohol, which is consumed legally, openly, and with great *Lebensfreude* in the out-of-doors.

"You guys!" I declared to the class on a Friday morning so blindingly sunny it occurred to me that I hadn't actually seen the sun—or felt remotely happy—since I could remember. "We need to have a *Picknick* tomorrow! Tiergarten park! Everyone come! Bring your friends!"

In the end, only a handful of the class showed up—Mu-Yuan had a full weekend of ironing her husband's ties, Katja was too busy studying for her language exam, and Goran, thank goodness, had skipped class on the day we planned the outing and didn't know about it. In the end, it was just Zoë the French Swiss, the Americans, Hsu the grammatically perfect slow talker, and me, feasting on *Butterbrot* and washing it down with room-temperature champagne. In honor of the warm day, I was wearing a backless cotton halter dress from Anthropologie, in a yellow-and-green floral print that was supposed to evoke 1970s glam but instead made me look like I had a starter case of hepatitis B. Few noticed the sallow tinge to my complexion, however, because everybody was looking at my boobs: the dress had a neckline that plunged halfway down my rib cage. It felt like a bit of a shame to be wasting it on *Oberstufe*—especially when Hsu so clearly disapproved: "If your skin is so pale and sensitive," he said in his measured, grammar-translation-method diction, "why do you wear *so little clothing*?" I took a little pleasure in noting that *Herr Perfektes-Deutsch* used the phrase *so wenig Kleider,* a literalism no German would employ in that context, because it evokes a mental picture of someone draping multiple garments all over her and then removing all but a few of them. (A German would technically say *so little,* but Germans would never say that to begin with, because they think *swimsuits* are for prudes, for chrissake.) Just as I was about to tell Hsu I had on plenty of SPF 50, he got a text and jumped up.

"I'm going to get my friend from the S-Bahn station," he said.

Huh, I thought. *Hsu has a friend. Must be French or Taiwanese, because otherwise how could they ever have a conversation?* To my immense surprise, fifteen minutes later he returned with an actual German dude, who introduced himself as Matthias and explained that he enjoyed meeting international students. Matthias was, we learned, in a *band*—with a name in nonsense-English, Assimilated Funk. He was twenty-four and in the final semester of an eighteen-month *Ausbildung,* or professional school, an alternative (or sometimes a supplement) to university that trains Germans for a specific vocation. This is because almost all jobs in Germany require some sort of certification. You shop for shoes in Germany, and the person who gets your size and makes officious recommendations about your foot shape is not some Al Bundy schmoe, but rather a graduate of an official certificate program in footwear retail. Matthias was training in *Werbeverkauf,* or ad sales. I made the silly mistake of asking what he was going to do when he was finished with his studies, and he looked at me like I didn't know how words worked and said: *"Ich werde Werbekaufmann."* (I'll work in ad sales.)

"Sorry," I said. "In my country, the *mythos* is that philosophy dropouts become multibillionaire CEOs, and people with eighth-grade educations grow real-estate empires." (*Oberstufe* was working really well. Apparently all it took to get better at German was, you know, to study German a lot. *Phantastisch.*)

"I thought everybody in America drove a package truck," Matthias said.

"A what?"

"A package truck. You know, like on *The King of Queens.*"

I told Matthias that despite my job as a *professionelle Fernsehzuschauerin* (professional TV watcher), I had only seen a few episodes of *The King of Queens* and I didn't like it.

"Echt?" he said in disbelief. "It's the funniest show *in the world.*" Germans love terrible American television for reasons I will never understand (I, in turn, love terrible German television), so this was not the deal-breaker it would have been on domestic soil. As the sun finally began to set, Matthias suggested we all meet up in a few hours out at Krumme Lanke, which sounds like "crummy lake," but it is actually a quite lovely place to go, down in the leafy southwestern suburb of Dahlem. "I can bring my guitar and some candles, and we can sing and hang out." This was exactly the kind of weird adventure I'd been expecting since I walked off the plane, and if I had to withstand some German-language recounting of Kevin James jokes, so be it.

Three hours later, I alighted at the Krumme Lanke station, the end of the U1 line that I used to ride to my Bertolt Brecht seminar. I expected to see the same ragtag crowd of internationals as before, but instead it was just Matthias. "Nobody else is coming," he explained. He was, as promised, carrying his guitar and three small tea lights. I had, as promised, brought a bottle of red wine and an opener. We were, I realized with what turned out to be a very slow mind, on a date. Berlin was nearly unrecognizable to me now, full of expensive boutiques and nightclubs with international reputations that wouldn't let someone like me in. (Not that I was a fan of German techno, which sounds like a Volkswagen and a record player challenging each other to a duel, or dancing to German techno, which primarily involves jumping up and down in one place.) I was older, too, no longer able to glom onto amorphous groups of students up to no good. But I was pleased to see that fortunes there could still turn in forty-five seconds, that a picnic with a bunch of dorks could morph into a romantic lakeside date with no warning. What's better, I could do the whole thing in German, which would be great practice. The competitiveness of my early youth had recently resurfaced, and since I had recently discovered that German wasn't actually that hard to learn if only one actually spent any time studying, I'd shot to the top of *Oberstufe*. This also had the pleasant side effect of unnerving Goran and Hsu, who were used to being the best at everything and, at least in Goran's case, distraught to be schooled by a *girl*. Who knew that the key to linguistic and academic success was, you know, effort? And now here I was on some top-notch cultural immersion, if I did say so myself.

Except then, as we settled in by the lake and Matthias asked me exactly why breaking up with my boyfriend had made me so sad, before I could answer, he said, in English: "You know what? Let's switch. I find it much easier to speak about my emotions in English."

God *dammit*. Turns out he'd spent a year of high school in Ireland and spoke English as well as I did. I wanted to say that I'd rather not speak about emotions if it was going to interfere with my linguistic process. But that sentence had some tricky subjunctive constructions I wanted to get *just* right—plus I had to search a second for the word for "progress," *Fortschritt*, literally "a step forward"—and I accidentally created about four seconds of awkward silence. Matthias took this as his cue to make a move, and asked, in English, if he could kiss me. I hesitated, but only for an instant. I knew that nothing about this evening would really take away any of my pain, my loneliness, my insecurity. *But,* I had also never had relations on the banks of a lake by candlelight before—and if I did, its adventure-cache would finally begin to make up for all the previous evenings spent watching German Phoebe sing "*Schmuddelkatz.*"

"How much longer are you going to be here?" Matthias asked later, as we rode the night bus back to Schöneberg and I inspected the abrasions on my knees caused by the rough sand.

"About two weeks," I said.

That was his German way of informing me that we would be dating for those two weeks. He introduced me to all of his friends and took me to hang out at a sort of unstaffed informal club near the FU, where I learned to play a board game called Therapy, which plays off the general German disapproval of the mental health profession and those who partake in its practitioners.

Matthias's friends were nice enough, with the exception of Hanno, who, when he learned that I was about to start a doctorate and enjoyed the fiction of Franz Kafka and the political theory of

Walter Benjamin, just kept shaking his head and going *"ACH DU SCHEISSE!"* When it was my turn to read off one of the questions in Therapy, he would mimic my slight accent until whatever confidence *Oberstufe* had bestowed was duly obliterated. *Scheiße* indeed.

There were a lot of downsides to my two-week relationship with Matthias. First of all, he was the opposite of Johannes and Paul—and for that matter, any German I had ever met—when it came to his cigarettes. I was under the impression that German smokers offered cigarettes to other smokers no matter what the pretense, but after I'd bummed about three, he turned to me and said, in poorly ordered English that was out of character: "Not to be an asshole, but, maybe you buy *also* cigarettes?" And he, like many twenty-four-year-old Germans, still lived with his parents. This meant that if I ever wanted to have relations with him indoors, I would have to do so in his childhood twin bed. Whereas the act of bringing home a sex-companion about whom one is decidedly unserious, and parading her in front of one's parents, is the subject of many a prudish American advice column, adult Germans who live with their parents often enjoy a relationship more akin to flatmates (except the parents still pay for all the rent and the food, and, in Matthias's case, still cleaned and ironed his underwear).

That is why, on my penultimate morning in Berlin, as I tiptoed petrified into Matthias's living room, he couldn't *at all* see what the big deal was.

"It's just my *mum*," he scoffed in English. "She's nice."

I tried to take it as yet another opportunity to interact Germanically with Germans in their natural milieu. *Germans* are not uptight Puritans about sex. *German* TV plays soft-core porn after 10:00 P.M.! *Germans* expect their adult children to be *adults*. This is acceptable. Here goes. Mattias's *Mutti,* on the other hand, had apparently not been told anything about me except that I was American. So when I shuffled into her dining room and mustered up my least-awkward *"Morgen,"* she replied at about ninety-billion decibels and a speed slower than my classmate Hsu.

"GUTEN MORGEN!!!" She pointed outside to the sky, so that I could figure out, from its morningness, what she meant.

"Hallo," I answered, *"ich bin die Rebecca."* This is the excellent way that Germans casually introduce themselves, because it contains the definite article. "I am THE Rebecca," as if I am the only one. All foreigners immediately start doing this all the time as soon as they learn how, because everyone wants to be THE only one of themselves, and also everyone wants to signal to their interlocutor that they are no *Mein Bett ist geschlossen*–mumbling beginners. I might not be a native speaker—as Matthias's dick friend Hanno never stopped pointing out—but I was fluent in German, goddammit, and I would have the friendly German *Frühstück* (breakfast; literally, "early piece") that I'd squandered back at the Herrmanns', and if I had to do it with a *King of Queens* fan to accomplish this, so be it, goddammit.

"OH!!!" Matthias's mother answered, again with the face-splitting grin of the person who conflates being foreign with possessing a severe intellectual hindrance. *"SPRICHST DU ETWAS DEUTSCH?!?!"*

"Ach, Mama," Matthias said sheepishly. "She studies *Germanistik;* of course she speaks German."

"Ich spreche eigentlich ziemlich fließend Deutsch," I said, but with the most confidence I could muster. ("I actually speak fairly fluent German.")

"SURE YOU DO, DEAR!" she replied. "WE HAVE *BREAK-FAST* IN THE OTHER ROOM FOR YOU! *FRÜHSTÜCK?* DO YOU KNOW WHAT *'FRÜHSTÜCK'* MEANS?"

The good news, I realized as I sipped Matthias's mom's fortu-itously strong coffee and affixed cheese to my *Brötchen* with a healthy slathering of butter, was that I had at long last managed to chip away just slightly at my Love Grief. This would have made the trip to Berlin a rousing success, if only I were about to go for a Ph.D. in being on the rebound. But alas, the linguistic confidence for which I had just paid a healthy sum still eluded me, and I re-turned to the U.S., left New York, moved—at the age of twenty-eight—back in with my parents for the summer, and moped about Eugene, fairly sure that I was about to begin doctoral-level study in a language in which nobody would believe I knew the word for "breakfast."

8.

Ereignis

n. event, from the nominalized form of the verb to befall.

ex. In the OC, it is a major Ereignis to walk more than a city block. (Or to see an actual city, divided into blocks.)

Irvine, California, is not so much a city as an amorphous blob of identical carpeted apartments and prefab miniature mansions built in at least three clashing architectural styles, located about fifty miles south of Los Angeles. It is a mass that sprawls indistinguishably into the never-ending tangle of freeways and strip malls that make up parched, moneyed Orange County. Irvine's streets are twisting, highway-fast arterials that often go two miles without a turnoff or turnaround, punctuated only by cul-de-sac planned communities and chain businesses, all with addresses like 50955 Vista Bonita Drive, where the eponymous view has long been bulldozed away to build a SoulCycle studio.

Surrounded on all sides by four of these mini-highways is the campus of the University of California at Irvine, which is second-arily famous for being the ninth-ranked public research university in the United States, and primarily famous for its excellent (or ter-rifying, depending on your aesthetic) examples of brutalist archi-tecture. The William Pereira originals that comprise most of the core campus were so futuristic-looking at the time they were built, in the 1960s, that they were used as set pieces in a 1972 *Planet of the Apes* sequel. The squat, concrete assemblages of cubbyhole win-dows are arranged in a circle around a large, hilly park shaded by towering and fragrant eucalyptus trees. This park is beautiful, but according to campus lore, it was designed in the early 1960s to be inhospitable to students hanging out in large numbers—you know, to prevent protesting, sitting-in, troublemaking, rabble-rousing, communism, etc. Today, almost all of Irvine's graduate students live in subsidized housing on the outskirts of campus, because they can't afford private apartments anywhere near the place. As a result, the university is an isolated haven of research and angst, inchoate but nevertheless hermetically sealed, inside one of the most vacuous communities in the world.

Moving to Southern California from New York to start gradu-ate school in German at the age of twenty-nine was like being bur-ied alive in Chanel logos. For the past eight years, I'd just had to step out the door of my building to be surrounded by diversity and energy and life. I'd been a cheap subway ride away from interest-ing things—and if I found myself tipsy and alone in a strange neighborhood in the middle of the night, I could get into a cab and feel relatively confident about getting home safe. Now, suddenly, I was living in that subsidized grad housing—whose primary con-struction materials seemed to be particleboard and not giving a shit—surrounded by twenty-two-year-old strangers. My randomly assigned roommate, Beryl, was a tiny beauty from Turkey who spent most of her time lighting hookah coals on our electric stove and complaining about how cold it was; our ever-present neighbor, Elena, was an unrepentant semifunctioning opiate addict from Boston whose gaunt body and giant brown eyes attracted every burnout and predatory dickbag within a ninety-mile radius. I'm not saying this in judgment of them; quite the contrary: they were wonderful people, really, and they gave the place its only character.

And that was fortunate, because I was trapped at home a lot of the time, dependent as I was on my 1990 Volvo, my long-dormant driving abilities, and my nonexistent gasoline budget to go anywhere outside of campus—and, further, since Orange County's businesses primarily catered to the cosmetically augmented housewives of wealthy Republican businessmen (often themselves cosmetic surgeons), there wasn't much of anywhere to go. There were no dive bars or cool coffee shops within walking distance of campus, both because if you asked where a cool coffee shop was, OC residents would say "You mean, like, Panera?" and because nothing was within walking distance of anything, and nobody walked anywhere. Despite living in beautiful walking weather literally every single day of the year, people in Orange County regularly—I mean *regularly*—drove to different points in the same shopping mall.

Living in the OC was like being stuck in the backseat of a car with a too-smooth automatic transmission and overpowering new car smell, on a road trip through an airless nothing-space, for infinity, because (in true Kafkan fashion), the road trip was the destination. The only recreation my fellow grad students seemed to enjoy was an identical series of house parties held in identical flimsy apartments, where we sipped identical putrid glasses of Charles Shaw wine ("Two-Buck Chuck," purveyed for $1.99 plus tax at Trader Joe's), out of identical red Solo cups.

So what in the ever-loving fuck was I doing there? Well, besides the small matter of the hundred thousand dollars the German department had given me to come be allegedly smart in their midst, the OC did have its selling points, even to someone as pale and surly as me: the vegetarian food was spectacular; there were pockets and exurbs that weren't inhabited only by surgically enhanced wealthy white assholes, if you knew where to look; I could ride my bike to the same beach that the Bluths visit on *Arrested Development*; it was never, ever, ever, ever, ever, ever, ever, *ever* cold. And, as a special bonus, after being dumped and disillusioned, I could start my life over not knowing a single soul.

And yet. Were those good enough reasons? Where was my all-consuming love for the German canon? A reverence that hovered somewhere between religious and sexual ecstasy, culminating in the steadfast knowledge that even if nobody ever paid me a cent, I would sit around writing lengthy research essays about Goethe and Schiller and Rilke in my spare time for fun? I wasn't sure I had it. Yet? At all? I certainly found German literature interesting—and German philosophy, and language, and culture, and art, and architecture; I was a grown-up now with a modicum of intellectual curiosity and maturity, and had legitimate favorites in each of those categories. (Nietzsche's "On Truth and Lying in an Extramoral Sense"; the word *angeblich,* or "allegedly"; tiny eyeglasses and ubiquitous bicyclists; Otto Dix's *Portrait of the Journalist Sylvia Hardin;* anything Bauhaus.) I also, in my intellectually mature adulthood, actually enjoyed working through very difficult texts that few other people had heard of (much less understood), simply for the challenge and the uniqueness. I even enjoyed this enough to do it for thirteen hours at a time, which was lucky, because that is often how my days went down. (Good thing I had nowhere to go and no money to get there.)

But still: Was any of this sufficient? *Should I really make German studies a career?* I thought. *Could a person even do that?* But I was staring down thirty and had not, as of yet, found anything I wanted to do enough to keep doing it for more than a few years. I quit jobs, I moved out of apartments, relationships self-destructed (or I destroyed them), and now suddenly here I was at the age most people are at least in middle management. All I knew, as I began a journey that would last at least a half-decade and likely shrink my career prospects to even smaller than they already were, was that I wanted to dedicate myself as fully as possible to something really, truly rigorous. Or at any rate, I didn't *not* want it badly enough not to do it.

"I cannot fathom why anyone would want to do this," said Anja, the Irvine German department's newest professorial hire, on the first day of my first graduate seminar ever, of the education that she herself had recently finished and the academic position that she herself had. "The job market is terrible—I mean, *terrible*. There are no jobs. And this is such a difficult and obscure subject. So I'd like to know, really know—why are all of you here, studying this subject, at this time?" Anja was German, and—as everyone from the Herrmanns of Münster and the unemployed room-renters of Berlin had helpfully informed me over the years—nobody has less understanding of why non-Germans want to study Germans than Germans.

But she was right. The doctorate was a massive commitment. One hundred thousand dollars is a lot of money to get paid to read and learn (and teach, when you don't know how to teach)—but divide it by several years, and then subtract the cost of tuition, fees, and health insurance, and suddenly you're looking at a living stipend of less than fifteen grand a year. (*"Technically* it's only for the nine months you're here," our professors bristled if anyone dared mention penury. "In the summer, you'll have to wait tables or something." How we were supposed to do that while studying thirteen hours a day for our comprehensives was left to our imaginations.)

On that first day of Anja's seminar, my classmates—they were named Eileen, Evan, and Christiane—all dutifully reported their Germanist creation stories. Evan was a former opera singer who had begun studying German as part of his training as a *Heldentenor*—and then read one Schiller play and couldn't resist the lure. He had a ponytail that reminded me a little too much of the one Bart cuts off a Ph.D. student in an episode of *The Simpsons*. ("I'm a grad student! I'm thirty and I made six hundred dollars last year," says Bart, wiggling the hair behind his own head. Then Marge says: "Bart, don't make fun of grad students. They just made a terrible life choice.") Eileen had moved to Germany after college to be with her German boyfriend, gotten super-fluent, but then became bored teaching English for a corporate language school; she would use her student loans to finance summer trips back to the *Vaterland*. Christiane was German, so her reasons weren't questioned. It got to be my turn, and my throat squeezed itself shut. I didn't know what to say. I cycled between rage and panic. My relationship with German literature was private and intimate, goddammit, and none of these strangers' beeswax. And, also—two contrary opinions at once, Herr Dr. Kafka—my relationship with German literature, especially vis-à-vis pursuing it as a permanent profession, was completely unclear. So what should I say?

How about: *I am here because I wanted health insurance for five years while I figured out what to do with myself, and I thought I'd be supported by my movie-star boyfriend, but now I'm not, and I guess I better make a real fucking go of it?*

How about: *I am here because my childhood boyfriend was into Franz Kafka, and then he dumped me, and I figure by becoming a successful Kafka scholar I will somehow show him once and for all?*

How about: *I am here because I want a really difficult challenge that means something to me intellectually and emotionally, and someone among you apparently thought I'd be up for it, and that I'd belong with you people, but I do not know if this is the case?*

In the end, I said: "I'm sorry. It's personal."

Anja shrugged, said, "Interesting. Fair enough." My classmates stared at me uneasily. I'd made two grave grad-school faux pas by showing any sort of unexpected emotional vulnerability and by defying authority. The move to the OC had been one form of culture shock, but it was inconsequential compared to induction into the doctoral-study milieu.

There were so many new behavioral conventions I wasn't sure I could adopt them all fast enough. For starters, I had to start dressing differently. Worse. Much, much worse. On my wooing visit to Irvine, I'd spent three hours sitting in on a seminar called "Poetics of Punishment," whose intellectual rigor made my M.A. courses seem like the fourth grade, but whose sartorial rigor was somewhere on the continuum between halfway house and unintentional self-parody. Students in my M.A. program had the same priorities as Maya Rudolph's old Donatella Versace character on *SNL*: to smoke and look cool. Do you know what the Irvine crowd thought was cool? A special weight you drape across a book to hold its pages open.

Franz Kafka was always telling people that he had made an "unshakable" judgment about Felice Bauer within thirty seconds of meeting her. Within two minutes of this seminar starting, I had come to the unshakable realization that real graduate students had reached new levels of not-giving-a-fuckness about their outward appearances. Of course, my future cohort had also made an unshakable judgment about me: I was a snobby, image-obsessed flake who maligned Los Angeles having never lived there, and my research interests in philosophical approaches to Kafka were somehow both "trendy" *and* "tired." When we became friends, I assured them that my snooty facial expression was actually displaying crippling intellectual inadequacy, and they explained to me that in graduate school, dressing like a middle-school guidance counselor in 1993 was a mark of intellectual commitment.

Granted, the irony of my vanity during my campus visit was not lost on me, promising literary scholar that I was. For I had, during the second half of my twenties, aggressively cultivated a look that was supposed to show that *I* didn't give a fuck what I looked like. This is because if the fashion world had a Geneva Convention, the early aughts in New York would have violated it, so I chose conscientious objection. Every subway ride displayed a nauseating mélange of three-hundred-dollar whisker-faded jeans that exposed butt cleavage, elbow-length hair blown out ruler-straight, and stilettos whose toes were so pointy, they made the wearer look like the Wicked Witch of the East after the house gets dropped on her. So I invented my own aesthetic based on the last time I was cool, and adopted a late-nineties Berlin fashion ethos of Look Like You Slept in Makeup and Sword-Fought with Your Clothes. I honestly believed that there was nobody on earth who gave less of a fuck about looking attractive than I. But that was before I set foot in a real graduate seminar in German, when I would soon realize that I "didn't care" about my looks in the same way Gustav von Aschenbach "doesn't care" about his looks in *Death in Venice.*

The other crucial cultural truth I learned about grad seminar was that the more confident a student sounded, the fuller of shit he probably was. Shortly thereafter I also learned that the professor, brilliant as she may be, is but a human being who has either written, or is in the process of writing, an article or book on the text you're discussing, and is testing out her thesis on you. But nobody tells you this when you're just starting out, so the first day of seminar leaves even the brightest young intellectuals feeling like impostors—or at any rate, that's how I felt.

I'm not supposed to be here, I thought.

All these people know what they're talking about, and I most certainly do not.

How can anyone have thought I was smart enough to be here?

What the fuck is a subaltern?

I would kill for a decent bagel.

Oh, God, pay attention! Did someone just say "subaltern" again? Gah.

Impostor Syndrome is like one of those antibiotic-resistant superbugs, in that no matter what remedies you try, it mutates and flares up anew—that is, the second I figured out one difficult thing (thanks to untold hours of reading and intermittent weeping), I immediately decided that that thing must thus be something kindergartners could parse. This went for the entire graduate-school cycle: seminar papers, comprehensive exams, even the dissertation. Soon, it all just seemed like a soup of easy stuff any idiot could do. And I was no outlier—I learned that behavior from what I saw around me. And *this,* friends, is why so many academics are pompous dickheads, because they are all scared out of their damn minds that someone who actually knows what they're talking about will come along and recognize that the impostors have been in charge the whole time.

The only antidote to Impostor Syndrome (which is actually not an antidote, but rather, in Kafkan fashion, exacerbates it), is posturing—well, that and eyeball-peeling amounts of work. But I was already doing that, and I still felt like a fake. So all that left was faking it better. *Do not ever let anyone know anything is difficult for you, Schuman.* I could not betray weakness to anyone, even if that person was allegedly my friend. I could not let on for a second that I felt like a water-treading fraud who was ten seconds from drowning at all times. If someone referenced a book I hadn't read, I learned to say, "I should really read that *again*." (Then I checked that book out and read its introduction, index, and two most relevant chapters for future name-dropping.) If someone asked if I was familiar with a theorist whose name might as well be in Kyrgyz, I just said what everyone else said, which was: "Oh, I haven't read *him* since undergrad." If the person responded, "Actually, Xyvltz Yqctullzxll is a woman," I dialed it all the way up: "*Obviously*, but I genderqueer names at random as a performative act. You mean to tell me you don't?" (I looked the theorist up on the *Stanford Encyclopedia* later in the privacy of my room, with *Law & Order* on in the background.) If I had to write a lengthy essay on a subject that perplexed me beyond all reasonable measure, I just gave it a proper academic title so nobody would be the wiser: *MILDLY CLEVER THING: Three-Part List, "Incomprehensible Scare Quotes," and an Extremely Convoluted Explanation with at Least One Made-Up Word.* (Then I employed my all-consuming and overly complex essay-writing system, which involved color-coded index cards.) And, when in doubt, I made a reference to Martin Heidegger. Because what better way to counter a bunch of my own gibberish than a bunch of *someone else's* gibberish?

I was in an especially good position to become the greatest of grad students, because I took two Heidegger seminars in a row as soon as I arrived in Irvine. Dear old Martin is primarily famous for being an active Nazi, but he is somehow also the unabashed go-to favorite thinker of every progressive literary theorist on earth. He is secondarily famous for *schtupping* Hannah Arendt. He is tertiarily famous for finding human earth language—even German, with its infinite repository of untranslatable compound words—incapable of expressing the most important ideas of his wide-ranging and prolific philosophical career. As a result, he made up a bunch of his own, such as *Dasein* ("being-there"), *Sein-Zum-Tode* ("being-toward-death") or *Zeit-Spiel-Raum* ("time-play-space"); *Gelassenheit* ("released-ness"), *Geworfenheit* ("thrown-ness"), *vorhanden* ("present-at-hand")—and my department chair's personal favorite, *Ereignis,* which literally means "event," but in Heideggerese means something more akin to "a coming-into-view" (i.e., something coming into view—you know, a *noun*). (Heidegger is 100 percent the German language's fault.)

The word *Ereignis* was also, I learned in seminar, pretty much directly relevant to Goethe, who pretty much (almost) used it to describe the German *Novelle,* or novella. English speakers will call something a "novella" if it's too long to be a short story but too short to be published on its own, but for Goethe the sole criterion was that it describe one "single unheard-of event," or *sich ereignete unerhörte Begebenheit.* Crash course in what passes for fun in a Ph.D. seminar: the compound adjective Goethe uses here contains the adjectival version of the verb *sich ereignen* ("to occur"), which is the root of the word *Ereignis,* and so he and Heidegger were pretty much best friends, even though one of them was born fifty years after the other one died. At any rate, thanks to my department chair's enthusiasm for orthography (and, I suppose, ontology), I cut my Ph.D. teeth on a seminar about Heidegger and the *Novelle,* a seminar I took in the winter quarter of my first year that turned my feeble *Dasein* into what Heidegger might term *putty-silliness.*

It wouldn't have been so bad had I not decided to double down on impossible-to-read German philosophers that quarter—but I did, with the only German philosopher who is even more difficult to read than Heidegger: Immanuel Kant, the man whose four-page-long sentences made me yearn for something as simple as a Heideggerian made-up hyphenate. Specifically, I bookended the Heidegger seminar with a course offered by the philosophy department, whose only text was the interminable *Critique of Pure Reason.* Since the material terrified me and the class was full of people I didn't know, on the first day, I did what three months of grad-school inculcation had taught me to do: I distinguished myself as a complete pompous posturing twit.

"Do you have a preferred translation we should read?" one of the philosophy students had asked, a guy whom everyone called Jack Osbourne because he looked just like Jack Osbourne.

"That's a good question," answered Will, our professor, an awkward and exceedingly kind guy who couldn't have been more than two years older than me. I didn't pay attention to the answer he gave, because I was too busy screwing up my courage to ask my own question.

"Yes?" he said.

"Uh," I said, "do we have to read it in translation?" I tapped nervously on my own ancient used copy of the *Kritik der reinen*

Vernunft, which I'd snagged for $7.50 at a used bookstore in Oregon over Christmas break.

"Of course not! If you *can* read it in German, *do.*"

What I didn't say was that since reading the *Critique of Pure Reason* was, to me, like performing a Jazzercise routine in hardening cement, I might as well not-understand it in its original glory. What the rest of the seminar heard was me upping the ante on their sad little monolingual philosopher asses, and for years after that people in the philosophy department would refer to me as the Girl Who Reads Kant in German, protagonist of the world's most stultifying Stieg Larsson novel.

Luckily for me, the seminar was what the philosophy department called a "piggyback," a graduate reading group that met as part of an advanced undergraduate course, so I had the good fortune of attending a twice-weekly lecture for younger people that went slowly and used middle-sized words. By the time graduate section each Friday rolled around, I had amassed a passable (if temporary) grasp on "synthetic a priori judgments," the "transcendental dialectic," and the "pure concepts of the understanding." I was thus left free to sit in the seminar circle and space out, as the philosophy graduate students did their goddamnedest to word-salad away whatever tenuous understanding Will's undergrad lecture might have imparted.

I liked to stare around the room at the faces of my classmates and wonder what these philosophy types were like. By six weeks into the quarter, I'd already made a Kafka-style unshakeable judgment about most of them—Maya the gorgeous Iranian probably belonged in Comp Lit; the guy with the Indiana Jones hat and the old-timey book-strap was a jackass; the Jack Osbourne–looking motherfucker wasn't a dick, he was just really insecure. (I knew nothing about that.) That didn't stop me, however, from making my lone contribution to discussion, which was to interrupt him as he pontificated on a passage in which Kant discussed "two modes of understanding" and say: "Well, *Brad*, in the *German*, it says *zweierlei Erkenntnissart*, which literally means 'twofold mode of understanding,' and I'm not *exactly* sure that's the same thing." Recommence silent staring. All of this silence and staring, combined with the fact that none of those philosophy people ever talked to me—indeed, some days nobody talked to me at all, and I didn't talk to anyone else, and I briefly feared that it might be because I was a ghost, and it made me long for some kid who sees dead people to come hang out with me—gave me the decided impression that nobody in philosophy would ever want to hang out with me.

This, it turns out, was not a correct impression—someone in that class did want to hang out with me, but I almost didn't realize it because of my terrible habit of skipping breakfast. One Friday, about seven weeks into the ten-week winter quarter of my first year—so, mid-February, and thus a perfect and sparkly day of about seventy degrees—the clock somehow managed to strike the 1:00 P.M. start of Kant seminar and I still hadn't eaten anything. I'd *bought* a bran muffin, and I was desperate to chomp it down, but nobody else was eating, so I chickened out. Real intellectuals didn't need any further sustenance than the theory of Apperception, goddammit. By the time the clock inched its way to three, I was what Heidegger might term *the Ready-to-eat-my-own-hand*.

As I rushed to the door, I noticed that one of my classmates—a strong-jawed silent type who always sat in the back and had recently started showing up with his arm in a sling—had stopped dead in my path. With the muffin halfway to my gaping maw, I damn near ran into him, which would have pushed his slung arm directly into the doorway. Instead I stopped short, said: "Gah! Sorry!" and prepared to maneuver around him, with my food, at long last now, six or seven inches from my quivering yap. He, however, turned to face me and addressed me directly, almost like he knew I existed. "So," he said, "you're in the German department?"

"Yes?" I said.

Did he want to have, like, a conversation or something? With me? Why? My mind suddenly entering what Heidegger might call a *Disappearing-of-all-smart-talkiness,* all I could come up with was the same damn question as everyone else.

"I realize this is probably the last thing you want to talk about," I said, which is of course an excellent way to begin a conversation, "but what happened?"

"Oh," he said. "I dislocated my shoulder." He pointed to the wrist braces I wore for my carpal tunnel syndrome. "What's with you?"

"This? It's from too much typing and writing. How did you *dislocate* your shoulder?"

"I was bodysurfing," he explained.

"Like, in the *ocean*?"

"Yep. Big wave caught me and slammed me into the sand."

I was terrified of the ocean and all the things that could go awry in its merciless salty grasp (most of them shark-related), so I winced and gasped. I also noticed that, arm sling and head grease aside, he looked like a goddamned matinee idol, all broad shoulders and dramatic brow and sensitivity-inflected eye crinkles. Green eyes. Bright ones. How did I not notice this from six weeks of staring? Jack Osbourne's big fat head must have been in the way. "I'm just impressed that you have *time* to go to the beach with all the Kant we have to read," I said.

"Oh, I'm just auditing this course for fun."

"*Excuse* me?" Reading the *Critique of Pure Reason* was like knocking down a brick wall with only my own skull and a ten-gallon bucket full of my tears.

"Yeah," he said. "I'm almost done with my dissertation, which has some chapters on the first *Critique*. So, you know."

"Oh, yeah. I know." I barely knew anyone who had passed their comprehensives, much less almost finished a dissertation, so I did *not* know.

"Anyway," he said, "you're probably right. I should stop spending so much time at the beach and spend more time at home. You know, *typing*." He smiled at my bound wrists. I smiled back at his shoulder, snuck only a *fleeting* glance at my food. "Well," he said, "my department is having a colloquium, so I should go. Enjoy your muffin." I hadn't asked his name, and he hadn't asked mine.

"Hey," I said at a party later that night when I ran into Jeff, a philosophy student in the Kant seminar who happened to enjoy the love that dare not speak its name, by which I mean he was going out with someone in the German department, and thus, unlike the rest of his classmates, he had to acknowledge my existence. "Who's that guy with the greasy hair and the arm sling in your department?" I demanded.

"Oh, you mean *VEE*-told?" he asked.

"Vee-what?"

"W-I-T-O-L-D. Some European thing. What about him?"

"No reason," I said nonsensically and a little too fast. "I mean, nothing."

Jeff went back to his gin and tonic.

"Wait," I said. "What's his deal?"

"I don't really know," he answered. "He's not in my department. He's in that Logic and Philosophy of Science program, where they hate Hegel and insist that all 'philosophy' is really math or something. They're weird. Witold is, like, a sixth year or something."

Sequestered once again in my hermetic study chamber before bed, I performed the kind of perfunctory cyber-stalk available to the masses in 2006: I looked him up on his department website— his picture was devastating—and then cross-referenced that with Friendster. According to his department profile, Witold Romanoff was an NYU alum as well—and on Friendster he listed his hometown as New York City. *Ach,* we already had *so* much in common and he didn't even *know* it. He was listed as "single," and his favorite TV show was *The Simpsons.* (As long as he meant the pre-2000 *Simpsons,* this was excellent.) His "research interests" were a bunch of gobbledygook that made my eyes glaze over. (Also acceptable; all graduate students' "research interests" are gibberish.) One of his Friendster "testimonials" proclaimed: "Witold is more into simplicity than anyone I've ever known. He'd have to try to be less put-upon than he is, which would defeat the purpose." Uh-oh. Did that mean he prized simplicity in others? I was asking for no reason.

No, seriously, I was asking for no reason. The week after the Muffin Conversation, Witold apparently came to his senses and determined that sitting through two hours of Jack Osbourne and Indiana Jones butchering the Transcendental Dialectic was not, actually, fun, and he stopped auditing the Kant seminar. We crossed paths on campus every week or so, as our routes to and from class intersected between UCI's different retrofuturistic edifices, but that was cause for little more than a flicker of recognition and a nod (from *me*, I mean; I am very cool. I managed not to yell out HELLO HOT LOGICIAN WITH WEIRD NAME, I AM ALSO FROM NEW YORK, WELL NOT REALLY BUT I USED TO LIVE THERE, SO, YOU KNOW—WAIT, WHERE ARE YOU GOING? So I pretty much deserve a trophy). Eventually, my seminar papers eclipsed all other pursuits; the one about Heidegger and Heinrich von Kleist was just called "—," after the "substantive Nothing" that allows the "unheard-of event" of sexual assault to take place in *The Marquise of O,* so it was obviously very important. I forgot all about the hot logician with the weird name.

One day shortly after the start of the spring quarter of my first year in Irvine—thirteen months after the Schillerian-genius actor had broken up with me; not that I was counting—I was in the midst of a severely undermotivated elliptical-trainer workout at the student gym, and I caught sight of Witold talking to some girl. *No fair!* I thought. Didn't the hot logician with the weird name understand that I was mulling him over still? And so, since he was conveniently standing somewhere in the general vicinity of the cubby where I had stashed my student ID and keys, I swerved on over to say hello under that completely feasible pretense. He paused, taking in my ratty workout pants. (They were from one of those ill-begotten early-aughts velour tracksuits that everyone wore out to legitimate establishments because they cost two hundred dollars. Mine were knockoffs.) His eyes then swept my excellent New Kids on the Block shirt (vintage 1988, worn in pretend-irony but actual fandom), and alighted upon my visage, which he appeared not to recognize. After ten eternities, he finally said *hey.* Victory! Once at my cubby, I realized I had nothing to do there—I was actually planning on returning to the elliptical to make my workout a full eighteen minutes—so I pretended to futz with my stuff and then bolted for the drinking fountain.

Once I returned to the machine, however, I noticed that Witold had extricated himself from conversation with the other girl—*my nemesis!*—and was walking in my general direction. Toward me? Maybe. Possibly not, as behind me stood all of the gym's other equipment, and it is entirely probable that he was there to exercise and not to search, day after day and with a longing beyond human words, for the mythical Girl Who Reads Kant in German, whose name he didn't know and whose tender overworked carpal tunnels he had mocked so roundly. But I already looked like an overeager jackass, so I figured I might as well try for a conversation that involved neither injuries nor breakfast goods. I made eye contact and ripped out an earbud as he passed me by—but just *one,* you know, keeping it mysterious.

"How's it going?"

He looked surprised. "Not bad," he answered. "Taking any more philosophy courses this quarter?"

Excellent. He *did* remember me. Because I am unforgettable. Obviously. "Well, in my Enlightenment and Counter-Enlightenment course in the German department, we're reading a lot of Johann Georg Hamann," I offered, referring to a little-known Kant antagonist who disputed the very idea of "pure reason" with the extremely cogent assertion that language must precede thought, because all language is metaphorical approximation of the *language of the angels.* "Does that count?"

He managed a small smile. I returned to watching the seconds count backward on my elliptical machine. But he hadn't left yet.

"Hey," he said. "Do you know Eli Bergman?"

Of course I did; Eli was the German linguistics professor in my department, which was small enough that you could count all faculty and grad students on two hands.

"I took an undergraduate class from him last quarter," said Witold. "You know, for—"

"—let me guess, fun? I have to say, you have a somewhat bizarre concept of fun."

"I was *going* to say, to improve my German, which I need for my research."

That made a little more sense. All of the philosophers Witold researched, he explained, wrote in German.

"What, Heidegger?"

He smiled. "More like Frege." I would soon learn that exactly no analytic philosophers read Heidegger—not even for alleged fun—and that simply by not floating out of the nearest window on a miniature dirigible powered by his own smugness, Witold was proving to be among the nicest philosophers in the world. Meanwhile, the guy he was talking about, Gottlob Frege (I discovered via Dr. Wikipedia half an hour later), was the founder of first-order symbolic logic, otherwise known as the math class everyone in college takes when they don't want to take math (except it pretty much *is* math; burn). I had never heard that name in my life—as far as I knew it could be spelled *Freyga,* and he could have been Estonian or something, and just written in German for kicks. But, now having two entire quarters of graduate school behind me, I behaved accordingly, which is to say I nodded sagely.

"Anyway," Witold said, "in Eli's class we read *Der Verschollene.*"

I was impressed—most Anglophones used the English name for Kafka's least-known novel, *Amerika.* "I really liked it," he said. "Every sentence was like its own adventure."

That might have been the most exactly correct thing I'd ever heard, and from a fucking amateur, no less. And then, Witold opened his mouth and these words came out of it: "Do you like Kafka?" Did this person seriously just ask this question? So overwhelmed was I with the different options of expressing how much I *did,* indeed, like Kafka that my brain coagulated into a dollop of goo, of the sort the frat guy on the elliptical next to me had slathered liberally into his hair. So I did what I always do when I'm overwhelmed, which is make the worst choice possible. (This is why, if I make the error of entering a New York City bodega hungry, I will always, always exit with a bag of Bugles.)

I hopped down off the elliptical machine, which, let's face it, was little more than an unwieldy prop covered in undergrad germs, and with no prelude whatsoever, I lifted up the back of my NKOTB shirt far enough for him to see that two-inch-high к. I'd had inked on the small of my back when I was living in Williamsburg in 1999, nihilistic and jubilant to be free of a bad relationship.

"*I,*" I said, "have a *tattoo.*" Witold cleared his throat.

"Well, I'm, uh, interested in reading more by Kafka in German," he said. "Do you have anything to recommend?"

"I would be *honored* to make you an itemized *list,*" I said, approximately seventy-five times faster than I had heretofore been exercising. "Annotated, of course. I'll try not to make it too long. I'll just put the best stuff on there. I promise. Just the best stuff. A list!"

"Sure," he said. "Oh," he added, as I returned to my nominal evening of exercise, "what's your name?"

Two excruciatingly paced days later, I got his e-mail address off the Logic and Philosophy of Science website and thanked the thousand spires of Prague that academics are so easy to stalk. I began composing the first volley of a full-court e-mail charm offensive—and they said the years I spent studying Kafka's letters to Milena and Felice were wasted—but then I realized two things. One: If I wrote in *German,* that would be both more charming and excellent pretense for corresponding all quarter, because Witold wanted to work on his German, right? I'd be a free tutor and all he'd have to do was pay attention to me. Two: I still hadn't asked *his* name, so he was going to realize I'd looked him up. All the more reason to write in German; I made sure the sentence wherein I admitted to having asked Jeff his name was extremely convoluted and possibly above his level (or, at any rate, enough of "its own little adventure" that he'd enjoy reading it so much that he'd have to give me a chance). After much agonizing, I explained to him, I would like to recommend the following Kafka works, with the following annotations:

> *The Trial,* his best-known work, although a bit more difficult than *Der Verschollene* and it drags a bit in the middle; also, DID YOU KNOW that the order of its chapters is an editorial reconstruction, because Kafka never finished it and skipped all over the place in his notebook?

> "In the Penal Colony," short story of about thirty-five pages about a torture machine; extremely violent and bloody, several possible allegorical parallels to the industrial revolution. (P.S.: DO NOT pay attention to ANYONE who compares this story to the HOLO-CAUST because it was written in 1915! They do NOT know what they're talking about!)

"A Hunger Artist," short story about a guy who starves himself for sport but nobody comes to see him anymore. Very sad.

"A Country Doctor," I bet you can guess what it's about. Gross scene depicting an open wound full of worms. Common assignment in upper-level German courses for undergraduates.

"The Bucket Rider," possible critique of capitalism. Two pages long.

"The Judgment," about a guy and his dad and their pretty bad relationship; odd sex joke at the end.

"Contemplations," my personal favorite, collection of few dozen paragraph-length mini-stories, all enchanting. Favorites: "The Trees," "The Next Village," "Resolutions."

Several agonizing days later, my breath caught in the back of my throat as the name *Witold Romanoff* appeared in my inbox, with a message composed in careful German, thanking me very much for my suggestions and saying that he would choose *The Trial*, because he happened to own it already. (Oh, how the tables had turned since 1993.) Would I, he wrote, like to get together and talk about it when he finished? Of course! I wrote back, while thinking *God DAMMIT, man, why did you have to choose the longest and most difficult of all those things? "A Country Doctor" is six pages* long! "*The Trees*" is THREE SENTENCES! We could be discussing it NOW! By the time you get through the interminable Lawyer-Manufacturer-Painter chapter it's going to be 2010! Gah!

I had to think of something. Handsome, nice, well-adjusted, not-jerkish, not-pompous single male graduate students were rare enough at UC-Irvine that I'd spent all year there without running across one. (Not that I'd been looking. Heidegger was all the boyfriend I needed.) But still, hadn't I already seen at least one other girl making a move? Possibly an *undergraduate,* who of course would lack my intellectual gravitas and life experience but in their place would have youth, which at the decrepit age of twenty-nine I sincerely believed I no longer possessed? It was entirely possible that by the time Witold finished *The Trial,* he could have impregnated that girl, and they'd be moved into family housing, and I'd see him pushing a stroller down the bike path and pretend not to know him.

What could I possibly have to offer Witold the hot logician with the weird name that an undergraduate girl did not? I did a quick scan around my room: Improperly hung black curtains to block out the merciless morning sun? Possibly. A minifridge full of hard cider and Becherovka, a spicy-sweet Czech liqueur that is supposed to cure all ailments? Maybe, but the undergrads probably had Jell-O shots in their minifridges, and also no cellulite. What did I have that could possibly override cellulite?

My eyes finally alighted upon a DVD of *Triumph of the Will* sitting on top of my TV, floor model tube set I'd talked the guy at Best Buy into selling me for fifty-two dollars. I'd seen *Triumph of the Will* before—or at least I'd convincingly pretended to—but I was supposed to watch it "again" as an assignment for my Violence and Modernism course. So, here was what I had to offer. Would anyone else, ever, think to ask someone on a first date to view the world's most famous Nazi propaganda film, helmed by the world's most famous person who never returned my fax? It was worth a shot. In the invitation I sent, I matter-of-factly included the sentence *Hier ist meine Telefonnummer,* like it was a business necessity and not a substantial overture, a feat made entirely possible by the majestic default officiousness of the German vernacular. (A pretty fair trade-off for Heideggerese, I supposed.)

And it worked! Witold called. Later that week, I dragged my friend Eileen away from her fifteenth reading of Johann Georg Hamann's *Aesthetica in nuce* to come help me pick the perfect outfit for my nebulous maybe-date. ("Put down the 'angel speak' and come give me some 'human speak' about how to do my hair, please," I implored.) We sat on the foot of my bed watching *Law & Order* and drinking hard pear cider from my minifridge; I figured I'd have one or two while I was waiting for the hot logician with the weird name to show, and then the two of us would clear out the rest of my stash while we heckled Nazis—and then we'd, you know, see what happened. By the time the doorbell of my prefab student apartment rang, I was a few ciders deep as I left Eileen in my room and elbowed my roommate and Elena out of the way to get to the door. (Wonderful women both, but third-date introductions for sure.)

As the door swung open, my slightly buzzed brain immediately began doing calculations: Clean shirt (*yes*). Scraggly week-old stubble (*no*). Came bringing something (*yes*). Came bringing a half-eaten bag of Trader Joe's cookies (*no*). To be fair, said cookies were a special kind of chocolate-dipped macaroon only available at certain Southern California Trader Joe's during the years of 2005–2008, and they were spectacular, but I didn't know this yet. So when he said, quite gamely and cleverly, "I thought macaroons would be a good companion to Nazi propaganda," because it was *Jewish food,* because he, like me, is part Jewish, I was so busy wondering why he didn't like me enough to shave his face that I didn't even appreciate the joke, and I forgot about the macaroons entirely.

I tried to beat back the tide of panic that was rising in my torso. Eileen was still in my room at this point, as per my instructions, so that it would be apparent that I was cool and popular and had many exciting engagements per evening from which to choose. "Hello," she said, like a normal person.

"This is Eileen!" I interjected. "She's in the German department with me. She is my friend. WE ARE FRIENDS."

She gave me a duly impressed look as she showed herself out. All right, so not the effervescent demonstration of my popularity I'd hoped, but I still had one more armament in the Schuman arsenal of seduction: minifridge. "Can I offer you something to drink?" I asked.

"I'll just take some water," he said.

Oh, no. "Wait," I said, "check out what I have, and *then* tell me if you just want water."

I opened it with a flourish to show off my collection of hard ciders, Trader Joe's brand Hefeweizen, Becherovka, vodka, and two Vitamin Waters.

"Really," he said. "Water's fine."

Fuck. Had I misjudged the entire evening? Was he planning on chugging a perfunctory sip of agua and *politely* watching ten minutes of Heinrich Himmler prancing around *out of politeness,* before running off to go on his real date of the night? Because he was too nice to say *nein* outright to the Girl Who Reads Kant in German, with the big sad staring eyes and the gnarled wrist tendons? *Was this a carpal tunnel syndrome pity date?* I supposed there was only one way to find out. I at least had the wherewithal to switch to Vitamin Water, and I popped in the movie as Witold perused my bookshelf, removed his jacket (he'd been living in California long enough to wear a jacket outdoors at night, which I still refused to do), and made himself comfortable at the foot of my bed, which was the best and also only place to watch my television.

As the never-ending opening credits of *Triumph des Willens* played—*twenty years after the World War . . . sixteen years after the beginning of German suffering . . . nineteen months after Germany's rebirth*—the pear cider wore off, and Witold and I slipped into conversation. Riefenstahl's creepy masterpiece is, after all, dialogue-free for long stretches (unless you count the roar of seven hundred thousand people yelling *Heil Hitler*)—thus, although it was somewhat strange to have *der Führer* smiling creepily at his teenaged fans as a backdrop, the movie afforded plenty of opportunity for us to begin getting to know each other.

Witold had been born and raised in Brooklyn, the oldest child of Polish immigrants. His father was also named Witold. His parents had had sincere plans to name their firstborn son Michael, an unobtrusive American name that nobody would ever misspell or mispronounce. Once he was born, however, his father took one look at him, naked and covered in slime (Witold left out this part, but I think it's important not to romanticize childbirth), and became so overcome with emotion that he decided to give the boy his own name, despite the playground taunts, butchering, and general onerousness that would surely follow. "I hated my name when I was a kid," Witold said. "I went by Willy for all of middle school. Now that I'm an adult, though, I like it." I liked it, too. We talked about everything in the world but graduate school: Disneyland (which he hated); the beach (which he loved); vegetarian food (which we both ate); this one bodega near the NYU campus that makes terrible sandwiches (which we both remembered); and the time that I was rearranging my bag on the subway platform to accommodate one of said terrible sandwiches and dropped my wallet right onto the tracks, and when I got it back I felt lucky but also kind of pissed because the sandwich had, of course, been awful. Bodega food was terrible, we agreed, but we missed every single one of those bodegas anyway, because there was nowhere in Irvine with any character. He mentioned the fact that Irvine left him feeling "dead inside" with such gentleness and good humor that I almost didn't realize what he meant. I quickly forgot that we weren't drinking—in fact, I quickly forgot about everything, including my Kramer-style neighbor Elena, who poked her sweaty head in around 1:00 A.M. to tell us to "keep it down." This was not because we were being loud, but because our regular-volume conversation was drowning out the voices in her head.

I excused myself to the bathroom and beckoned her to follow so she would not be left alone with Witold to find out that he studied the philosophy of math, and thus would ostensibly want to hear all about her dissertation plans, which involved Henri Bergson and "like, fractals and stuff; I don't know, the math shit will be easy, I'll figure it out later."

"You've got to cool it down in there," she said as I washed my hands.

"Get your mind out of the gutter! We're just *talking.*"

"No," she said. "I mean you're laughing, like, way too much and way too hard. I can hear it from my *apartment.* It sounds really overeager. Like, be *cool,* Rebecca. Be cool."

I splashed some water on my face. "First off," I said, "I'm *not* cool, so I wouldn't want to give the wrong impression. And also, this happens to be what I sound like when I'm happy. Which probably seems unusual because you've never heard it before."

By the time Witold left with a chaste hug, it managed not to send me into paroxysms of insecurity because it was four in the morning, and I figured that even the nicest Polish New Yorkers with weird names would probably find reason to extricate themselves from a hellish garbage nightmare situation before the break of day, if they so desired. After he walked out the door, I noticed that he'd left that light California jacket by my bookshelf. *Score!* A George Costanza–type leave-behind. We'd even talked about *Seinfeld*, so, *obvious*. I had no choice but to e-mail him to arrange a handoff, which then facilitated the procurement of a second date— this time to view my second-favorite documentary, *Hell House*, which is about a conservative evangelical church's haunted house of sin. This date involved no alcohol whatsoever, also ended at four in the morning, and didn't end in a hug.

For those next few months in 2006, which then turned into years that spooled out after 2006 like so much sun-baked Orange County asphalt, Witold and I ended up having quite a few small adventures with each other, sometimes even setting out into the dread OC on purpose: to the *Borat* movie at the mall we called "the Speculum," where it took us half an hour to find a parking space and I was just happy to spend the time with him; to an Indian restaurant in Tustin where the food was so spicy that I had a beet-red face for two days afterward; on a series of increasingly subversive walks in our unwalkable neighborhood, one of which had us scrambling along for an hour in a drainage ditch; on a road trip to Los Angeles on a gloriously clear day, where we sat in the garden of the Getty Museum talking for so long that the guard had to come kick us out; to many mornings and afternoons spent on the beach, some even in the frigid, terrifying water, where he demonstrated how to jump into the waves head-on so that they couldn't smash me down on the sand (he'd learned that, of course, the hard way).

By March of my second year of grad school, I was no longer scared by Martin Heidegger or admitting I didn't know what the fuck I was talking about, and Witold and I had been going out for almost a year, so I was also no longer scared that nobody would ever love me again. And then, my family experienced a sudden and traumatic event—an *Ereignis,* if you will. My grandfather drowned in a canoeing accident. On the surface, if you hear someone explain that her ninety-four-year-old grandpa just passed away, it doesn't sound shocking—but the grandpa in your mind's eye is not *my* grandpa, who still went canoeing every day, who built entire tree houses in an hour, whose bare adoration of his grandchildren could power a small train. Every kid thinks her grandpa is immortal, but it's rare that a thirty-year-old *adult* believes this to be so with such tenacity—because her grandfather, who has survived Nazis, and heart disease, and even an unfortunate dalliance with two-week-old corned beef, goddamned near *was* immortal. Before I had to leave for a three-day trip to Chicago for the funeral, Witold drove us to the beach and sat with me while I looked out on the water and thought about drowning, with his arm around me, staring out at those waves.

As he dropped me off at the airport later, he told me he admired what he called my "stubborn insistence" on facing my grief directly. When I returned, he picked me up, and we drove home as the setting sun turned the sky a vibrant purplish pink. I was exhausted from sadness, from so many grieving Schumans in one place, and from withstanding the mind-bogglingly tone-deaf insistence of my cousin's asshole husband that we get together again someday when I wasn't "so stressed out." ("I am not *stressed out*," I told that fucker. "My grandfather just died. *I'm sad*.") As we drove on, and the sky and the burnt desert hills around us grew brighter and then darker, I began to feel the first stirrings of relief, of knowledge that yes, my immortal grandpa was dead and it had ripped a gaping and permanent hole into my family, but somehow, with enough care and gentleness from the people who loved me, old and new, I would be all right eventually. "I don't know what it is," Witold said, as we stopped at a traffic light, "but these past months I've been feeling a lot more alive."

"Yeah," I said. "I think I know what you mean."

We drove in silence for two more stoplights—so, it being Orange County, three more miles—and watched the sky soften together.

It was, I thought but didn't say aloud, a moment of pure human joy, just coming into view.

9.

Schadenfreude

n. malicious happiness, from damage *and* joy.

ex. You could say I should have seen all this coming,
but that would be unnecessarily *schadenfroh*. (And
I've heard it all before.)

The Schumans are big cremators, but if I buck tradition and get a
tombstone, I'd like it to have on it nothing but my name and a line
of Kafka's "A Little Fable," which is a tiny story about a mouse who
gets stuck in a maze. "Alas," the mouse says, "the world gets smaller
every day." At first she was relieved when she saw walls appear in
the distance. "But," she continues, "these long walls closed in so fast
that I'm already in the last room, and there in the corner is the trap
into which I must run."

Then, a surprise: the story's most important character—lurking
the whole time, unbeknownst to all of us—appears and changes the
game entirely, furnishing me with my epitaph:

> "You've simply got to run the other direction," said
> the cat, and ate it.
> Rest in peace, me.

I think that last line is meant to be funny, but I fully expect all
who visit my interred remains to think it's stern and somber, and
to leave the cemetery with at best a new insight into futility and
mortality, and, if I'm lucky, a full-blown existential crisis.

Speaking of graves, and cemeteries, and cities where the dead
outnumber the living two to one, I spent my penultimate year
of graduate school in Vienna, Austria, crown jewel of Central
Europe—*Zentralfriedhof* corpse pop. 3 million; living pop. 1.7 million. I was there on a Fulbright grant, as a "fellow" at a lovely
cultural studies institute where I attended a lot of lectures by
Austrians who talked way too quickly, and got unlimited free
room-temperature mineral water. My other activities during the
year were staring awkwardly into my webcam at Witold back in
the U.S., where he had a non-tenure-track job teaching philosophy
in St. Louis; riding the tram; shuffling mournfully around perfectly preserved old neighborhoods; getting jacked up on six-euro
cups of coffee; being depressed in the birthplace of psychoanalysis;
and pecking away at my dissertation on Wittgenstein and Kafka.
At the end of the year, I gave a forty-five-minute talk on my research
in carefully enunciated German, then braced myself for a Q&A
courtesy of the city's notoriously literate and grumpy populace. It
turns out my most perplexing query was from the director of the
cultural-studies institute, Herr Boltzmann, who, after I illustrated
part of Wittgenstein's *Philosophical Investigations* with that "Little
Fable," insisted that he'd never heard the story with that last sen-

tence before. "Are you sure it doesn't just end with 'you've got to change direction'? Are you entirely, *entirely* sure?"

"I'm pretty sure," I said.

"I could swear I've read that fable a hundred times and there's no cat in it."

"You're like the person whose mom takes *Old Yeller* out of the VCR before the dog gets shot," I said, to raucous laughter, either because the audience appreciated that I'd stolen a joke from *Friends,* or because—in a triumph of assimilation—the audience thought it was a legitimately good bit of Austrian humor, what the Viennese call *Schmäh.* I'll never know.

I do, however, know exactly why Herr Boltzmann wanted the "Little Fable" to end before the cat appeared, because then the story would have had a discernible moral. But doesn't that kind of miss the entire point of Kafka? Kafka is parables without a lesson. "A Little Fable" is kind of the granddaddy of his oeuvre, given that it's not a parable without a moral so much as a parable whose moral is that there are no real morals to be had in parables.

I cared a lot about all this in 2009, because this sort of the-answers-are-nonanswers stuff was what linked Kafka together with Wittgenstein. Wittgenstein liked to demonstrate that instead of answering a so-called question of philosophy, it was more important to prove how wrong that question was in the first place. He didn't solve problems so much as *dis*solve them. As far as I was concerned, *I'm not going to answer because your question can't be asked* summed up Kafka quite nicely—that, and the use of stunning German prose to insist that language couldn't express anything important. To me, the connection between the two nominal

Austrians who never met each other was the stuff of true scholarly epiphany. And yet, as I rounded the final year of grad school—on another paid fellowship, one that allowed me to live in St. Louis full-time—I was starting to feel like my own journey to the Ph.D. was itself a parable with no answer or moral.

This made me a real hit at Witold's department parties, where the philosophers treated literary studies as at best an amusing trifle and more often than not a jargon-riddled, pseudointellectual farce. (Philosophy, of course, is nothing like this.) Witold's colleague Viktoria, for example, was a very enthusiastic and inquisitive Russian who for some reason enjoyed inviting us to dinner.

"Tell me," she said one glum autumn evening, as St. Louis's scraggly vegetation began its annual metamorphosis into angry-looking twigs, "what is it you love about Kafka?"

"Give me a second," I said, and excused myself to the bathroom.

I locked the door behind me and took a breath. This wasn't a fucking book club. I wasn't doing this dissertation to talk about what I *loved*, to feed into that pernicious rhetoric of intellectual vocation—the "calling"—that enables hundreds of thousands of part-time professors in the United States to qualify for fucking food stamps because at most of our universities, the inner rewards of soaring exegesis are now expected to count as pay. My research wasn't about *love*. It was about—

—and therein lay the rub. What was it about? There was no question that I had loved Kafka once. I had loved him a lot. I had loved him in place of a living person who broke my heart; I had loved him through college and young adulthood. But now, after half a decade of graduate school, at the age of thirty-three, 250 pages deep in a dissertation (times six drafts), I could think of no reason for what I was doing, other than that in 2005, a German department had offered me $100,000 to be a full-time student.

Back in Oregon for a Christmas visit to my family, I was at the health-food store with my mother and ran into Victor, a family friend I'd known since I was five.

"I heard you're finishing your dissertation!" he said.

"Yep." I developed a sudden interest in reverse-osmosis kale water.

"What's it about?" he asked.

"Oh," I said, "it's boring. You don't want to hear about it."

Victor shrugged and went back to his perusal of sprouted wheat berries.

As I loaded our groceries into the car, my mother said: "I think you hurt Victor's feelings. Why do you do that?"

"Honestly," I said, "I have no fucking idea."

"Do you really think your own dissertation is boring?"

"That's a ridiculous question, because dissertations are inherently boring, as you *well know*."

"That's different. Mine really *was* boring."

"See?"

"But I didn't tell everyone it was boring at the *time*."

"Well, maybe you were deluded and I'm not."

Her eyes were in the rearview as she spoke, but I could see her looking thoughtful.

"Do you even *want* to be an academic?" she said.

"Sure I do," I said. "I'm good at it. Or, you know, better at it than I was at anything else I tried before."

"I'm not asking if you're good at it."

"All right, how about this? I'm well into my thirties, and have spent the better part of the last decade working harder than I ever have, in training for one specific career at the expense of all others, and I don't think anyone is going to want to hire a thirty-four-year-old German Ph.D. to be an editorial assistant, and at least I've had dental insurance this whole time."

My mother pulled into our carport and sighed. "You'll figure it out, Bekibek," she said. "You always do."

"Actually, I never do, but somehow I still manage." This despite having a mother who calls me *Bekibek* and has done so since 1990.

She was right, though. I had to quit telling everyone my research was boring and terrible, even if doing so was for purely altruistic purposes, to spare them a quarter-hour of bloviation about the rule-following paradox and whether controversial Wittgenstein scholar Saul Kripke ruined it or blew it right open. (If you want to know the answer to that, then I hate to tell you this, but that's the wrong question.) If I wanted to succeed on the job market, I'd have to start assuming everyone else should find my dissertation as interesting as I did back when I started it.

The academic job market is not the kind of thing you enter for fun, thinking maybe you'll apply for a job as a professor, because *what could it harm?* Because it does—and in my case did—a tremendous amount of harm. How? Let me count the ways. First, the job market destroyed my time, time that would have been better spent on my dissertation, or making out with Witold, or submitting my résumé at the Gap. (Not really. I'd never be hired at the Gap, because I was too old.) Applying for a single academic job—and mine was but one application out of two hundred for each position—requires about thirty hours of work up front to compile an eighty-page dossier, customized for each institution, with a meticulous cover letter and an extensive portfolio of teaching and research materials. This was bad enough, but then every place I applied also required I use a specific online portal that demanded, from all two hundred of its applicants, two more hours of irrelevant HR paperwork aimed at people with regular jobs. ("Phone number of current supervisor"? "Years spent in current position"? "Reason for leaving this position"? How about: *TA positions and dissertation fellowships are all for a single year each, as per industry standard, you fucking dicks?*)

Back when I reluctantly took the GRE, and despite barricading myself in the NYU library for three days with nothing but black coffee and quadratic equations, I scored a 710 on the math portion. This sounds like it was good but was actually very bad. Engineers and physicists take the GRE, too, and so I scored in the thirty-third percentile. (I guess I am bad at math after all. At least for an engineer.) But even my feeble thirty-third-percentile brain knew that a one-out-of-two-hundred shot at the two dozen open tenure-track German positions in the country was what professional statisticians call *extremely fucking shitty odds.*

And yet, when the rejections came, I could barely see through the hurt of it. It wasn't just that I didn't get a job. Sometime during the past five years, my academic self had snuck up on my personal self and eaten her whole. (I suppose it might have had something to do with spending most of my waking hours being an academic, even if I didn't "love" it or entirely know why.) Being passed over for a professorship was Dylan Gellner my high-school boyfriend dumping me all over again—I'd bared the fruits of the hardest intellectual work I'd ever done before these search committees, essentially shown them my soul, and they'd been unmoved. I'm sure, like Dylan Gellner, they *liked me fine*—but once again, the whole of my thinking, feeling self had fallen short. Actually it was even worse than getting dumped by Dylan Gellner, because going out with Dylan Gellner didn't pay for my rent, food, and utilities.

The totalizing sense of existential failure that emanated from the rejections then infected my household, and a pall of uncertainty took root about every aspect of my future. It wasn't just *Where would I be working?* (Or, for that matter, *Would I be working?*) It was: Where would I be living in the next year—or, foreseeably, for the rest of my life? Would it be somewhere Witold could get a job and move? Would he want to? It was simply expected that if I was a serious enough scholar, I would happily sacrifice my relationship. Who needs a love life when you've got the Life of the Mind? Academic job applicants are cautioned on a regular basis to remove wedding rings at interviews, not to speak of a spouse (or, if female, children), and to appear married only to the Profession (and yes, they call it "the Profession," capitalized, in utter seriousness).

People with no experience in academia wonder why their cousins or friends with Ph.D.s are on the brink of nervous collapse, when nowadays it's hard for everyone to find a job, thank you very much. What they don't realize—and they have no reason to know this, of course—is that academia expects its aspirants to sacrifice everything for even the slightest, smallest chance at full membership in the club. The rhetoric is painted cheerily—*Be flexible and willing to move!*—but the reality is pernicious: *Give up everything, expect nothing—and you just might get something.* Discovering all of this for the first time, while sequestered in a strange town with no day job, made me a truly delightful partner. So much so, in fact, that one day, Witold did what he does best, which is use math to express difficult concepts.

"Your job market woes," he said, "have sucked ninety-five percent of the fun out of this relationship."

"I'm surprised you're leaving the five," I said. "That's pretty generous."

"I know it is."

But I couldn't help myself. I couldn't so much as run a comb through my hair without sinking into terror and self-doubt, so frayed were my nerves for the entire year. This was due to the extended nature of the academic hiring cycle, where listings appeared in early fall and weren't filled until April or May. This meant nine months of prostration, waiting, rejection, and, worst of all, hope both legitimate and false (but mostly false). *Plenty of hope,* as Kafka allegedly once said. "An infinite amount of hope. Just not for us." Or, at any rate, not for me. So, *what could it harm,* indeed.

As I probably should have expected, my first try on the market yielded exactly bupkes. It was as if I'd screamed those eighty-page dossiers into a yawning chasm, a void that wasn't even kind enough to be the Nietzschean abyss and actively glare back at me. Ludwig Wittgenstein told everyone that the most important part of the *Tractatus* was the part he didn't write. Was the most important part of the job market the things the search committees didn't say? I pondered this as I spat bile onto Facebook and refused to leave (or clean) our grimy one-bedroom in St. Louis, rising from bed only to make chocolate-chip pancakes that began to favor the chocolate chips over the pancake batter so aggressively that in the end I was just drowning molten goo in syrup. I pondered it as, after several months of this excellent use of my time, I pulled what had once been a roomy pair of Katharine Hepburn–style wide trousers over my behind, only to clasp them with protracted effort and create what I believed the youngsters called a "muffin top."

"I think," I said to Witold on a soaking-wet February morning, another set of form rejections from Southeastern Evangelical College and Semi-Pro Football Team et al. piled up in the mailbox as I waddled into the living room, "that I might have been eating my feelings a little bit."

He looked up from grading his two hundredth logic assignment of the weekend and smiled a sly Witold smile, this thing he does when he really wants to say something smart-ass but isn't sure he should.

"Go on," I said, lower lip quivering. "Just say it."

"You know what's *really* good exercise?" he said.

"CrossFit?" I sniffled.

"Cleaning the bathroom."

"Why don't *you* clean the bathroom, then?"

"I *do* clean the bathroom—but I also work forty hours a week, and pay eighty percent of the rent, and I thought that *perhaps*, with you on fellowship and home all day, you might, you know, notice your surroundings a little bit."

"I'll have you know," I said, "that the *job market* is a full-time job."

"Perhaps," he said, "but the pay is fucking terrible. And the benefits seem chiefly to be a bottomless vortex of misery."

I scowled at him and made a big show of throwing all the half-empty shampoo bottles across the bedroom while I limply smeared some Simple Green around the bathtub.

When I read "Before the Law," all I wanted to do was jump into the page and tell the man from the country to just go back home. *What do you need the Law for, really? I would say. The Doorkeeper is an asshole, and he's just the most minor of the assholes—he said so himself—so what do you think is going to happen to you, even if you get in there? You won't have won anything. You'll just be surrounded by assholes, just like in* Spaceballs. *Don't listen to him with* his "*maybe later*" *and* "*try again.*" *He was created to tell you* "*maybe later*" *disingenuously! Go home!*

A reasonable person would, in a similar vein, have spent that one year on the job market, taken one look around, gone *Jesus H. Christ, this is ridiculous,* and beaten feet out of there. But I had other plans. Other excellent, fun plans. You would think, at the very least, if I hadn't gleaned the appropriate lessons from "Before the Law," I'd at least have paid attention to an even more important part at the end of *The Trial,* when the Priest explains to Josef K. the real moral of that very parable: that the Court's case against K. *isn't* actually personal. "The Court wants nothing from you," the Priest says—doors created for the sole purposes of slamming in faces notwithstanding. "It takes you when you come and lets you out when you leave." And that's all. Of all his unknown crimes, K.'s worst was the egocentricity of assuming he was being persecuted.

I knew this intimately from my work, and I of all people should have let art bleed into life. And yet, I couldn't help but assume that an academic search committee happening to choose another applicant, for reasons that ultimately had nothing to do with me (or my 198 best friends), was a swift personal judgment upon my inherent unworthiness as a scholar. Or, worse, somehow these search committees knew I'd been a nineteen-year-old lazy-ass, and no amount of sincere intellectual labor in my thirties could compensate. Making the job market personal in this way wasn't just egocentric, though—it was also easier than the reality, which was that being selected for a particular academic position required an alchemic combination of "correct" qualities that was largely out of my control: a perfectly in-need specialization (one that stepped on no toes, but was familiar enough to everyone not to be dismissed as vogueish gibberish); a CV that struck the *exact* correct balance between teaching and research (different, of course, for every institution); and, most importantly, some sort of transcendental intangible that made one person the right "fit" and another the wrong one.

The reality was that my CV was probably near-identical to everyone else's: a handful of publications in the "right journals"; a dissertation under contract to become a book; an impressive-sounding list of conference presentations in far-flung locations; a stack of glowing teaching reviews and another stack of glowing letters of reference. What made me "not good enough" (and someone else good enough) largely came down to factors I'd never be able to identify, much less control. Academia wasn't weeding *me* out personally for my past or current sins, real or imagined. The job market wasn't out to get me. It wanted nothing from me. It took me when I arrived—and it would let me leave when I left.

Except I wouldn't leave. Sometimes, after all, you want the impossible precisely because it's impossible. Also it was just so much less terrifying to decide that it was all my fault for being lazy fifteen years ago—or any number of other character shortcomings, academic and otherwise. All I had to do, I decided, was be better. Publish more. Work harder. Be even more willing to move anywhere, and do anything. I decided to attempt the job market for three more years. Every single person I knew in academia who held a position I respected told me in no uncertain terms that this was exactly the right thing to do—if not, perhaps, too few years. (Many suggested five. Some suggested ten. A few suggested "as long as it takes.")

"It's hard out there, no doubt," they said. "But there are always jobs for good people." Yes, an infinite amount of jobs. (Well, twenty-four jobs.) But not for me.

Keep trying.
Come back.
Maybe later.

In the meantime, I was both lucky and unlucky to land some stopgap academic employment, a day job to pay the bills while I continued on the market. I was lucky, because the difference between unemployed and employed is of course vast. I was unlucky because the job was as an adjunct, the academic equivalent of the Land-Surveyor in Kafka's *Castle*, a sort of shifty mercenary who's summoned to the ivory tower but not really let inside, who effectively both belongs to the Castle and doesn't.

Adjuncts are real professors in that they have teaching responsibilities that are, in most cases, more or less identical to those of their full-time, tenure-track or tenured counterparts. (To students, they're exactly the same, save for the fact that they always show up in the course listing as "staff.") But they're also *not* real professors, in that they aren't listed in a department roster, don't have offices (or if they do, they share with multiple other adjuncts), often don't have use of the copier or the library, don't have building keys, aren't invited to faculty meetings, and are generally regarded by their full-time colleagues somewhere between invisible and gonorrhea incarnate. Adjuncts teach on a course-by-course, semester-by-semester basis for as little as seventeen hundred dollars per class (per *three-and-a-half-month semester*), and can be fired at any time for any reason. They are academia's dirtiest little secret—not because they keep quiet (they don't; many form unions and agitate); it's more that for some reason, students and their parents don't seem to care that they're paying $250,000 to be taught by someone who has to eat at the soup kitchen.

The adjunct job I was offered at the small honors college asso-

ciated with Witold's university was a few sections of the introductory freshman literature course, which contained no German texts,
but for which I had trained as a TA back in Irvine, when I taught
a section of the humanities core sequence. That had been a welcome diversion from my normal duties, of teaching German 101
to half-snoozing freshmen who used Google Translate for most
of their assignments, which is not as intellectually fulfilling as you
might think. But the literature courses I taught, both in Irvine and
then as an adjunct in St. Louis, were different. Demystifying texts
with students—difficult ones that they never would have chosen
for themselves, that they approached with trepidation or sometimes hostility—was, it turned out, even more enjoyable than
demystifying them alone in my room.

After every semester, I would rip into my student evaluations
like they were a plate of the chocolate-chip pancakes I now rarely
allowed myself.

It was a surprisingly enjoyable class to go to.

If I could take any class at college over again, I'd pick this one.

*One of the most interesting classes I've taken, and one I will
never forget.*

*Dr. Schuman is pretty much the smartest person I've ever met
ever.*

*Dr. Schuman is the best teacher I have ever had, not just here,
but in my life.*

The good news was that I clearly and at long last had found the
place I belonged. The bad news was: What if nobody would let me
do this for a living wage, ever? If I stopped teaching college, I'd feel
destroyed—but if I kept adjuncting, I'd *be* destroyed. So that is
why I couldn't just leave. That is why I couldn't just tell the Doorkeeper to go fuck himself, and get Botox so I could be hired at the

Gap. That is why, after another market cycle again yielded no tenure-track offers, I kept waiting outside that door for two more years—even though it damn near killed me.

I don't mean this existentially. I almost died courtesy of an appropriately Kafkan disease. But let's backtrack a second: What if the Doorkeeper allowed the man from the country in to the Law for exactly two years, with the promise that almost everyone who has been allowed to do this got full and permanent access afterward? That's what happened to me. I applied for—and won—a postdoctoral fellowship from a high-profile granting institution, one that was for "promising scholars" who were in danger of Leaving the Field, a fate worse than death.

"Many of our fellows have had their positions converted into tenure-track jobs," explained the program's director during a terrifying orientation webinar (largely terrifying because of the word *webinar*). "Just work hard and make yourself *indispensable*." Sounded feasible enough.

I was placed at a massive research university in Ohio, in a department whose chair sold me on four impending retirements (nudge nudge, wink wink), and "collegiality" (academic shorthand for "we actively pretend not to hate each other"). *This is it,* I thought. I was going to go to Ohio alone, take advantage of my solitude and turn that dissertation into a book, crank out articles, overprepare for class, and suck up to my collegial new colleagues with such believable sincerity (believable because they, being so collegial, would be nice people I'd enjoy pleasing) that they'd have no choice but to look at each other and go: *Why even bother with a stupid national search to replace these retirements, when Rebecca is right here being indispensable?*

When I arrived, the department manager pointed to the unopened box of books and teaching materials I'd had mailed to my-self and told me I might as well take it home. "We thought about petitioning the Dean of Space for an office for you—but for such a short time, will it really be worth it?"

All I could think to say in answer was: "You have someone called a Dean of Space?"

After I held office hours with unimpressed students in the de-partment storage room for several weeks, one of my new colleagues took pity upon me: since he had *two* offices, he'd allow me to use one of them—so long as I didn't make him clean it out. That had been a true moment of collegiality, yes—one that almost made up for the start-of-semester party, when the department's most emi-nent professor came up to me and said: "Amy! It's nice to meet you. It must be so nice to be almost finished with your disserta-tion."

"It's nice to meet you too," I said. "My name is, uh, actually Rebecca, and I am happy to report that I finished my dissertation two years ago."

She looked at me like she wanted to spit poison. I was reminded of the scene in *The Trial* where Josef K. has his first interrogation, and the magistrate says, "So, you're a house painter!" This isn't true, and K. tries to set the record straight—but that actually just ends up making him look worse in the eyes of the ever-shifting Court.

"Rebecca is our new faculty fellow!" said the chair, in a good-faith effort to rescue me. "Remember? She's going to be here for the next year."

"Thank you," I said. "But I'm actually going to be here for two."

"Oh, but you'll find a job before then," she said. "Surely, you will."

I had hoped to find a job *there*—I'd already been investigating a spousal hire for Witold, since this was finally a big institution with money (or at any rate a very rich football team). I had been led to believe a job there wasn't out of the question. Perhaps I was wrong. Perhaps this whole thing was going to turn out differently than I thought. If only some force in Wittgenstein's ineffable realm of the transcendent would give me a signal as to what to do next. If only.

Seven months later, I got pneumonia.

It started out like a bad cold. Witold was visiting for the weekend, and on Friday night I declared, midway through an episode of *Homeland* (which was currently "our show"), that I would be taking to bed. Witold harrumphed around my cavernous living room—the apartment was too big for one person, furnished in matching red and black décor via one frantic trip to an IKEA a hundred miles away, loneliness radiating from every particleboard surface—unsure exactly why he drove the four hundred miles if I was just going to slink off alone. When he finally slipped in beside me, he recoiled.

"I'm *sorry*," I said.

"No," he said, "you're burning up."

I couldn't eat. I could barely sit. I would sweat through my clothes every hour, overcome by shaking chills. On Sunday afternoon, Witold had to leave, due in the classroom the next morning at nine.

"Go, go. I'm fine. It's probably a flu."

"Are you sure?"

What was he going to do? Take FMLA so he could keep me company while I did the world's most cursory course prep and gnawed halfheartedly on frozen waffles?

"Can't you get a friend to cover your classes for you?" he asked.

"My colleagues are *German*. It takes like seven years to become someone's actual *friend*. You know that. I'll be fine. Go home."

I waved him out the door, but I wasn't actually sure I'd be all right. In fact, I was pretty sure that with Witold gone, I could die in my apartment and nobody would notice for days. So I took his advice and composed what I thought was a fairly brave (and desperate) e-mail to my colleagues, quickly reminding them of my name and rank, and asking if anyone might be able to pop into my class the next day, just to hand out a group activity (*"Worksheet attached!"*) and then leave again.

Those who didn't ignore me sent back apologies: There was a bigwig visiting that week, a finalist for the "Eminent Scholar" position. Everyone was too busy showing him the racquetball courts and attending his mini-seminar on Nietzschean semiotics. What did I expect? They didn't know me. I can't imagine I would have done a thing different in their places. And so, I forced down two more Tylenol, dragged jeans over my legs and a semirespectable shirt over my head, and wrapped a cashmere scarf around my neck a half-dozen times, before walking—grandpas everywhere, take note—a half-mile, in the sleet, with a 103-degree fever, to go teach my fucking class.

As the week progressed, my condition deteriorated past the point that my last flu had started to improve. My dad called up with the radical suggestion that I seek the counsel of a medical doctor.

"I don't have a doctor," I explained. "I just moved here."

"Then just go to one of those rent-a-docs at Walgreens," he begged.

"Those are such a rip-off!" I said, before dissolving into coughs.

"I will spot you whatever it costs," he said. "Just go."

Twenty minutes and a delirious bus ride later, I shuffled into a Minute Clinic looking every bit the pill-scheming druggie: skin that had progressed from waxy to hanging off my craggy visage; eyes that had disappeared into the sunken purple caverns that surrounded them; hair that had touched neither suds nor comb in a week; breath that could have caused a conflagration had I exhaled too forcefully in the nail-care aisle.

"I think," I said to the nonplussed nurse-practitioner, "I have the flu."

"You *think* you have the flu?" she said. "The *flu,*" she said with a resigned exhale, "is a high fever that lasts for—"

"I've had a temperature of a hundred and three for eight days," I said.

"Oh dear," she said. "You need to go to the emergency room."

At the hospital, I was spirited into a cozy cot with clean sheets, in my very own partitioned-off room with its own TV and everything. *The Fresh Prince of Bel-Air* kept me company while I waited for test results. Once they plied me with enough Tylenol and Motrin to get my fever down, I even kind of enjoyed the break. I had been too out of it to bring my laptop with me, and so now, for the first time since I'd arrived in Ohio, I couldn't feel guilty about the few hours per day I didn't spend working on my godforsaken book or answering student e-mails about whether or not I could "just bump up" their grades from an A-minus to an A. Nurses flanked me with warmed blankets, soup, hot water, more Tylenol, and care. Yes, I know they were being paid to care, but after a week alone in my apartment shivering into my soaked pillow, I didn't give a shit.

The doctor attending me was also named Rebecca, and looked about twelve. That's the thing about academia; because you're thirty-five and still applying to entry-level positions, you forget that most thirty-five-year-olds are already established in their careers. Forget middle management; they're partners in their law firms and medical practices. They're upper management or even executives. So you get administered to by medical residents of perfectly average medical-resident age, but suddenly they're all Doogie Howser. Anyway, teen wonder medical-doctor Rebecca surmised that since I'd flunked—or perhaps passed—the flu test (whichever it was, I didn't have the flu), I probably just had "some other virus" that apparently couldn't be pinpointed, and was about to be sent home.

"But I guess we'll do a chest X-ray, just to cover our bases."

"I always appreciate some perfunctory radiation," I said, before falling into a brief fever dream about doing the Carlton dance in front of my Intro to German Prose class. The next thing I knew, medical-doctor Rebecca was nudging me awake, telling me I had *pneumonia*.

"Holy shit!" I said. "The walking kind?"

"Nope," she said, "the regular kind. I guess that chest X-ray wasn't a bad idea."

Pneumonia. An actual *Lungenkrankheit,* a "lung disease," not unlike the sort that killed Franz Kafka. The kind of illness that, if left untreated—if, for example, its sufferer is a reclusive German professor in a new town with no primary care provider—kills people even today. I sent out an unsolicited but searing follow-up e-mail to my colleagues, explaining that I would have to cancel class for a few days—"given the pneumonia," I said, lest they have not read the first two sentences, most of which were comprised of the word *pneumonia,* nor the subject line, which was "PNEUMO-NIA."

After I got better, I went onto Etsy, where you can purchase jewelry in the shape of literally anything, and found a necklace in the shape of lungs. I wore it to remind me, not of the pneumonia per se, but of the helplessness that went with it. And of the fact that out of my seventeen colleagues, one taught at the same time as I did, one was pregnant and couldn't come within thirty feet of me, and the other fifteen did not know me well enough to think I was anything other than a melodramatic hypochondriac.

Was contracting a 1920 disease—the result, according to my teen doctor, of stress—sign enough for me to find something else to do with my life? It was not. Here's why: What if, instead of just being told *maybe later,* the man from the country had actually and legitimately gotten a little bit closer to the Law every time he tried to get past the Doorkeeper? Like, to use a random example, let's say the first time, he was ignored completely; the second time he was granted a preliminary interview of sorts for admittance to a low-level Law anteroom; the third time he got an even better interview—*for full access to the Law*—and the fourth time, he even got a follow-up invitation to come and spend two days hanging out with all of the Doorkeepers as a sort of final audition. In this case, it would seem like the man from the country was making progress and shouldn't give up, no?

The year after my first attempt's gaping void, I got a single non-tenure-track interview (for a position that was later canceled); the year after that, I was at last granted an uncomfortable seat at the foot of a hotel bed at the Modern Language Association conference (an interview I blew by "having a personality," as one of them put it). Finally, the year after that, my personality and I somehow made it past the interview stage to the coveted position of finalist at another university in Ohio not far from where I already worked. That meant I was invited on a campus visit, which is a two-day gauntlet of more interviews, teaching demonstrations, and "casual" meals where every gesture would secretly communicate to the search committee the innermost nuances of the quality of my mind and my likelihood to remain in rural Ohio forever.

The visit was an unmitigated disaster, largely because I bombed my teaching demo. It wasn't just the worst German class I'd ever taught; I was pretty sure it was the worst class of any sort that anyone had ever taught. To be fair, I never stood a chance: it was nine on a Friday morning at a school known for its fraternity culture, on a day that was both in the single digits temperature-wise and on which the students had an essay due. You couldn't have come up with a better formula for calamity if you tried: *day everyone wants to skip + reason they have to be there anyway.* But, to be fair to them, I did whatever the opposite of rising to the occasion is: their resistance threw me off so terribly that I flubbed every exercise, and ended the class near tears.

In hindsight, I now know that teaching demonstrations in foreign-language classrooms are an impossible minefield. The students are timid about speaking in front of strangers; they've got their own stresses and commitments (and poorly timed essay assignments and frat parties) without a visibly terrified, overenthusiastic, suit-wearing rando plunking name plates down in front of them. I should have come in with five games aimed at total beginners that would have immediately made them feel smart and relaxed, and just played the whole time—of course, then I wouldn't have gotten to demonstrate my precious *pedagogy,* and I still wouldn't have gotten the damn job. One option was the mousetrap and the other was the cat. I just wanted to go home, sink into my wobbly red IKEA couch I put together myself, and wait for the slow embrace of death.

But first, I had four more interviews and what's creatively called a "job talk," a brief lecture about research that's supposed to be the final tribunal, where the candidate is lobbed a bunch of withering criticism and, if she vanquishes her opponents properly, is then deemed worthy to join their ranks. Mine was called THE CASE FOR A LOGICAL MODERNISM: the *Tractatus,* Kafka's 'The Judgment,' and the Ineffable. (Mildly Clever Thing; three-part list; made-up word, check check check.) I gave it to a tiny smattering of the faculty, most of whom spent it texting. Afterward, nobody lobbed me any scathing *This isn't a question so much as a comment* questions, which a normal person might take as a good sign, but which a seasoned academic knows to mean that nobody is taking you seriously. *Jesus, word about my Chernobyl of teaching demos must have gotten around fast.* After that, even though at that point nobody was even pretending I was still under serious consideration, I still had one last dinner, where allegedly I could *just be myself,* which my mentors were clear to warn me meant *be nothing like yourself.*

Sometime on the glacial walk between my on-campus hotel and the restaurant—where, since I had no need to impress these people further, I decided to see how much free food I could get and ordered an appetizer, main course, and dessert—it dawned on me that I didn't want this. I wanted to be *offered* the job, yes. I wanted to be good enough to get a tenure-track job, and more than that I wanted everyone else to know that I was good enough, too. But I didn't want *this* job. I didn't want to move to rural Ohio alone in the agonizing hope that someday Witold would get laid off and have no choice but to come move in with me and be an adjunct, the exact reverse of what I'd done two years before. I didn't want to wade through knee-deep snow on a Friday morning just to be glared at by twenty future Mitt Romneys of America who still reeked of booze and called me *our Frau,* with an unrolled American *r.* I didn't want to spend every waking second I wasn't prepping for class churning out meticulous thirty-page articles that, best-case scenario, would appear three years later in some journal with a circulation of 125.

In other words, dinner went great.

"What would you tell one of your students if he asked you to recommend good Ph.D. programs in German?" asked my never-to-be-future-colleague Boris, as I ripped into my bread pudding with chocolate sauce.

"Honestly? I would say: *Under no circumstances should you do this.*"

Two weeks later, I got a kindly worded e-mail from the department chair letting me know they'd made a hire, a woman who already worked there as a well-liked visiting professor (visiting from nowhere; it's a euphemistic title for "adjunct with health insurance"). In academic parlance, she was an "inside candidate." That explained everything: the finalist from a short drive away who wouldn't need airfare; the awkward teaching slot, as I wouldn't have been allowed to take over the insider's class or even be on campus at the same time she was; the lack of attendance at my talk. There was never any mousetrap. There was never any wrong direction to run. There was only the cat.

Yes, I had spent the past four years getting incrementally closer to the goal of becoming a German professor. Sure, I liked being a German professor fine (with my own students, who didn't hate me).

I was also pretty good at it, despite the two days I'd just spent proving that I was bad at it. But I was now a thirty-six-year-old apprentice who would be expected to keep apprenticing for as long as it took. How did I get here? Who the hell was I? Where was the person who'd spent her nights playing on the indoor swing hanging from the ceiling of her Kreuzberg loft? The person whose Friday nights were not spent writing her book's seven hundredth footnote until one in the morning—not because she was behind in her work, but because she could think of nothing else to do with herself? The person whose relationship had a fun-percentage higher than five? Who, for that matter, had any human contact whatsoever, outside of her nineteen-year-old students and emergency-room personnel? I know "A Little Fable" doesn't really have a moral, but I still think the cat was onto something. Yes, of course I was just going to die in the end—we all are—but somewhere between declaring a German major in college and pulling on my ill-fitting Banana Republic suit for that campus visit, I had gone severely off track. And the walls were closing in.

Or were they? Because here's the thing. That cat, carnivorous four-legged embodiment of *Schadenfreude* that she was, also had another good point. It wasn't just that I'd made bad choices, which everybody does. It was that I was looking at the maze all wrong. Understanding something and misunderstanding the same thing can happen at the same time. The mouse insists that the walls closed in on her until there was no room left. But what happens, really, when those walls close all the way in? They disappear.

And guess what else, cat? Every German compound word is easily distilled back into the words that made it, and *Schadenfreude* is no different. If your life is somehow, either through your own ignominious choices or bad luck, subject to malicious happiness, either from others or yourself, you still have a choice. You can choose the *Schaden*, the misfortune, the pewter lungs around the neck. Or you can say *fuck it*, and go for the *Freude*—decide, after all of that, in spite of (perhaps because of) everything, on joy.

Which did I choose? The answer is simple. And just on the other side of this door.

Nachwort

n. epilogue, from after *and* word.

All right. I'm not Franz Kafka, and I'm now to the point in my life where I know that's a good thing. I'm not going to leave this like he did *The Castle,* at an unceremonious dropping-off midsentence. I'm going say that everything turned out fine in the end.

Around the time of my doomed campus visit, I got back in touch with a long-lost acquaintance from New York, who was a senior editor at an online magazine with a very large readership (now, it seemed, it was writing for print that didn't count). He suggested I expand some of my bile-shooting Facebook posts about the job market into fifteen hundred words, which he would both publish on the Internet and exchange for actual money. What resulted was an article that implored readers who thought it might be fun to get a Ph.D. in literature to, well, maybe *not* do that, on account of it would ruin their lives. To my shock, the article racked up hundreds of thousands of views, and in the space of two days I went from wishing that any academic anywhere knew my name to wishing that more of them didn't. Still, though, it was for the best: with those fifteen hundred words, I had at long last silenced everyone who had spent all those years insisting I keep trying.

In *The Notebooks of Malte Laurids Brigge,* Rainer Maria Rilke describes a nineteenth-century practice to ensure that you didn't bury someone alive. Namely, if you were pretty sure someone was dead but not 100 percent sure, you stuck a needle through his heart. That way, if he had still been alive (but barely so, and not fooling anybody), he wasn't anymore. I had known my academic career was dead for some time, and I was sick of everyone I knew insisting I keep trying to perform CPR on a corpse.

"I assure you I am not going back on the job market ever again," I would say.

"Don't put that on your Facebook!" they'd say. "A search committee might see it."

"I'm not ever going back on the job market," I'd say. "I don't give a fuck what any search committee thinks about my Facebook."

"Shh!" they'd say. "*Rebecca!* What would a search committee think if they heard you say that?"

I put a stop to that shit at last by creating an indelible paper trail of unhireability—in academia, and possibly everywhere else.

But with that article, I'd also committed my last (to date) act of Kafkan perspective shift. I went from professional failure—as in, failure *at* my profession—to professional failure, as in failure *as* a profession. Antipathy and loserdom were my new business, and business was terrible, which meant it was great. And indeed, a few months after my questionable debut, the magazine brought me on as a columnist. It was now my job to detail my failures and academia's vicissitudes—and, when it was newsworthy, I could write about Germany, Austria, and even Franz Kafka.

My new career as a professional train wreck also meant I could dwell in wreckage wherever I wanted—preferably somewhere very cheap, as Internet magazine writing is enjoyable but not lucrative. As it happened, Witold was in year six of his one-year job in St. Louis. He'd won Non-Tenure-Track Faculty of the Year; he'd been made director of undergraduate studies—basically, barring a cataclysm, his job would be lived out in one-year increments in perpetuity. (That, by the way, is what we call "the new tenure.") Before I moved to Ohio, he'd even bought a two-bedroom condo in a lovely neighborhood, in cash, for approximately the price I paid for my top-of-the-line Discman in 1996. No mortgage for him equaled no rent for me—not to mention, perhaps, the return of cohabitation, which might tick the fun percentage of a certain relationship up into the double digits.

"This place," he said in the spring of 2013, as I grappled with being newly "academic-famous" (that is, not at all famous), and we lugged what remained of my personal effects out of the beat-up 2000 Saturn on the back end of our very last stultifying four-hundred-mile journey down I-70 from Ohio, "is exactly the right size for a young family."

"Wow," I said. "Are you proposing?"

"No!" he said.

"We've only been together seven years. Wouldn't want to do anything rash."

"Are you serious?" he said. "I thought you weren't the marrying sort."

I shrugged.

"And I quote: 'I have no interest in participating in a patriarchal ownership ritual, thank you very much.'"

"Well, it's not like I'd take your *name*."

"'I am nobody's help-meet!'"

"All I'm saying is that I could really use some health insurance."

On the heels of that grand romantic gesture, Witold and I were married at City Hall in a ninety-second ceremony. He did not shave for the august occasion. By our first anniversary, and shortly before my thirty-eighth birthday, that health insurance had already come in quite handy, given that I was three months pregnant. (Six months after that, it came in handier still, when the Schuman progeny had to be wrested from my uncooperative torso by brute surgical force.)

Our daughter was born in St. Louis on what would have been my grandfather's one hundredth birthday. We gave her a weird Polish name. When she is old enough to withstand an international flight (or, more accurately, when she is old enough for me to withstand bringing her on an international flight), we will take her to Germany, and Austria, and Prague. I will point out the window of the train as the landscape rolls by—craggy mountains and defunct nuclear power plants; painfully bucolic villages and electric-green rolling hills; buildings that look older than God and that will make her think about believing in Him. I will show her Kafka's grave (but probably not the mental-institution-turned-hotel where I nearly conceived her twenty-years-older sibling with a guy I didn't even like). I will remind her that the ground floor is "Floor Zero" and the first floor is the second floor. I will extol the virtues of room-temperature mineral water. I will show her how to skin cooked potatoes with a knife and fork, and how to weigh her produce at the supermarket before checkout, so as not to get yelled at. When we invariably still do get yelled at, I will explain to her that it's not personal; she's not really in trouble; that's just how Germans express their love. That will be both true and a lie at the same time, and someday, I will explain to her that understanding something and misunderstanding the same thing are not mutually exclusive. Someday, I will tell her all about it, but only when she's much older. And only after the first time she's waited outside a door that was created for the sole purpose of slamming in her face.

Acknowledgments

Many unsuspecting (and suspecting) individuals appear in this book, in forms they may or may not recognize, and it is them I thank most of all. They are not mere supporting characters in some loser's narrative. (Especially the Germans: *Ganz vielen Dank, und es tut mir Leid*.) They are complex and real, with their own stories, and I hope that they do not object too strenuously to their roles in mine.

My oldest friend, most unjudging confidante, and staunchest supporter, Amy Boutell, good-naturedly hectored me to write a memoir "about all those losers you dated, etc." For *years*. Well Amy, as you can see, I have many *serious problems*, and now they're immortalized in print, *like this*.

Alia Hanna Habib is the fiercest and smartest literary agent in the world. I wish I could mail-order her a Sachertorte every day. Bob Miller, Big Boss at Flatiron Books, was willing to bet that readers might actually be interested in Germany. Colin Dickerman, my editor, is as insightful and supportive as he is merciless; the cohesive work of narrative nonfiction that you hold in your mitts is due to his sharp, diligent eye. (What is *legally classifiable as nonfiction*, that is—a distinction, among others, I learned from ace lawyer Mark A. Fowler.) I also owe an infinite debt to James Melia, who is better at his job than I once was at a very similar job in the same building; he is a wonderful and incisive reader, whose delightful well-bred Gentile millennial maleness also prodded me to clarify such mysteries as youth hostels, public school, Eastern European Jewish immigration, and urinary tract infections. The cover design for this book is by Darren Haggar, and the illustration is by Alice Pattullo who was given direction to "make the cockroach cuter" and did not resign on the spot. The lovely production design is by Donna Noetzel, and the production manager, David Lott, is the only reason this is an actual book and not a collection of chicken-scratches on a stack of index cards. Greg Villepique went above and beyond his job as copy editor. Steven Boriack has the not-enviable task of organizing publicity for an inveterate misanthrope who can't go anywhere without a miniature person in tow. And Kersten Horn managed not to be a condescending pedant about my German, whilst still saving me from claiming that his *Landsleute* regularly go around saying, "Hey, you: shit!"

Dan Kois, my first editor at *Slate*, is my hero, and I'm sorry that I was Max Brod to his Kafka and disobeyed his only (VERY REASONABLE) wish, which was that he be credited as Bob Ass. David Haglund allowed me to file at least a dozen *Slate* posts about utterly random German things, which provided the basis for this book. Jean Tamarin, Brock Read, Gabriela Montell, and Denise Magner have been wonderful to work with at the *Chronicle of Higher Education* and *Vitae*.

In my very first conversation with Kai Evers, my doctoral dissertation adviser at UC-Irvine, he said to me: "I like to read things that punish me." I hope this qualifies. John H. Smith's *Ereignis* seminar proved stimulating long beyond the classroom; David

Tse-Chien Pan still insists that I could get an academic job if I really wanted one; Gail K. Hart taught me about Schiller's skull and the *Bürgerliches Trauerspiel* (and the unfortunate fact about force-lactating suspected infanticides); Anke Biendarra never bullshat about the job market; Glenn Levine taught me to teach. My associates at the IFK in Vienna (special shout-out to Björn Blauensteiner) were lovingly described in a chapter that got cut; my associates at USML and OSU made it in; thank you (or sorry). Karen Zumhagen-Yekplé, Samuel Frederick, and Bob Lemon kept me from wanting to set the entire profession of academia on fire, *Michael-Kohlhaas*-style (or possibly *Billy-Madison*-style); Sarah Kendzior, Karen Kelsky, William Pannapacker, Joe Fruscione, Liana Silva, Annemarie Perez, Dorothy Kim, and Adeline Koh remind me that I did the right thing when I left.

RTV survivors, you will always be my crew, even though I can't throw down anymore and never will again. Ed, Akil, Patricia, Scalise, Adam B, Catherine, Emily, Josh, Dylan, Nicole, Nate, Eva, Raven, Mike G, Mace & Co. ("Wait, was it an AMPERSAND in the Character Bible? Or an 'and'? I CAN'T publish until I know!"). You will forever be the most talented people I have ever worked with, who were simultaneously made to do the most mind-numbing bullshit at work imaginable.

Love and thanks to my oldest and closest friends: Brittany and Matt (and Huck); Frank and Audrey (and Zelda and Gus); Jacob; Jessicca and Caleb (and Olias and Apollo); Jill, Jeff, and Eleanor; Gretchen (and Adam, Juniper, and Hazel) and Liliana. Dana Lemlein, Willow Schrager, and Judy Sznyter all searched through *actual photo albums* to provide a richness of embarrassments from my years abroad.

Eunjae Lee, the wonderful caregiver for my daughter who had the nerve to go off to medical school, gave me four to six priceless guilt-free uninterrupted hours every week to work.

Readers of *Slate*, the *Chronicle*, and my blog, Pan Kisses Kafka, thank you for alternately puffing my head up and puncturing it down to size. And I'm forever grateful to the authors who took pity on a plaintive first-timer: Dave Barry, Pamela Druckerman, Rosecrans Baldwin, Simon Kuper, J. Ryan Stradal, and Mike Scalise.

My in-laws: Jolanta, Adam and Lauren, Lisa and Ken, and Monica and Sean (and Asher). Please do not read this book. Babcia Wanda, Grazyna, and Uncle Richie: *PLEASE* do not read this book. My extended family: the Schumans (read at your own risk); the Johnsons (remember that only He can judge me in the end). My nuclear family: David, Sharon, Billy Budd (yes, that's a dog), my brother Ben (who, in accordance to disownment-threats, does not appear *anywhere*), Lani, Charlie (another dog), Milly, and Forthcoming Issue #2. In memoriam: Stephanie Green, Stanton Schuman, and Sam Schuman.

My husband, who listens (and listens, and listens . . .) and, more importantly, taught *me* to listen: you are the realest and best heart I know, and you passed that on to the small human who lives with us now—and then you cared for that small human while I wrote, and rewrote, this book. And, finally, my daughter, who was tormenting me from the inside when I got the idea, threatening to bust out when I got the contract, and cleaved onto my bosom, a sleeping succubus, for much of the composition.